Lecture Notes in Computer Science 12120

More information about this series at http://www.springer.com/series/7412

Žiga Špiclin · Jamie McClelland ·
Jan Kybic · Orcun Goksel (Eds.)

Biomedical
Image Registration

9th International Workshop, WBIR 2020
Portorož, Slovenia, December 1–2, 2020
Proceedings

Editors
Žiga Špiclin (iD)
Faculty of Electrical Engineering
University of Ljubljana
Ljubljana, Slovenia

Jan Kybic (iD)
Faculty of Electrical Engineering
Czech Technical University in Prague
Prague, Czech Republic

Jamie McClelland (iD)
Centre for Medical Image Computing
University College London
London, UK

Orcun Goksel (iD)
Computer Vision Lab
ETH Zurich
Zurich, Switzerland

ISSN 0302-9743   ISSN 1611-3349   (electronic)
Lecture Notes in Computer Science
ISBN 978-3-030-50119-8   ISBN 978-3-030-50120-4   (eBook)
https://doi.org/10.1007/978-3-030-50120-4

LNCS Sublibrary: SL6 – Image Processing, Computer Vision, Pattern Recognition, and Graphics

This Springer imprint is published by the registered company Springer Nature Switzerland AG
The registered company address is: Gewerbestrasse 11, 6330 Cham, Switzerland

Preface

The 9th International Workshop on Biomedical Image Registration (WBIR 2020, https://wbir2020.org) was to be held in Portorož, Slovenia, June 16–17, 2020. At the time of writing, the global crisis and the Covid-19 pandemic are in full swing. To ensure the safety and well-being of all participants the Organization Committee decided to postpone the meeting to December 1–2, 2020. We sincerely hope that the global situation will improve over time and permit us to host the meeting at the set date so that we can enjoy WBIR 2020 together.

The WBIR 2020 meeting is a two-day special session in conjunction with the 8th European Medical and Biological Engineering Conference (EMBEC 2020), organized by the Slovenian Society for Medical and Biological Engineering. Preceding editions of WBIR have been running mostly as standalone two-day workshops at various locations: Bled, Slovenia (1999); Philadelphia, USA (2003); Utrecht, The Netherlands (2006); Lübeck, Germany (2010); Nashville, USA (2012); London, UK (2014); Las Vegas, USA (2016), and Leiden, The Netherlands (2018). As with previous editions, the major appeal of WBIR 2020 is its scientific program in a relaxed two-day format, allowing for a lot of interaction and discussion among peers. As everyone's mindset is on image registration, it makes it easier for students to approach and meet their distinguished colleagues. The workshop program includes both oral and poster presentations in a single track, two keynote lectures, and ample opportunities for discussion.

The WBIR 2020 proceedings, published in the *Lecture Notes in Computer Science*, were established through a rigorous peer-review process in a double-blind fashion, with each submission evaluated by at least three members of the Program Committee. The International Program Committee consisted of 29 senior scientists in the field of medical image registration. From a total of 22 submissions, 16 were selected for oral and poster presentation. In this edition topics of papers varied, including five registration initialization and acceleration, two on interventional, two on landmark based registration, five on multi-channel image registration, and two on sliding motion. Submissions of one-page abstracts are also invited in addition to full-paper submissions. The one-page abstracts do not appear in the proceedings, but are set to be presented at the workshop. The aim is to give scientists the opportunity to present early work and to get feedback from workshop attendees on recently published or submitted journal papers not presented previously.

We expect two excellent keynote speakers at WBIR 2020. With rich experience in translating and commercializing image analysis algorithms, Prof. Dr. Sébastien Ourselin from King's College London will speak about translating medical imaging research towards real-world clinical applications. This subject is highly relevant since, from our observation, a large and ever-growing number of exciting clinical applications and solutions that utilize advanced medical image analysis are proposed each year, however, few seem to penetrate into the clinical world. As the adoption of machine and deep learning tools for the image registration tasks seems to finally be gaining traction in the research community, Prof. Dr. Mattias Heinrich from University of Lübeck will discuss how to make deep learning work in medical image registration, and present current advances, pitfalls, and remaining challenges.

Many contributed to the organization and future success of WBIR 2020. In particular, we would like to thank the members of the Program Committee for their work that assures the high quality of the workshop. We also thank the organizers of EMBEC 2020, especially the general chair Prof. Dr. Damijan Miklavčič, for the organizational effort and kind support of WBIR 2020. We thank the UCL Institute of Healthcare Engineering for their financial support and the MICCAI Society for their endorsement. Finally, we would like to thank all authors and prospective participants of WBIR 2020 for their contributions.

June 2020

Žiga Špiclin
Jamie McClelland
Jan Kybic
Orcun Goksel

Organization

General Chairs

Žiga Špiclin — University of Ljubljana, Slovenia
Jamie McClelland — University College London, UK
Jan Kybic — Czech Technical University in Prague, Czech Republic
Orcun Goksel — ETH Zurich, Switzerland

Program Committee

John Ashburner — University College London, UK
Brian Avants — University of Virginia, USA
Kristy Brock — The University of Texas, MD Anderson, USA
Gary Christensen — University of Iowa, USA
Olivier Commonwick — Inria Rennes, France
Adrian Dalca — Massachusetts Institute of Technology, USA
Sune Darkner — University of Copenhagen, Denmark
Benoit Dawant — Vanderbilt University, USA
Stanley Durrleman — Inria Paris, France
Ali Gholipour-Baboli — Harvard University, USA
Ben Glocker — Imperial College London, UK
Mattias Heinrich — University of Lübeck, Germany
Yipeng Hu — University College London, UK
Stefan Klein — Erasmus Medical Center, The Netherlands
Georg Langs — Medical University of Vienna, Austria
Boudewijn Lelieveldt — Leiden University Medical Center, The Netherlands
Marc Modat — King's College London, UK
Jan Modersitzki — University of Lübeck, Germany
Josien Pluim — Eindhoven University of Technology, The Netherlands
Karl Rohr — University of Heidelberg, DKFZ, Germany
Julia Schnabel — King's College, UK
Gregory Sharp — Massachusetts General Hospital, USA
Dinggang Shen — University of North Carolina, USA
Stefan Sommer — University of Copenhagen, Denmark
Marius Staring — Leiden University Medical Center, The Netherlands
Matthew Toews — École de technologie supérieure, Canada
Jef Vandemeulebroucke — Vrije Universiteit Brussel, Belgium
Tom Vercauteren — King's College London, UK
Wolfgang Wein — Technical University Munich, Germany

Contents

Registration Initialization and Acceleration

Nonlinear Alignment of Whole Tractograms with the Linear
Assignment Problem 3
    Emanuele Olivetti, Pietro Gori, Pietro Astolfi, Giulia Bertó,
    and Paolo Avesani

Learning-Based Affine Registration of Histological Images 12
    Marek Wodzinski and Henning Müller

Enabling Manual Intervention for Otherwise Automated Registration
of Large Image Series 23
    Roman Grothausmann, Dženan Zukić, Matt McCormick,
    Christian Mühlfeld, and Lars Knudsen

Towards Segmentation and Spatial Alignment of the Human Embryonic
Brain Using Deep Learning for Atlas-Based Registration 34
    Wietske A. P. Bastiaansen, Melek Rousian,
    Régine P. M. Steegers-Theunissen, Wiro J. Niessen, Anton Koning,
    and Stefan Klein

Learning Deformable Image Registration with Structure Guidance
Constraints for Adaptive Radiotherapy 44
    Sven Kuckertz, Nils Papenberg, Jonas Honegger, Tomasz Morgas,
    Benjamin Haas, and Stefan Heldmann

Interventional Registration

Multilevel 2D-3D Intensity-Based Image Registration 57
    Annkristin Lange and Stefan Heldmann

Towards Automated Spine Mobility Quantification: A Locally Rigid CT
to X-ray Registration Framework 67
    David Drobny, Marta Ranzini, Amanda Isaac, Tom Vercauteren,
    Sébastien Ourselin, David Choi, and Marc Modat

Landmark Based Registration

Reinforced Redetection of Landmark in Pre- and Post-operative Brain Scan
Using Anatomical Guidance for Image Alignment 81
    Diana Waldmannstetter, Fernando Navarro, Benedikt Wiestler,
    Jan S. Kirschke, Anjany Sekuboyina, Ester Molero, and Bjoern H. Menze

Deep Volumetric Feature Encoding for Biomedical Images   91
Brian Avants, Elliot Greenblatt, Jacob Hesterman,
and Nicholas Tustison

Multi-channel Registration

Multi-channel Image Registration of Cardiac MR Using Supervised Feature
Learning with Convolutional Encoder-Decoder Network   103
Xuesong Lu and Yuchuan Qiao

Multi-channel Registration for Diffusion MRI: Longitudinal Analysis
for the Neonatal Brain   111
Alena Uus, Maximilian Pietsch, Irina Grigorescu, Daan Christiaens,
Jacques-Donald Tournier, Lucilio Cordero Grande, Jana Hutter,
David Edwards, Joseph Hajnal, and Maria Deprez

An Image Registration-Based Method for EPI Distortion Correction Based
on Opposite Phase Encoding (COPE)   122
Hester Breman, Joost Mulders, Levin Fritz, Judith Peters, John Pyles,
Judith Eck, Matteo Bastiani, Alard Roebroeck, John Ashburner,
and Rainer Goebel

Diffusion Tensor Driven Image Registration: A Deep Learning Approach . . .   131
Irina Grigorescu, Alena Uus, Daan Christiaens,
Lucilio Cordero-Grande, Jana Hutter, A. David Edwards,
Joseph V. Hajnal, Marc Modat, and Maria Deprez

Multimodal MRI Template Creation in the Ring-Tailed Lemur
and Rhesus Macaque   141
Frederik J. Lange, Stephen M. Smith, Mads F. Bertelsen,
Alexandre A. Khrapitchev, Paul R. Manger, Rogier B. Mars,
and Jesper L. R. Andersson

Sliding Motion

An Unsupervised Learning Approach to Discontinuity-Preserving
Image Registration   153
Eric Ng and Mehran Ebrahimi

An Image Registration Framework for Discontinuous Mappings
Along Cracks   163
Hari Om Aggrawal, Martin S. Andersen, and Jan Modersitzki

Author Index   175

Registration Initialization and Acceleration

Nonlinear Alignment of Whole Tractograms with the Linear Assignment Problem

Emanuele Olivetti[1,2], Pietro Gori[3], Pietro Astolfi[1,2,4(✉)],
Giulia Bertó[1,2], and Paolo Avesani[1,2]

[1] NeuroInformatics Laboratory (NILab) Bruno Kessler Foundation, Trento, Italy
{olivetti,pastolfi}@fbk.eu
http://nilab.fbk.eu
[2] Center for Mind and Brain Sciences (CIMeC), University of Trento, Trento, Italy
[3] LTCI, Télécom Paris, IP Paris,
Palaiseau, France
[4] PAVIS, Italian Institute of Technology, Genova, Italy

Abstract. After registration of the imaging data of two brains, homologous anatomical structures are expected to overlap better than before registration. Diffusion magnetic resonance imaging (dMRI) techniques and tractography techniques provide a representation of the anatomical connections in the white matter, as hundreds of thousands of streamlines, forming the tractogram. The literature on methods for aligning tractograms is in active development and provides methods that operate either from voxel information, e.g. fractional anisotropy, orientation distribution function, T1-weighted MRI, or directly from streamline information. In this work, we align streamlines using the linear assignment problem (LAP) and propose a method to reduce the high computational cost of aligning whole brain tractograms. As further contribution, we present a comparison among some of the freely-available linear and nonlinear tractogram alignment methods, where we show that our LAP-based method outperforms all others. In discussing the results, we show that a main limitation of all streamline-based nonlinear registration methods is the computational cost and that addressing such problem may lead to further improvement in the quality of registration.

1 Introduction

Image registration is a cornerstone of brain imaging applications. After registration of the data of two brains, homologous anatomical structures are expected to overlap better than before registration. Typically, brain images are registered to atlases, or between different subject, for different purposes, such as: conducting group-studies, guiding segmentation, or for building new atlases [9].

Diffusion magnetic resonance imaging (dMRI) techniques measure the orientation of diffusion of water molecules in biological tissues. By means of tractography techniques on dMRI data from the brain, it is possible to obtain a

© Springer Nature Switzerland AG 2020
Ž. Špiclin et al. (Eds.): WBIR 2020, LNCS 12120, pp. 3–11, 2020.
https://doi.org/10.1007/978-3-030-50120-4_1

representation of the anatomical connections in the white matter, as hundreds of thousands of streamlines, forming the tractogram.

The linear or nonlinear transformation to register the tractogram of one subjects to that of another subject can be estimated in two main ways: from volumetric data, such as T1-weighted, fractional anisotropy (FA), or orientation distribution functions (ODFs), see [3,4,11], or directly from streamlines. In this last case, the literature on nonlinear methods addresses the registration of bundles, which are just a portion of the tractogram, usually because of the very high computational cost of the algorithms, see [5,17,18,20,21]. Differently, in the case of linear methods, solutions to compute an affine transformation from whole tractograms are available, see [7,9].

Recently, a new concept has been proposed to accurately align tractograms, based on the idea of streamline correspondence [10] and formalized as a graph matching (GM) problem. There, the building block of the methodology is to compute which streamline of the first subject corresponds to which streamline of the second subject, as in a combinatorial optimization problem. The principle of streamline correspondence has also been used for the problem of bundle segmentation [6,8,12,13,19].

In this work, we present two contributions: first, we propose the use of the linear assignment problem (LAP) as computational building block to align *entire* brain tractograms from streamline information, extending the work of [12], which addressed only bundles and segmentation. The alignment obtained with LAP acts locally, as in a nonlinear transformation. Second, we quantitatively compare the proposed method against some methods in the state of the art for tractogram alignment, for which the implementation is freely-available. To the best of our knowledge, it is pretty infrequent to find *quantitative* comparisons between tractogram alignment methods, in the literature.

In order to carry out the quantitative comparison, we designed an experiment where, given the tractograms of two subjects, we computed the transformation of the first in order to match the second one. Similarly to [10], we quantified the accuracy of the whole tractogram alignment by estimating the degree of overlap between homologous bundles. The reason behind it is that, after registration, the anatomy of the white matter of the two subjects should match more accurately than before. On 90 pairs of subjects from the dMRI dataset of the Human Connectom Project [14], we compared the registration obtained with 5 different methods, using 10 main bundles as landmarks for the quantification.

The results show that the proposed method outperforms voxel-based methods and streamline-based methods in almost all cases. Moreover, as expected, linear methods are outperformed by nonlinear methods. The Symmetric Normalization (SyN) algorithm of the Advanced Normalization Tools (ANTs, see [1]), despite being designed for volumetric images, shows excellent results against streamline based methods, outperforming them in some cases. The main limitation of streamline-based methods is the high computational cost, which requires to resort to approximations.

In the following, we briefly describe the proposed method. Then, in Sect. 3, we describe the details of the experiments. In Sect. 4 we discuss the claims in the light of the results.

2   Methods

Let $s = \{\mathbf{x}_1,\ldots,\mathbf{x}_n\}$ be a *streamline*, i.e. a sequence of points in 3D space, i.e. $\mathbf{x}_i = [x_i, y_i, z_i] \in \mathbb{R}^3, \forall i$. Let $T = \{s_1,\ldots,s_N\}$ be a tractogram and $b \subset T$ the set of streamlines corresponding to a white matter bundle of interest, e.g. the cortico-spinal tract (cst). With $|\cdot|$ we indicate the number of objects in a set. Typically, $|T|$ is in the order of 10^5–10^6. Several distances has been defined between streamlines, see [9] In this work, we adopt the commonly adopted mean of closest distances, $d(s_a, s_b) = \frac{d_m(s_a, s_b) + d_m(s_b, s_a)}{2}$, where $d_m(s_a, s_b) = \frac{1}{|s_a|} \sum_{\mathbf{x}_i \in s_a} \min_{\mathbf{x}_j \in s_b} ||\mathbf{x}_i - \mathbf{x}_j||_2$.

2.1   Streamline Correspondence

Given two tractograms, T_A and T_B, the problem of aligning them can be framed as finding the correspondences between each streamline in T_A the corresponding one in T_B, see [10]. If $s_i^A \in T_A$ corresponds to $s_j^B \in T_B$, the transformation obtained from such correspondence is the one that returns s_j^B when given s_i^A. The set of correspondences will provide a good alignment of tractograms if, after the transformation, homologous anatomical structures will match. Previously, the task of finding a good set of correspondences has been formulated as graph matching [10].

2.2   Linear Assignment Problem

Given two sets of objects, e.g. T_A and T_B, of the same size N, and a $N \times N$ cost matrix C, whose element $c_{ij} \in \mathbb{R}$ is the cost of assigning $s_i^A \in T_A$ to $s_j^B \in T_B$, e.g. $c_{ij} = d(s_i^A, s_j^B)$, then the linear assignment problem (LAP) is the combinatorial optimization problem that attempt to optimally assign each element of T_A to each element of T_B, with a *one-to-one* assignment, minimizing the total cost:

$$P^* = \underset{P \in \mathcal{P}}{\operatorname{argmin}} \sum_{i=1}^{N} \sum_{j=1}^{N} c_{ij} p_{ij} \tag{1}$$

where $\mathcal{P}$ is the set of all possible one-to-one assignments, each represented as a $N \times N$ permutation matrix, i.e. $P \in \mathcal{P}$ is a binary matrix where each row and column sum up to 1 and the element $p_{ij} = 1$ if s_i^A is assigned to s_j^B and 0 otherwise. Notice that LAP for streamlines, the minimization of the total cost is the minimization of the distances of corresponding streamlines and, in many cases, the one-to-one constraint forces the correspondences to follow the local differences between the anatomical structures, see [13]. When $|T_B| > |T_A|$, the problem is called *rectangular* LAP (RLAP), which seeks the best assignment of $\{s_1^A, \ldots, s_N^A\}$ to subset of size N of T_B. The most efficient algorithm to find the optimal solution of LAP and RLAP is LAPJV, see [2], whose time complexity is $\mathcal{O}(N^3)$ and space complexity is $\mathcal{O}(N^2)$. In practice, even LAPJV is unfeasible to be executed on problems where $N > 10^4$, both in terms of time and memory required.

2.3   Large-Scale Approximation

The correspondence between entire tractograms cannot be computed even with LAPJV, because of the excessive computational cost. Here, we adopt a hierarchical two-steps procedure that exploits the geometrical structure of tractograms. In the first step, both T_A and T_B are clustered into k clusters, named $\{\alpha_i\}_{i=1\ldots k}$ for T_A and $\{\beta_j\}_{j=1\ldots k}$ for T_B. Then, each tractogram is simplified with k streamlines, i.e. the centroids of the respective clusters. Then, LAP is computed between the two simplified tractograms, as explained above, i.e. a $k \times k$ LAP is solved. This first step aims at finding corresponding clusters across the two tractograms, e.g. α_i corresponds to β_j. In the second step, given two corresponding clusters, the correspondence of streamlines is computed by solving the RLAP between the streamlines of the two clusters[1]. Details are given below. In total, the two-steps procedure requires to solve 1 LAP with a $k \times k$ cost matrix and k RLAPs each with, approximately, a $\frac{N}{k} \times \frac{N}{k}$ cost matrix. For this reason, the resulting time complexity is reduced from $\mathcal{O}(N^3)$ to $\mathcal{O}\left(k^3 + \frac{N^3}{k^2}\right)$ and space complexity from $\mathcal{O}(N^2)$ to $\mathcal{O}(k^2 + \frac{N^2}{k})$.

   In the second step of the procedure, assuming cluster $\alpha_i \subset T_A$ to correspond to cluster $\beta_j \subset T_B$, there are two possible scenarios: either (i) $|\alpha_i| \leq |\beta_j|$, for which finding the corresponding streamlines of α_i in β_j is a straightforward RLAP, or (ii) $|\alpha_i| > |\beta_j|$, for which there are not enough streamlines in β_j to set up a LAP or RLAP. In this last case, we propose to compute the corresponding streamlines of α_i by violating the one-to-one constraint and assigning one or streamlines of α_i to each of β_j. The procedure is the following: first we solve the reverse RLAP, i.e. we compute the optimal assignment of all the streamlines in β_j to (some of) those in α_i. In this way, a subset of the streamlines in α_i will obtain their corresponding ones in β_j. We denote such subset of assigned streamlines as $\alpha_i^a \subset \alpha_i$ and that of the remaining ones, i.e. the non assigned streamlines, as $\alpha_i^{na} \subset \alpha_i$. Then, for each non assigned streamline $s \in \alpha_i^{na}$, we compute its nearest neighbor in α_i^a. Finally, we define the corresponding streamline of $s \in \alpha_i^{na}$ as the one corresponding to its nearest neighbor in α_i^a.

3   Experiments

We selected 30 healthy subjects at random from the publicly available Human Connectome Project (HCP) dMRI dataset [14] (90 gradients; b = 2000; voxel

---

[1] In general, the number of streamlines of the two corresponding clusters is different, thus leading to a RLAP.

size $= 1.25$ mm isotropic). For each subject, tractograms of 400–500 thousands streamlines were obtained using the constrained spherical deconvolution (CSD) algorithm [15] and the local deterministic tracking algorithm implemented in DiPy[2] (step size $= 0.625$ mm, 1 seed/voxel from the white matter). We segmented 14 major bundles from each tractogram, using the TractQuerier/white matter query language (WMQL, see [16]) and we used some of them as ground truth. In order to reduce the impact of poor segmentations obtained in some cases, we jointly selected 10 subjects and 10 bundles in order to minimize the differences in number of streamlines for each bundles across the subjects. These bundles are (both left and right): cingulum (cb), cortico-spinal tract (cst), inferior fronto-occipital fasciculus (ifof), thalamo prefrontal (thpref) and uncinate fasciculus (uf). We visually inspected the resulting bundles to avoid outliers. The experiments were then conducted on the 90 pairs of different tractograms that can be obtained from the selected 10 subjects.

3.1   Comparison

We quantified the quality of alignment between two tractograms as the degree of overlap between the voxel masks of homologous bundles, after registration, see [7,10]. The degree of overlap was quantified as dice similarity coefficient (DSC): $DSC = \frac{2 \times (|v(\hat{b}_A) \cap v(b_B)|)}{|v(\hat{b}_A)| + |v(b_B)|}$, where $v(\hat{b}_A)$ is the voxel mask of the bundle $b_A \in T_A$ after the alignment of the entire tractogram T_A to T_B. In other words, $v(\hat{b}_A)$ attempts to approximate the voxel mask of the homologous bundle of the target subject, $v(b_B)$, considered as ground truth. In the comparison, we considered the following methods to align tractograms: 1) registration based on anterior and posterior commissures (AC-PC), directly provided within the HCP dataset, used as baseline. 2) Streamline linear registration (SLR, from DiPy, see [7]): in [10], SLR has shown slightly superior quality of registration with respect to other linear methods, so we considered it as a good representative of the linear methods. 3) The voxel-based nonlinear registration method of ANTs[3], see [1], used with default values. As reference volume, we considered the T1w images of the two subjects and the fractional anisotropy (FA) volumes. 4) Deformetrica[4] [5], a diffeomorphic streamline-based registration method for bundles. Streamlines were modeled as varifolds and we used 7 mm and 15 mm for the varifolds and diffeomorphic kernel bandwidths respectively. 5) Correspondence between streamlines as graph matching (GM[5], see [10]). 6) Correspondence between streamlines as linear assignment problem (LAP) (Sect. 2). Some of the methods have too high computational cost when computed on whole tractograms. For this reason, tractograms were simplified for such methods following the simplification step described in Sect. 2.3, using the fast mini-batch k-means

---

[2] http://nipy.org/dipy.
[3] http://stnava.github.io/ANTs.
[4] http://www.deformetrica.org/.
[5] https://github.com/emanuele/graph_matching_tractograms.

algorithm, as described in [10]. For each tractogram, we computed the approximate k-means clustering on streamlines, with $k = 1000$ and $k = 5000$. The simplified tractogram consisted of the k centroid streamlines. Note that such values of k ensure an extensive coverage of the brain, which we can assume to be enough to guarantee reasonable one-to-one assignments. We provide code and datasets of all experiments under a Free/OpenSource license here: https://github.com/FBK-NILab/WBIR2020_experiments.

3.2   Results

In Table 1 we report degree of overlap (higher is better) between homologous bundles after whole tractogram registration, with different methods. The DSC value is averaged over 90 pairs of subjects. The standard deviation of the means is always below 0.01. All computations were executed on a modern desktop computer, i.e. Intel Xeon E5 8 cores, 3.50 GHz, 16 Gb RAM, always using only CPU[6]. In Fig. 1, we show an example of matching between homologous bundles (IFOF left) after whole tractogram alignment for some of the methods.

Table 1. For each of the 10 bundles considered in this study (one per column), the table reports the degree of voxel-overlap after whole brain tractogram alignment, quantified as DSC (higher is better) and averaged over 90 pairs of subjects, across different methods - one per row. In each cell, the standard deviation of the mean is always below 0.01. In bold face are reported the highest values for each bundle, as well as those within 0.01 from them. The last column reports the computational time in minutes for aligning a pair of tractograms.

	cbL	cbR	cstL	cstR	ifofL	ifofR	thprefL	thprefR	ufL	ufR	Time
AC-PC	0.42	0.38	0.41	0.43	0.32	0.29	0.38	0.38	0.21	0.19	–
SLR	0.47	0.43	0.46	0.50	0.38	0.37	0.44	0.45	0.27	0.25	5
ANTs (T1w)	**0.61**	**0.56**	0.56	0.59	0.54	0.51	0.54	0.55	0.37	0.35	30
ANTs (FA)	**0.62**	**0.57**	0.56	0.61	0.57	0.53	0.55	0.56	0.38	0.36	30
Deform ($k = 1000$)	0.46	0.42	0.44	0.48	0.41	0.38	0.44	0.44	0.28	0.27	170
GM ($k = 1000$)	0.46	0.45	0.57	0.59	0.62	0.64	0.56	0.57	0.39	0.35	480
LAP ($k = 1000$)	0.52	0.48	0.60	0.63	0.63	0.64	0.56	0.57	0.40	0.34	60
LAP ($k = 5000$)	0.56	0.52	**0.63**	**0.66**	**0.66**	**0.67**	**0.60**	**0.60**	**0.43**	**0.39**	120

4   Discussion and Conclusions

In this work, we describe the use of the linear assignment problem (LAP) to align entire tractograms of two different subjects, by introducing approximations as computational shortcuts. The LAP acts locally, as a nonlinear registration method. In Table 1, we compare the proposed method with some linear and nonlinear methods in the literature. The results show that LAP ($k = 5000$)

---

[6] To note that Deformetrica has also a GPU implementation.

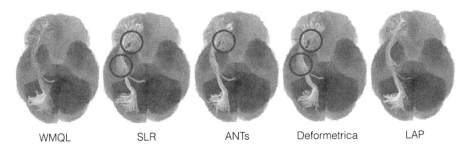

| WMQL | SLR | ANTs | Deformetrica | LAP |

Fig. 1. Example of homologous bundles after tractogram registration of T_A (HCP subject ID: 199655) to T_B (HCP subject ID: 599671). In green, on the left, the IFOF left of the static T_B, as segmented by WMQL. In yellow, the IFOF left of the moving T_A, after tractogram registration with four different methods. Red circle indicates the location of major differences with respect to the (green) IFOF left in T_B. (Color figure online)

outperforms other methods on almost all bundles. The only exception is the cingulum (cbL, cbR) for which ANTs provides significantly better DSC, with LAP second in the ranking.

The results also show a number of other interesting facts and confirm basic sanity checks: despite the limited quality of the ground truth provided by the WMQL, the values of DSC increase steadily from AC-PC registration, to linear registration and to nonlinear methods. 90 pairs of subjects selected as described in Sect. 3 are enough to keep the standard deviation of the means low enough (≤ 0.01) to clearly see differences between the methods. It is also reassuring that, for each bundle, the results are sufficiently similar across the two hemispheres, e.g. ifofL and ifofR obtain almost the same score, for all methods. Nonlinear methods outperform linear methods in all cases, with the exception of Deformetrica, most probably because we could not perform a large model selection for the user-selected parameters due to the high computational time. Furthermore, the introduced approximations might interfere too much with the underlying method, which is tailored to register bundles. ANTs provided excellent results, given the fact that it does not operate on streamline information. Most probably this occurs because the grid on which ANTs operates, i.e. the voxel grid, is much more dense than what the simplified tractograms offer. The results between graph matching (GM) and LAP are not very different, for the same level of approximation ($k = 1000$), with LAP in advantage. This advantage can be explained by the fact that LAPJV computes the *exact* solution of the RLAPs, while in the case of GM the underlying algorithm, DSPFP (see [10]), provides only an approximate solution. Notably, LAP is 8 times faster than GM for this size of tractograms, see Table 1 last column, which allowed us to run LAP with $k = 5000$ in a reasonable amount of time and to obtain substantially superior scores.

All this evidence supports the hypothesis that the results are limited also by the level of approximation and that, by improving algorithms and implementations to reduce computational cost, some of the methods may reach even better results.

References

1. Avants, B.B., Epstein, C.L., Grossman, M., Gee, J.C.: Symmetric diffeomorphic image registration with cross-correlation: evaluating automated labeling of elderly and neurodegenerative brain. Med. Image Anal. **12**(1), 26–41 (2008). https://doi.org/10.1016/j.media.2007.06.004
2. Bijsterbosch, J., Volgenant, A.: Solving the rectangular assignment problem and applications. Ann. Oper. Res. **181**, 443–462 (2010). https://doi.org/10.1007/s10479-010-0757-3
3. Christiaens, D., Dhollander, T., Maes, F., Sunaert, S., Suetens, P.: The effect of reorientation of the fibre orientation distribution on fibre tracking. In: MICCAI 2012 Workshop on Computational Diffusion MRI, CDMRI 2012, pp. 33–44 (2012)
4. Du, J., Goh, A., Qiu, A.: Diffeomorphic metric mapping of high angular resolution diffusion imaging based on Riemannian structure of orientation distribution functions. IEEE Trans. Med. Imaging **31**(5), 1021–1033 (2012)
5. Durrleman, S., Fillard, P., Pennec, X., Trouvé, A., Ayache, N.: Registration, atlas estimation and variability analysis of white matter fiber bundles modeled as currents. NeuroImage **55**(3), 1073–1090 (2011). https://doi.org/10.1016/j.neuroimage.2010.11.056
6. Feydy, J., Roussillon, P., Trouvé, A., Gori, P.: Fast and scalable optimal transport for Brain tractograms. In: Shen, D., et al. (eds.) MICCAI 2019. LNCS, vol. 11766, pp. 636–644. Springer, Cham (2019). https://doi.org/10.1007/978-3-030-32248-9_71
7. Garyfallidis, E., Ocegueda, O., Wassermann, D., Descoteaux, M.: Robust and efficient linear registration of white-matter fascicles in the space of streamlines. NeuroImage **117**, 124–140 (2015). https://doi.org/10.1016/j.neuroimage.2015.05.016
8. Labra, N., et al.: Fast automatic segmentation of white matter streamlines based on a multi-subject bundle atlas. Neuroinformatics **15**(1), 71–86 (2016). https://doi.org/10.1007/s12021-016-9316-7
9. O'Donnell, L.J., Wells, W.M., Golby, A.J., Westin, C.-F.: Unbiased groupwise registration of white matter tractography. In: Ayache, N., Delingette, H., Golland, P., Mori, K. (eds.) MICCAI 2012. LNCS, vol. 7512, pp. 123–130. Springer, Heidelberg (2012). https://doi.org/10.1007/978-3-642-33454-2_16
10. Olivetti, E., Sharmin, N., Avesani, P.: Alignment of tractograms as graph matching. Front. Neurosci. **10**, 554 (2016)
11. Raffelt, D., Tournier, J.-D., Fripp, J., Crozier, S., Connelly, A., Salvado, O.: Symmetric diffeomorphic registration of fibre orientation distributions. NeuroImage **56**, 1171–1180 (2011). https://doi.org/10.1016/j.neuroimage.2011.02.014
12. Sharmin, N., Olivetti, E., Avesani, P.: Alignment of tractograms as linear assignment problem. In: Fuster, A., Ghosh, A., Kaden, E., Rathi, Y., Reisert, M. (eds.) Computational Diffusion MRI. MV, pp. 109–120. Springer, Cham (2016). https://doi.org/10.1007/978-3-319-28588-7_10
13. Sharmin, N., Olivetti, E., Avesani, P.: White matter tract segmentation as multiple linear assignment problems. Front. Neurosci. **11**, 754 (2018). https://doi.org/10.3389/fnins.2017.00754

14. Sotiropoulos, S.N., et al.: WU-Minn HCP consortium: advances in diffusion MRI acquisition and processing in the human connectome project. NeuroImage **80**, 125–143 (2013)
15. Tournier, J.D., Calamante, F., Connelly, A.: Robust determination of the fibre orientation distribution in diffusion MRI: non-negativity constrained super-resolved spherical deconvolution. NeuroImage **35**(4), 1459–1472 (2007). https://doi.org/10.1016/j.neuroimage.2007.02.016
16. Wassermann, D., et al.: On describing human white matter anatomy: the white matter query language. In: Mori, K., Sakuma, I., Sato, Y., Barillot, C., Navab, N. (eds.) MICCAI 2013. LNCS, vol. 8149, pp. 647–654. Springer, Heidelberg (2013). https://doi.org/10.1007/978-3-642-40811-3_81
17. Wassermann, D., et al.: White matter bundle registration and population analysis based on Gaussian processes. In: Székely, G., Hahn, H.K. (eds.) IPMI 2011. LNCS, vol. 6801, pp. 320–332. Springer, Heidelberg (2011). https://doi.org/10.1007/978-3-642-22092-0_27
18. Waugh, J.L., et al.: A registration method for improving quantitative assessment in probabilistic diffusion tractography. NeuroImage **189**, 288–306 (2019). https://doi.org/10.1016/j.neuroimage.2018.12.057
19. Yoo, S.W., et al.: An example-based multi-atlas approach to automatic labeling of white matter tracts. PloS One **10**(7), e0133337 (2015). https://doi.org/10.1371/journal.pone.0133337
20. Ziyan, U., Sabuncu, M., Grimson, W., Westin, C.F.: Consistency clustering: a robust algorithm for group-wise registration, segmentation and automatic atlas construction in diffusion MRI. Int. J. Comput. Vis. IJCV **85**(3), 279–290 (2009). https://doi.org/10.1007/s11263-009-0217-1
21. Ziyan, U., Sabuncu, M.R., O'Donnell, L.J., Westin, C.-F.: Nonlinear registration of diffusion MR images based on fiber bundles. In: Ayache, N., Ourselin, S., Maeder, A. (eds.) MICCAI 2007. LNCS, vol. 4791, pp. 351–358. Springer, Heidelberg (2007). https://doi.org/10.1007/978-3-540-75757-3_43

Learning-Based Affine Registration
of Histological Images

Marek Wodzinski[1]([⊠]) and Henning Müller[2]

[1] Department of Measurement and Electronics,
AGH University of Science and Technology, Krakow, Poland
`wodzinski@agh.edu.pl`
[2] Information Systems Institute, University of Applied Sciences
Western Switzerland (HES-SO Valais), Sierre, Switzerland
`henning.mueller@hevs.ch`

Abstract. The use of different stains for histological sample preparation reveals distinct tissue properties and may result in a more accurate diagnosis. However, as a result of the staining process, the tissue slides are being deformed and registration is required before further processing. The importance of this problem led to organizing an open challenge named Automatic Non-rigid Histological Image Registration Challenge (ANHIR), organized jointly with the IEEE ISBI 2019 conference. The challenge organizers provided several hundred image pairs and a server-side evaluation platform. One of the most difficult sub-problems for the challenge participants was to find an initial, global transform, before attempting to calculate the final, non-rigid deformation field. This article solves the problem by proposing a deep network trained in an unsupervised way with a good generalization. We propose a method that works well for images with different resolutions, aspect ratios, without the necessity to perform image padding, while maintaining a low number of network parameters and fast forward pass time. The proposed method is orders of magnitude faster than the classical approach based on the iterative similarity metric optimization or computer vision descriptors. The success rate is above 98% for both the training set and the evaluation set. We make both the training and inference code freely available.

Keywords: Image registration · Initial alignment · Deep learning · Histology · ANHIR

1 Introduction

Automatic registration of histological images stained using several dyes is a challenging and important task that makes it possible to fuse information and potentially improve further processing and diagnosis. The problem is difficult due to: (i) complex, large deformations, (ii) difference in the appearance and partially missing data, (iii) a very high resolution of the images. The importance

© Springer Nature Switzerland AG 2020
Ž. Špiclin et al. (Eds.): WBIR 2020, LNCS 12120, pp. 12–22, 2020.
https://doi.org/10.1007/978-3-030-50120-4_2

of the problem led to organizing an Automatic Non-rigid Histological Image Registration Challenge (ANHIR) [1–3], jointly with the IEEE ISBI 2019 conference. The provided dataset [1,4–7] consists of 481 image pairs annotated by experts, reasonably divided into the training (230) and the evaluation (251) set. There are 8 distinct tissue types that were stained using 10 different stains. The image size varies from 8k to 16k pixels in one dimension. The full dataset description, including the images size and the acquisition details, is available at [3]. The challenge organizers provide an independent, server-side evaluation tool that makes it possible to perform an objective comparison between participants and their solutions.

One of the most difficult subproblems for the challenge participants was to calculate the initial, global transform. It was a key to success and all the best scoring teams put a significant effort to do this correctly, resulting in algorithms based on combined brute force and iterative alignment [8,9], or applying a fixed number of random transformations [10]. In this work, we propose a method based on deep learning which makes the process significantly faster, more robust, without the necessity to manually find a set of parameters viable for all the image pairs.

Medical image registration is an important domain in medical image analysis. Much work was done in the area, resulting in good solutions to many important and challenging medical problems. Medical image registration can be divided into classical algorithms, involving an iterative optimization for each image pair [11] or learning-based algorithms where the transformations are being learned and then the registration is performed during the inference [12]. The main advantage of the learning-based approach over the classical, iterative optimization is a fast, usually real-time registration, which makes the algorithms more useful in clinical practice. During the ANHIR challenge the best scoring teams [8–10] used the classical approach. However, we think that it is reasonable to solve the problem using deep networks, potentially both improving the results and decreasing the computation time.

Deep learning-based medical image registration can be divided into three main categories, depending on the training procedure: (i) a supervised training [13,14], where a known transformation is applied and being reconstructed, (ii) an unsupervised training [15–17], where a given similarity metric with a proper regularization or penalty terms is being optimized, (iii) an adversarial training [18,19], where both a discriminator and a generator are being trained to not only find the correct transformation but also learn a correct similarity metric. All the approaches have their strengths and weaknesses. The supervised approach does not require to define a similarity metric, however, in the case of multi-modal registration, the images must be first registered manually or by using a classical algorithm. The transformations applied during training can be both synthetic or already calculated using the state-of-the-art algorithms. However, in the case of synthetic deformations, one must ensure that they correspond to the real deformations and in case of using deformation calculated by the state-of-the-art algorithms, it is unwise to expect better results, only a lower registration time. In the case of unsupervised training, a differentiable similarity metric must be defined which for many imaging modalities is not a trivial task [20]. However, if the similarity metric can be reliably defined, unsupervised training tends to provide a better generalization [17]. The adversarial approach, just like the supervised approach, does not require defining a similarity metric but it still requires a ground-truth alignment that for many medical problems can not be determined. The adversarial training provides much better generalization than the supervised one [19]. However, the disadvantage of the adversarial approach is the fact that training this kind of network is hard and much more time-consuming than the supervised/unsupervised alternatives because finding a good balance between the generator and the discriminator is usually a difficult, trial and error procedure.

We decided to use the unsupervised approach because: (i) the state-of-the-art similarity metrics can capture the similarity of the histological images well, (ii) it does not require ground-truth to train the network, (iii) it is easy to train and has a great generalization ability. Currently, the most widely used approach for training the registration networks is to resize all the training images to the same shape using both resampling and image padding. As much as resampling the images makes sense, especially considering the initial alignment where the fine details are often not necessary, the padding is usually not a good idea, especially when the aspect ratio is high. It results in a high image resolution with much empty, unused space that then requires a deeper network to ensure large enough receptive field [21]. Therefore, we propose a network that can be trained using images with substantially different resolutions, without the necessity to perform the padding, while maintaining a relatively low number of network parameters, almost independent of the image resolution.

In this work we propose a deep network to calculate the initial affine transform between histological images acquired using different dyes. The proposed algorithm: (i) works well for images with different resolution, aspects ratios and does not require image padding, (ii) generalizes well to the evaluation set, (iii) does not require the ground-truth transform during training, (iv) is orders of magnitude faster than the iterative or descriptor-based approach, (v) successfully aligns about 98% of the evaluation pairs. We achieved this by proposing a patch-based feature extraction with a variable batch size followed by a 3-D convolution combining the patch features and 2-D convolutions to enlarge the receptive field. We make both the training and inference code freely available [22].

2   Methods

2.1   General Aspects

The proposed method adheres strictly to the ANHIR challenge requirements, namely the method is fully automatic, robust and does not require any parameter tuning during the inference time. The method can be divided into a preprocessing and the following affine registration. Both steps are crucial for the correct registration. A step by step summary of the proposed registration procedure is described in Algorithm 1.

2.2 Preprocessing

The preprocessing consists of the following steps: (i) smoothing and resampling the images to a lower resolution using the same, constant factors for each image pair, (ii) segmenting the tissue from the background, (iii) converting the images to grayscale, (iv) finding an initial rotation angle by an iterative approach.

The smoothing and resampling is in theory not strictly mandatory. However, since the fine details are not necessary to find a correct initial alignment, it is unwise to use the full resolution due to high computational time and memory consumption. Both the resampling and the smoothing coefficients were determined empirically, without an exhaustive parameter tuning. The resampling preserves the aspect ratio. After the resampling, the size across the larger dimension varies from ~600 to ~2000 pixels, depending on the tissue type.

The next step is to remove the background. This procedure significantly improves the results for mammary glands or mice kidneys because there are staining artifacts in the background that have a strong influence on the similarity metric. In this work, we remove the background using smoothed Laplacian thresholding with a few morphological operations. It works for all the cases and more advanced background removal algorithms are not necessary. Nonetheless, this is data specific step. For other digital pathology data sets, this step may be unnecessary or can look differently (e.g. a stain deconvolution or deep learning-based segmentation).

Finally, after converting both images to grayscale, an initial rotation angle is being optimized. We decided to use a simple procedure similar to [8,9] because optimization of a single parameter can be done extremely fast and does not require any advanced optimization techniques. As a result, the network architecture can be much simpler and requires fewer parameters to capture the possible transformations. The initial rotation angle is being optimized by the iterative rotation of the source image around the translated center of mass, with a given, pre-defined angle step. Then, the angle with the largest global normalized cross-correlation (NCC) is used as the best one. In practice, this step calculation time depends on the predefined angle step and can be optimized by performing it using a GPU. However, even considering an unoptimized, single-core CPU implementation, the computational time of this step is negligible compared to the data loading, initial resampling, and background removal. The affine registration network was trained using the preprocessed data and therefore this step is required during inference.

2.3 Affine Registration

We propose a network architecture that is able to calculate the correct affine transformation in a single pass, independently of the image size and the aspect ratio. The idea behind the network is as follows. First, the images are passed to

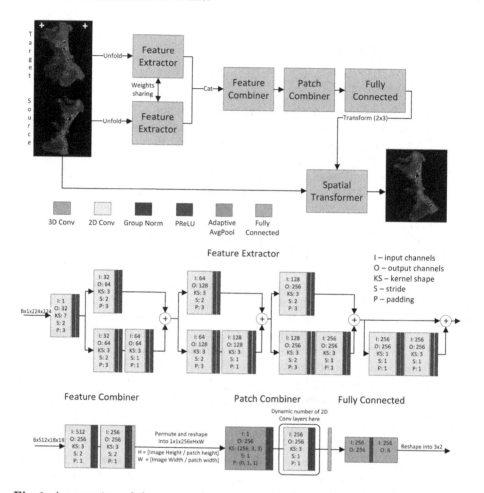

Fig. 1. An overview of the proposed network architecture. The source and target are unfolded and passed independently to the feature extractor where the batch size is equal to the number of patches after unfolding. Then, the extracted features are concatenated and passed to the feature combiner, patch combiner, and fully connected layers respectively. The whole network has slightly above 30 million parameters, independently of the input image size.

the network independently. They are unfolded to a grid of patches with a given, predefined size (224 × 224 in our case) and stride equal to the patch size, the patches do not overlap. Then, the patches are combined to a single tensor where the number of patches defines the batch size. This step is followed by a feature extraction by a relatively lightweight, modified ResNet-like architecture [23]. The feature extractor weights are shared between the source and the target. Then, the features are concatenated and passed through additional 2-D convolutions to combine the source and target into a single representation. Finally, the global correspondence is extracted by a 3-D convolution followed by a variable number of 2-D convolutions using the PyTorch dynamic graphs. The final step allows getting global information from the unfolded patches. The number of final 2-D convolutions depends on the image resolution and can be extended dynamically to enlarge the receptive field. In practice, on the resampled ANHIR dataset (the larger dimension contains from ~600 to ~2000 pixels) a single convolutional layer is sufficient. Eventually, the features are passed to adaptive average pooling and fully connected layers, which output the transformation matrix. The network architecture and the forward pass procedure is presented in Fig. 1. The number of parameters is slightly above 30 million, the forward pass memory consumption depends on the image resolution.

The proposed network is trained in a relatively unusual way. The batch is not strictly the number of pairs during a single pass through the network. The image pairs are given one by one and the loss is being backwarded after each of them. However, the optimizer is being updated only after a gradient of a given number of images (the real batch size) was already backpropagated. This approach makes its possible to use any real batch size during training but it requires an architectural change. Since all the image pairs have a different resolution, they are divided into a different number of patches during unfolding. As a result, it is incorrect to use the batch normalization layers because during inference they are unable to automatically choose the correct normalization parameters and strong overfitting is observed. Therefore, we replaced all the batch normalization layers by a group normalization [24], which solved the problem. One can argue that this approach significantly increases the training time. This is not the case because the batch size dimension after unfolding is sufficiently large to utilize the GPU correctly.

Algorithm 1. Algorithm Summary.

Input : M_p (moving image path), F_p (fixed image path)
Output: **T** (affine transformation (2x3 matrix)
1 **M, F** = load both the images from M_p and F_p
2 **M, F** = smooth and resample the images to a lower resolution using the same, constant factors for each image pair
3 **M, F** = segment the tissues from the background
4 **M, F** = convert the **M, F** images to the grayscale and invert the intensities
5 T_{rot} = find the initial rotation angle by an iterative approach which maximizes the NCC similarity metric between **M** and **F**
6 M_{rot} = warp **M** using T_{rot}
7 T_{aff} = pass M_{rot} and **F** through the proposed network to find the affine matrix
8 **T** = compose T_{rot} and T_{aff}
9 **return T**

The network was trained using an Adam optimizer, with a learning rate equal to 10^{-4} and a decaying scheduler after each epoch. The global negative NCC was used as the cost function. No difference was observed between the global

NCC and the patch-based NCC. Moreover, the results provided by NCC were better than MIND or NGF since the latter two are not scale-resistant and would require additional constraints. The dataset was augmented by random affine transformations applied both to the source and the target, including translating, scaling, rotating and shearing the images. The network was trained using only the training dataset consisting of 230 image pairs. The evaluation dataset consisting of 251 image pairs was used as a validation set. However, no decision was made based on the validation results. The network state after the last epoch was used for testing. Thanks to the augmentation, no overfitting was observed. Moreover, the loss on the validation set was lower than on the training set. No information about the landmarks from both the training and the validation set was used during the training. The source code, for both the inference and training, is available at [22].

3   Results

The proposed algorithm was evaluated using all the image pairs provided for the ANHIR challenge [1–3]. The data set is open and can be freely downloaded, so results are fully reproducible. For a more detailed data set description, including the tissue types, the procedure of the tissue staining and other important information, we refer to [3].

We evaluated the proposed algorithm using the target registration error between landmarks provided by the challenge organizers, normalized by the image diagonal, defined as:

$$rTRE = \frac{TRE}{\sqrt{w^2 + h^2}},\tag{1}$$

where TRE denotes the target registration error, w is the image width and h is the image height. We compare the proposed method to the most popular computer vision descriptors (SURF [25] and SIFT [26]) as well as the intensity-based, iterative affine registration [27]. All the methods were applied to the dataset after the preprocessing and the parameters were tuned to optimize the results. Unfortunately, we could not compare to initial alignment methods used by other challenge participants because the submission system reports only the final results after nonrigid registration. The cumulative histogram of the target registration error for the available landmarks is shown in Fig. 2. In Table 1 we summarize the rTRE for the evaluation set using the evaluation platform provided by the challenge organizers. We also show the success ratio and the affine registration time, excluding data loading and preprocessing time, which is the same for all the methods. As the success ratio, we define cases that are registered in a manner that can we followed by a converging, generic, nonrigid registration algorithm like B-Splines free form deformations or Demons. In Fig. 3 we show an exemplary case for which the proposed method is successful and the remaining methods failed or were unable to converge correctly.

Table 1. Quantitative results of the rTRE calculated using the ANHIR submission website [3] as well as the average processing time for the affine registration step. The success rate for the initial state shows the ratio of pairs not requiring the initial alignment.

	rTRE			Time [ms]	Success rate
	Median	Average	Max (Avg)	Average	[%]
Initial	0.056	0.105	0.183	–	31.15
Preprocessed	0.023	0.035	0.069	–	67.36
Proposed	0.010	0.025	0.060	4.51	98.34
SIFT [26]	0.005	0.085	0.174	422.65	79.21
SURF [25]	0.005	0.100	0.201	169.59	78.38
Iterative [27]	0.004	0.019	0.050	3241.15	97.30

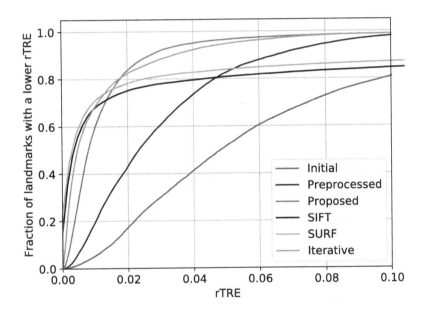

Fig. 2. The cumulative histogram of the target registration error for the proposed and compared methods. Please note that all the compared methods use the same preprocessing pipeline to make them comparable. We experimentally verified that the preprocessing does not deteriorate the results for the feature-based approach and significantly improves the results for the iterative registration.

Source   Target   Proposed   SIFT/SURF   Iterative

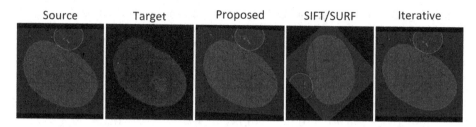

Fig. 3. An exemplary failure visualization of the evaluated methods. Please note that the calculated transformations were applied to the images before the preprocessing. It is visible that the feature-based approach failed and the iterative affine registration was unable to converge correctly.

4   Discussion and Conclusion

The proposed method works well for more than 98% of the ANHIR image pairs. It calculates a transformation that can be a good starting point for the following nonrigid registration. The registration time is significantly lower than using the iterative or feature-based approach. However, it should be noted that currently more than 99% of the computation time is spent on the data loading, initial smoothing, and resampling. This step could be significantly lowered by proposing a different data format, which already includes the resampled version of the images.

It can be noticed that both the iterative affine registration and the feature-based alignment provide slightly better results when they can converge correctly. However, the registration accuracy achieved by the proposed method is sufficient for the following nonrigid registration for which the gap between the proposed method and the iterative alignment is not that important. The proposed method is significantly faster and more robust, resulting in a higher success ratio, which in practice is more important than the slightly lower target registration error. The feature-based methods often fail and without a proper detection of the failures they cannot be used in a fully automatic algorithm. On the other hand, the proposed method does not suffer from this problem.

To conclude, we propose a method for an automatic, robust and fast initial affine registration of histology images based on a deep learning approach. The method works well for images with different aspect ratios, resolutions, generalizes well for the evaluation set and requires a relatively low number of the network parameters. We make the source code freely available [22]. The next step involves a deep network to perform the non-rigid registration, using the highest resolution provided by the challenge organizers. We think it is possible to solve this problem efficiently, even though a single image can take up to 1 GB of the GPU memory.

Acknowledgments. This work was funded by NCN Preludium project no. UMO-2018/29/N/ST6/00143 and NCN Etiuda project no. UMO-2019/32/T/ST6/00065.

References

1. Borovec, J., Munoz-Barrutia, A., Kybic, J.: Benchmarking of image registration methods for differently stained histological slides. In: IEEE International Conference on Image Processing, pp. 3368–3372 (2018)
2. Borovec, J., et al.: ANHIR: automatic non-rigid histological image registration challenge. IEEE Trans. Med. Imaging (2020)
3. Borovec, J., et al.: ANHIR website. https://anhir.grand-challenge.org
4. Fernandez-Gonzalez, R., et al.: System for combined three-dimensional morphological and molecular analysis of thick tissue specimens. Microsc. Res. Tech. **59**(6), 522–530 (2002)
5. Gupta, L., Klinkhammer, B., Boor, P., Merhof, D., Gadermayr, M.: Stain independent segmentation of whole slide images: a case study in renal histology. In: 2018 IEEE 15th International Symposium on Biomedical Imaging (ISBI), pp. 1360–1364 (2018)
6. Mikhailov, I., Danilova, N., Malkov, P.: The immune microenvironment of various histological types of EBV-associated gastric cancer. In: Virchows Archiv, vol. 473 (2018)
7. Bueno, G., Deniz, O.: AIDPATH: academia and industry collaboration for digital pathology. http://aidpath.eu
8. Lotz, J., Weiss, N., Heldmann, S.: Robust, fast and accurate: a 3-step method for automatic histological image registration. arXiv preprint arXiv:1903.12063 (2019)
9. Wodzinski, M., Skalski, A.: Automatic nonrigid histological image registration with adaptive multistep algorithm. arXiv preprint arXiv:1904.00982 (2019)
10. Venet, L., Pati, S., Yushkevich, P., Bakas, S.: Accurate and robust alignment of variable-stained histologic images using a general-purpose greedy diffeomorphic registration tool. arXiv preprint arXiv:1904.11929 (2019)
11. Sotiras, A., Davatzikos, C., Paragios, N.: Deformable medical image registration: a survey. IEEE Trans. Med. Imaging **32**(7), 1153–1190 (2013)
12. Haskins, G., Kruger, U., Yan, P.: Deep learning in medical image registration: a survey. arXiv preprint arXiv:1903.02026 (2019)
13. DeTone, D., Malisiewicz, T., Rabinovich, A.: Deep image homography estimation. arXiv preprint arXiv:1606.03798 (2016)
14. Chee, E., Wu, Z.: AIRNet: self-supervised affine registration for 3D medical images using neural networks. arXiv preprint arXiv:1810.02583 (2018)
15. de Vos, B., Berendsen, F., Viergever, M., Sokooti, H., Staring, M., Isgum, I.: A deep learning framework for unsupervised affine and deformable image registration. Med. Image Anal. **52**, 128–143 (2019)
16. Balakrishnan, G., Zhao, A., Sabuncu, M., Guttag, J., Dalca, A.: VoxelMorph: a learning framework for deformable medical image registration. IEEE Trans. Med. Imaging **38**(8), 1788–1800 (2019)
17. Dalca, A., Balakrishnan, G., Guttag, J., Sabuncu, M.: Unsupervised learning of probabilistic diffeomorphic registration for images and surfaces. Med. Image Anal. **57**, 226–236 (2019)
18. Fan, J., Cao, X., Wang, Q., Yap, P., Shen, D.: Adversarial learning for mono- or multi-modal registration. Med. Image Anal. **58**, 101545 (2019)
19. Mahapatra, D., Antony, B., Sedai, S., Garnavi, R.: Deformable medical image registration using generative adversarial networks. In: 2018 IEEE 15th International Symposium on Biomedical Imaging (ISBI), pp. 1449–1453 (2018)

20. Xiao, Y., et al.: Evaluation of MRI to ultrasound registration methods for brain shift correction: the CuRIOUS2018 challenge. IEEE Trans. Med. Imaging **39**(3), 777–786 (2019)
21. Luo, W., Li, Y., Urtasun, R., Zemel, R.: Understanding the effective receptive field in deep convolutional neural networks. In: Advances in Neural Information Processing Systems, pp. 4905–4913 (2016)
22. Wodzinski, M.: The source code. https://github.com/lNefarin/DeepHistReg
23. He, K., Zhang, X., Ren, S., Sun, J.: Deep residual learning for image recognition. In: Proceedings of the IEEE Conference on Computer Vision and Pattern Recognition (CVPR), pp. 770–778 (2016)
24. Wu, Y., He, K.: Group normalization. arXiv preprint arXiv:1803.084943 (2018)
25. Bay, H., Tuytelaars, T., Van Gool, L.: SURF: speeded up robust features. In: Leonardis, A., Bischof, H., Pinz, A. (eds.) ECCV 2006. LNCS, vol. 3951, pp. 404–417. Springer, Heidelberg (2006). https://doi.org/10.1007/11744023_32
26. Lowem, D.G.: Distinctive image features from scale-invariant keypoints. Int. J. Comput. Vis. **60**(2), 91–110 (2004)
27. Klein, S., Staring, M., Murphy, K., Viergever, M., Pluim, J.: elastix: a toolbox for intensity-based medical image registration. IEEE Trans. Med. Imaging **29**(1), 196–205 (2010)

Enabling Manual Intervention
for Otherwise Automated Registration
of Large Image Series

Roman Grothausmann[1,2]([✉]) [iD], Dženan Zukić[3] [iD], Matt McCormick[3] [iD],
Christian Mühlfeld[1,2], and Lars Knudsen[1,2]

[1] Institute of Functional and Applied Anatomy,
Hannover Medical School, Hannover, Germany
`grothausmann.roman@mh-hannover.de`
[2] Biomedical Research in Endstage and Obstructive Lung Disease Hannover
(BREATH), Hannover, Germany
[3] Kitware, Inc., Carrboro, NC, USA

Abstract. Aligning thousands of images from serial imaging techniques can be a cumbersome task. Methods ([2,11,21]) and programs for automation exist (e.g. [1,4,10]) but often need case-specific tuning of many meta-parameters (e.g. mask, pyramid-scales, denoise, transform-type, method/metric, optimizer and its parameters). Other programs, that apparently only depend on a few parameter often just hide many of the remaining ones (initialized with default values), often cannot handle challenging cases satisfactorily.

Instead of spending much time on the search for suitable meta-parameters that yield a usable result for the complete image series, the described approach allows to intervene by manually aligning problematic image pairs. The manually found transform is then used by the automatic alignment as an initial transformation that is then optimized as in the pure automatic case. Therefore the manual alignment does not have to be very precise. This way the worst case time consumption is limited and can be estimated (manual alignment of the whole series) in contrast to tuning of meta-parameters of pure auto-alignment of complete series which can hardly be guessed.

1 Introduction

The general approach to reconstruct 3D by 2D serial sections (also termed array tomography) is long known and can be applied with various imaging techniques [2,7,22,30]. This method has the common drawback that the images of the serial sections need to be aligned to the image of the adjacent slice. While this can be done manually with various programs (e.g. midas of IMOD, Fiji/ImageJ, VV, Gimp, PhotoShop), this can be very tedious labour. Although visual inspection seems easy, it often is hard to decide which transform is the "best", one reason being the fact that adjacent images in general contain similar but not equal

© Springer Nature Switzerland AG 2020
Ž. Špiclin et al. (Eds.): WBIR 2020, LNCS 12120, pp. 23–33, 2020.
https://doi.org/10.1007/978-3-030-50120-4_3

content due to the structure change in the 3rd dimension. This becomes of particular importance when employing registration allowing local deformations, because the natural 3D structure change is not meant to be corrected by local deformation.

Therefore, various procedures for digital automatic alignment have been investigated, which in general are based on finding a transformation that optimizes a metric (a well defined quantification in contrast to visually "best"). Many types of transformations, metrics and optimizers have been developed of which specific ones need to be chosen depending on the given data and desired results. Apart from the parameters of the transformation that get optimized during the processing, parameters of the chosen optimizer, metric and general ones such as denoising, size/shape of a mask and pyramid resolutions need to be set before the processing can start [4,10,32]. These parameters are referred to as meta-parameters and need to be tuned with expert knowledge in order to get an acceptable results for as many consecutive images as possible. The more serial sections the image series contains, the more difficult and time consuming this task can become. Experience shows, that for a series of a few hundred up to a few thousand realistic (i.e. non-ideal) images, the finding of suitable meta-parameters can take a few weeks, without a guarantee to succeed at all.

In order to have a better guarantee to succeed in practice, the procedure described in this paper limits the time consumption to that needed for a pure manual alignment of the whole series, while trying to use automation as much as possible.

2   Method

First Elastix [10], later SimpleElastix [16] was chosen as the framework that provides the means for automated registration. In general other implementation could be chosen, however Elastix (based on ITK [8]) already accepts initial transformations. Even if an initial transformation is provided by manual alignment, it can still enter the automatic optimization and therefore get improved quantitatively as in the default case of pure automated optimization. In other words, if the automated optimization gets trapped in a local optimum i.e. fails to find the global optimum, a manual initial transform provides a different start point for the optimization such that the global optimum is reached.

The work presented here is based on three distinct pieces of software:

1. The Python-implemented registration program `recRegStack.py` which employs SimpleElastix.[1]
2. Extra programs and commands needed to convert gigapixel slice scans from a Carl Zeiss slide scanner (in CZI fromat) to an image series usable by `recRegStack.py`.

---

[1] http://github.com/romangrothausmann/elastix_scripts/.

3. A build and invocation system to apply these to a full-size image series, with adjustments needed for the specific data at hand, using gnuplot [31] and GNU Parallel [29].[2]

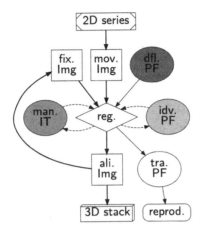

Fig. 1. Processing dependencies

Schematic flow graph to visualize the dependencies involved in the iterative process. Images are represented by squares, text-files by ovals. The parameters used by default (dfl. PF, dPF) during the registration (reg.) need to be tuned for the integral image series (2D series) in order to reduce the need for manual interactions. The first image at the start is copied unchanged. The last aligned image (ali. Img) is used as fixed image (fix. Img, fI) for registering the next image from the series (mov. Img, mI). In the case that the default parameters do not yield an acceptable result for an individual image pair, it is possible to supply a manual initial transform (man. iT, mIT) and/or provide individual registration parameters (idv. PF, iPF). Tuning the default parameters (dPF) is the most difficult (time consuming, red) task, adjusting some individual parameters less problematic (iPF, yellow) while creating a manual initial transform (mIT, green) with e.g. midas is easiest. In case some images need to be re-scanned (due to scan-artefacts, defocus, etc), the transform parameter files (tra. PF, tPF) can be used to register the new image exactly the same way (reprod.) or the registration process can be re-initiated to make use of the improved image quality.

recRegStack.py takes an Elastix/ITK parameter file (containing the definition of various meta-parameters) into account, which allows changing the default values used by SimpleElastix. The last transformed image is used to register the following one, see Fig. 1.

For the proof of principle, midas of the IMOD package [19] was chosen for manual alignment due to its superior precision and interaction possibilities. Manually created initial transform files (mITs, Fig. 1) will then be taken into account

---

[2] http://github.com/romangrothausmann/CZIto3D.

by `recRegStack.py` when continuing the automated alignment. In addition, it is possible to adjust the meta-parameters for individual image pairs (iPF, Fig. 1) in case the mIT together with the global defaults (dPF, Fig. 1) do not lead to a satisfactory result.[3] This can happen for example if the fixed image (fI) and the moving image (mI) come from different section bands, possibly differing significantly in focus quality.

3   Application and Results

The described approach was applied to an image series of about 2600 histological serial section of lung tissue (rat, details can be found in [27]), referred to as K2-dataset. An EM UC7 microtome (Leica, Germany) was used to cut semi-thin sections with a thickness of 1 μm connected to bands of about 1 to 20 sections. These bands were placed on 177 glass slides (where possible as a single row)

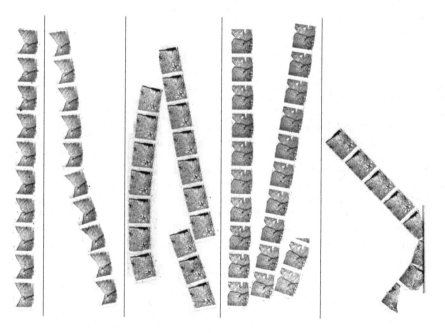

Fig. 2. Bands of serial sections of stained lung tissue on glass slides
Some exemplary thumbnails of slide scans with bands of serial sections of lung tissue stained on glass slides. Ranging from good (left, one band well aligned and no significant staining variations) to bad (right, broken bands with unobvious order, staining variations and slice loss due to folds and extending slide border). Lines indicate different glass slide.

---

[3] The iPF also allows to suppress further auto adjustments of an mIT in case the global optimum does not represent the correct transformation, which can happen for very destorted slices with repetitive, similar structures.

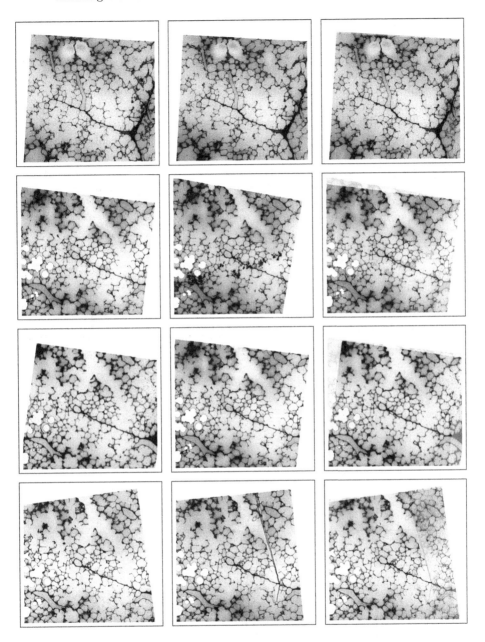

Fig. 3. Exemplary image pairs

Left column: fixed image, middle column: moving image, right column: Magenta-Green overlay of the image pair (similar to midas). Image pair rows:

1. ideal (no mIT or iPF needed).
2. dirt (mIT but no iPF needed).
3. defocus (no mIT or iPF needed).
4. folds (no mIT or iPF needed).

Metric for 3 without mIT is 34974 and with mIT 20214. (Color figure online)

see Fig. 2. After staining with toluidine blue, the slides were digitalized at a magnification of 10X by an AxioScan Z1 (Zeiss, Germany) using a single-channel fluorescence camera with a very low transmission light in order to get greyscale images (in CZI format) with a dynamic range above 8-bits.

The build and invocation system for this image series can be found in http:// gitlab.com/romangrothausmann/K2_fibrosis/. This git repository holds references to the raw-data (CZIs) in an annex (https://git-annex.branchable.com/), imports http://github.com/romangrothausmann/CZIto3D as a subtree for local adjustments as needed for the specific data and serves as processing protocol. `recRegStack.py` from http://github.com/romangrothausmann/elastix_scripts/ is invoked via a docker-image (http://www.docker.com/) containing all the needed libraries to reproducibly register the images. There is a short (downscaled) image series for testing in tests/recRegStack/.

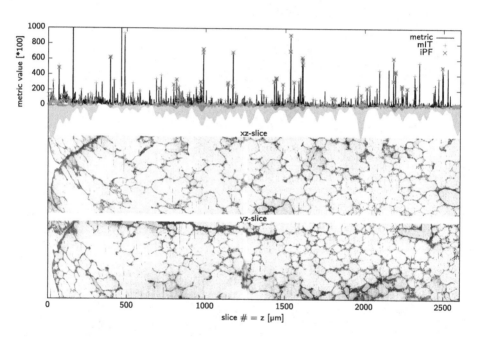

Fig. 4. Plot of metric values with markers for mIT and iPF
The point densities of mITs and iPFs are visualized with kernel density plots on the negative y-axis (unrelated to metric value, $\sigma = 10$). Mean of metric: ≈ 4100, Std. Dev.: ≈ 9300, some values are outside of the plot range, iPFs (52) are needed less often then mITs (621), mostly in cases of high metric values. The largest interval without any manual intervention (no mITs) is from 305 to 393 even though the default parameter file (dPF) was tuned at different locations (e.g. slice 929, 1266 and 1379). The centre xz- and yz-slice of the result stack (as shown in Fig. 5) are plotted for comparison. Distortions due to alignment drift can be seen, especially in the xz-slice up to slice 500.

Fiji [6] was used to roughly mark the centre of each section in thumbnail images of the gigapixel scans (czi2stack/Makefile). These centres were then used to automatically extract the region of each slice as its own image (3000 x 3000 pixel, PNG) with bfconvert [23] (czi2stack/Makefile). In case of broken bands, the ordering implied by the centre marks had to be adjusted to match the physical order (czi2stack/slides/slideOrder.lst, discrepancies often only visible after a registration). This order was then used to register the consecutive slices (czi2stack/Makefile). The mask for registration and the default parameter file (dPF) were adjusted to fit the K2-dataset, applying rigid registration using a "MultiResolutionRegistration" with "AdvancedMeanSquares" metric and "AdaptiveStochasticGradientDescent" as optimizer, see czi2stack/parameterFile.txt for details. Still, 621 mITs (in average every 4th image) and 52 iPFs (in average every 50th image) were needed to align all 2607 images, see Fig. 4. Some exemplary image pairs (good, dirt, defocus, folds) are shown in Fig. 3. Since the registration reconstructs the spatial correspondence in the 3rd dimension, the resulting image stack can then be regarded as a 3D dataset of 3000 x 3000 x 2607 voxel (about 44 GB @ 16-bit), see Fig. 5.

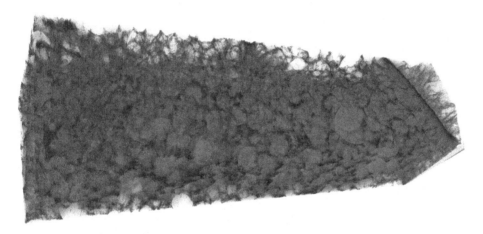

Fig. 5. Volume rendering of the 3D stack
Volume rendered visualization of the reconstructed 3rd dimension of the lung tissue block (sub-extent of $1000 \times 1000 \times 2607$ voxel). Tissue dark, resin semi-transparent grey (airspaces and blood vessels).

The volume in lung samples occupied by tissue is only about 10%–20% [3,7], so there is about 90%–80% mostly non-correlating texture in image pairs which disturbs the registration process. This is one reason why the registration of serial sections of lung tissue is challenging. A possible countermeasure is to "fill" the non-tissue space with (roughly) correlating data. This can be achieved by first auto-thresholding the image to roughly binarize tissue and non-tissue and then generating a distance map, which is implemented in the branch ot+dm and leads to image pairs as in Fig. 6. However, applying this version of `recRegStack.py` to the K2-dataset (K2_fibrosis@a5617581) showed, that more mITs are needed.[4] A reason for this might be that this approach is more sensitive to dirt, which ends up in the tissue segment and therefore causes significant disturbance in the distance transform, see Fig. 6. Another promising approach could be registration based on landmarks generated by SIFT [14, 15], similar to Fiji's "Register Virtual Stack Slices" [4] but using Elastix/ITK in order to keep the features of manual intervention (mIT and iPF)[5].

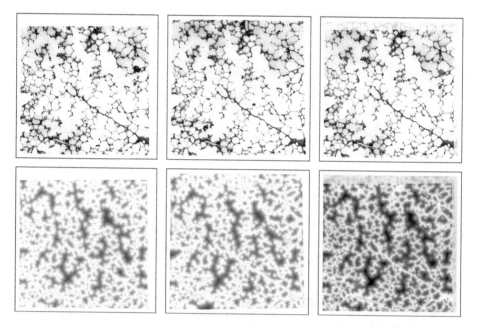

Fig. 6. Exemplary image pair for ot+dm variant
Top row: image pair as is (no mIT or iPF needed), fixed image, moving image, Magenta-Green overlay. Bottom row: ot+dm image pair for images on the left (blue-white-red LUT from -50 to 50, blue: air, blood space; red: tissue, dirt). (Color figure online)

---

[4] A full alignment with ot+dm was not pursued further because currently SimpleITK of SimpleElastix does not allow to set a mask for the otsu-threshold calculation (ot-mask). Therefore, the continuation feature of `recRegStack.py` cannot be used so that after each mIT creation the registration has to start from the beginning and therefore the whole procedure needs much more time. An alternative would be to port `recRegStack.py` to ITKElastix.

[5] The lack of the possibility for manual intervention and a trial of more than two weeks to find meta-parameters to register the K2-dataset with Fiji's "Register Virtual Stack Slices" was actually the motivation for implementing `recRegStack.py`.

4   Discussion

The described proof of principle combines automated alignment with manual intervention such that ideally the automation does the whole work but also ensures that "in the worst case" at least the result of a pure manual alignment will be achieved. This comes with a need to balance the two time consuming tasks: Either tuning the meta-parameters for the automated alignment of as many images in the series as possible (total time consumption can be unlimited) or helping the automation with initial manual alignments (total time is limited).

While the current implementation with Makefiles serves as a proof of principle, it can be further improved to a more intuitive and user-friendly program. For example, by incorporating the processing done by various commands into the Python code, as well as avoiding `midas` and other IMOD-tools or aborting auto alignment in order to provide a manual alignment to continue with. A graphical user interface (GUI) could provide visual feedback (similar to the image viewer `geeqie`), incorporate the needed `midas` functionality and offer a "manual intervention" button. In principle, a threshold on the final metric value could be used to automatically trigger the suggestion of a manual alignment.

Another variant of `recRegStack.py` (branch combT_01) accumulates all former transforms and adds the newly found transform of the processed image pair as in [21]. While the two approaches should yield similar results, accumulation of a few hundred transforms can become problematic but in return can avoid larger differences in case of already similarly recorded image pairs. A third variant (branch reg2tra+prevTra) uses both approaches and chooses the result with the better metric value finally achieved.

Ideally, a (non-destructive) tomogram or some form of markers should be used for guiding 3D reconstruction of serial sections (e.g. constrain local deformation corrections and avoid continuous drift), such functionality is offered by e.g. HistoloZee [1].

`recRegStack.py` provides the option to ignore some images of the series in case some slices are too distorted for registration or lost during the preparation (czi2stack/lostSlieds.lst). After aligning the next usable image of the series, a reconstruction of the lost slice can be created from the adjacent slices [14].

Acknowledgement. Special thanks go to Susanne Faßbender (for excellent technical assistance), Lena Ziemann (for slide scanning and creation of mITs and iPFs), Kasper Marstal, Fabien Pertuy, Stefan Klein and Marius Staring (for feedback on use of Elastix, SimpleElastix and debugging) and to David Mastronarde, Daniel Adler (for feedback on IMOD and HistoloZee details) and Oleg Lobachev (for feedback on the general approach).

References

1. Adler, D., Yushkevich, P.: HistoloZee, Penn Image Computing and Science Laboratory (PICSL), University of Pennsylvania. http://picsl.upenn.edu/software/histolozee/

2. Arganda-Carreras, I., Fernàndez-Gonzàlez, R., Muñoz-Barrutia, A., Ortiz-De-Solorzano, C.: 3D reconstruction of histological sections: application to mammary gland tissue. Microsc. Res. Tech. **73**(11), 1019–1029 (2010). https://doi.org/10.1002/jemt.20829
3. Buchacker, T., et al.: Assessment of the alveolar capillary network in the postnatal mouse lung in 3D using serial block-face scanning electron microscopy. Front. Physiol. **10**, (2019). https://doi.org/10.3389/fphys.2019.01357
4. Cardona, A., Arganda-Carreras, I., Saalfeld, S.: Register Virtual Stack Slices (Fiji). http://imagej.net/Register_Virtual_Stack_Slices
5. Cheung, W., Hamarneh, G.: n-SIFT: n-dimensional scale invariant feature transform. IEEE Trans. Image Process. **18**(9), 2012–2021 (2009). https://doi.org/10.1109/TIP.2009.2024578
6. Fiji/ImageJ development team: Fiji (ImageJ), see [25, 26]. http://fiji.sc
7. Grothausmann, R., Knudsen, L., Ochs, M., Mühlfeld, C.: Digital 3D reconstructions using histological serial sections of lung tissue including the alveolar capillary network. Am. J. Physiol.- Lung Cell. Mol. Physiol. **312**(2), L243–L257 (2017). https://doi.org/10.1152/ajplung.00326.2016
8. Ibanez, L., et al.: ITK, see [10, 33]. Kitware Inc. http://www.itk.org
9. Johnson, H.J., McCormick, M.M., Ibànez, L.: The Insight Software Consortium: The ITK Software Guide. Kitware Inc., Clifton Park (2018)
10. Klein, S., Staring, M.: elastix, see [12, 27]. Image Sciences Institute, University Medical Center Utrecht. http://elastix.isi.uu.nl/
11. Klein, S., Staring, M., Murphy, K., Viergever, M.A., Pluim, J.P.: elastix: a toolbox for intensity-based medical image registration. IEEE Trans. Med. Imaging **29**(1), 196–205 (2010). https://doi.org/10.1109/TMI.2009.2035616
12. Kremer, J.R., Mastronarde, D.N., McIntosh, J.R.: Computer visualization of three-dimensional image data using IMOD. J. Struct. Biol. **116**(1), 71–76 (1996). https://doi.org/10.1006/jsbi.1996.0013
13. Linkert, M., et al.: Metadata matters: access to image data in the real world. J. Cell Biol. **189**(5), 777–782 (2010). https://doi.org/10.1083/jcb.201004104
14. Lobachev, O.: The tempest in a cubic millimeter: image-based refinements necessitate the reconstruction of 3D microvasculature from a large series of damaged alternately-stained histological sections. IEEE Access (2020). https://doi.org/10.1109/access.2020.2965885
15. Lowe, D.G.: Object recognition from local scale-invariant features. **2**, 1150–1157 (1999). https://doi.org/10.1109/ICCV.1999.790410
16. Marstal, K.: SimpleElastix, see [18]. Image Sciences Institute, University Medical Center Utrecht. http://simpleelastix.github.io/
17. Marstal, K., Berendsen, F., Staring, M., Klein, S.: SimpleElastix: a userfriendly, multi-lingual library for medical image registration. In: Schnabel, J., Mori, K. (eds.) International Workshop on Biomedical Image Registration (WBIR). IEEE Conference on Computer Vision and Pattern Recognition Workshops, pp. 574–582, Las Vegas, Nevada, USA (2016)
18. Mastronarde, D.N.: Dual-axis tomography: an approach with alignment methods that preserve resolution. J. Struct. Biol. **120**(3), 343–352 (1997). https://doi.org/10.1006/jsbi.1997.3919
19. Mastronarde, D.N.: IMOD, see [21, 19, 13]. http://bio3d.colorado.edu/imod/
20. Mastronarde, D.N., Held, S.R.: Automated tilt series alignment and tomographic reconstruction in IMOD. J. Struct. Biol. **197**(2), 102–113 (2017). https://doi.org/10.1016/j.jsb.2016.07.011. SI: Electron Tomography

21. Mueller, D., Vossen, D., Hulsken, B.: Real-time deformable registration of multi-modal whole slides for digital pathology. Comput. Med. Imaging Graph. **35**(7–8), 542–556 (2011). https://doi.org/10.1016/j.compmedimag.2011.06.006

22. Ochs, M., Knudsen, L., Hegermann, J., Wrede, C., Grothausmann, R., Mühlfeld, C.: Using electron microscopes to look into the lung. Histochem. Cell Biol. **146**(6), 695–707 (2016). https://doi.org/10.1007/s00418-016-1502-z

23. Open Microscopy Environment: bftools (scripts using Bio-Formats), see [14]. https://docs.openmicroscopy.org/bio-formats/5.7.2/users/comlinetools/index.html

24. Schindelin, J., et al.: Fiji: an open-source platform for biological-image analysis. Nat. Methods **9**(7), 676–682 (2012). https://doi.org/10.1038/nmeth.2019

25. Schneider, C.A., Rasband, W.S., Eliceiri, K.W.: NIH Image to ImageJ: 25 years of image analysis. Nat. Method **9**(7), 671–675 (2012). https://doi.org/10.1038/nmeth.2089

26. Shamonin, D., Bron, E., Lelieveldt, B., Smits, M., Klein, S., Staring, M.: Fast parallel image registration on CPU and GPU for diagnostic classification of Alzheimer's disease. Front. Neuroinform. **7**, 50 (2014). https://doi.org/10.3389/fninf.2013.00050

27. Steffen, L., et al.: Surfactant replacement therapy reduces acute lung injury and collapse induration-related lung remodeling in the bleomycin model. Am. J. Physiol.-Lung Cell. Mol. Physiol. **313**(2), L313–L327 (2017). https://doi.org/10.1152/ajplung.00033.2017

28. Tange, O.: GNU parallel - the command-line power tool. Login: The USENIX Mag. **36**(1), 42–47 (2011)

29. Tange, O.: GNU parallel - the command-line power tool, see [29]. http://www.gnu.org/s/parallel/

30. Wang, C.-W., Gosno, E.B., Li, Y.-S.: Fully automatic and robust 3D registration of serial-section microscopic images. Sci. Rep. **5**, 15051 (2015). https://doi.org/10.1038/srep15051

31. Williams, T., Kelley, C.: gnuplot. http://gnuplot.sourceforge.net/docs_4.4/gnuplot.pdf

32. Yoo, T., et al.: Insight into Images: Principles and Practice for Segmentation, Registration, and Image Analysis. A K Peters Ltd., Natick (2004)

Towards Segmentation and Spatial Alignment of the Human Embryonic Brain Using Deep Learning for Atlas-Based Registration

Wietske A. P. Bastiaansen[1,2(✉)], Melek Rousian[2],
Régine P. M. Steegers-Theunissen[2], Wiro J. Niessen[1],
Anton Koning[3], and Stefan Klein[1]

[1] Departments of Radiology and Medical Informatics, Biomedical Imaging Group
Rotterdam, Erasmus MC, Rotterdam, Netherlands
`w.bastiaansen@erasmusmc.nl`
[2] Department of Obstetrics and Gynecology, Erasmus MC, Rotterdam, Netherlands
[3] Department of Pathology, Erasmus MC, Rotterdam, Netherlands

Abstract. We propose an unsupervised deep learning method for atlas-based registration to achieve segmentation and spatial alignment of the embryonic brain in a single framework. Our approach consists of two sequential networks with a specifically designed loss function to address the challenges in 3D first trimester ultrasound. The first part learns the affine transformation and the second part learns the voxelwise nonrigid deformation between the target image and the atlas. We trained this network end-to-end and validated it against a ground truth on synthetic datasets designed to resemble the challenges present in 3D first trimester ultrasound. The method was tested on a dataset of human embryonic ultrasound volumes acquired at 9 weeks gestational age, which showed alignment of the brain in some cases and gave insight in open challenges for the proposed method. We conclude that our method is a promising approach towards fully automated spatial alignment and segmentation of embryonic brains in 3D ultrasound.

Keywords: Image registration · Segmentation · Alignment ·
Embryonic brain · Ultrasound · Unsupervised · Deep learning

1 Introduction

Ultrasound imaging is prominent in prenatal screening since it is noninvasive, real-time, safe, and has low cost compared to other imaging modalities [10]. However the processing of ultrasound data is challenging due to low image quality, high variability of positions and orientations of the embryo, and the presence of the umbilical cord, placenta, and uterine wall. We propose a method to spatially align and segment the embryonic brain using atlas-based image registration in one unsupervised deep learning framework.

Ž. Špiclin et al. (Eds.): WBIR 2020, LNCS 12120, pp. 34–43, 2020.
https://doi.org/10.1007/978-3-030-50120-4_4

Learning based spatial alignment and segmentation in prenatal ultrasound has been addressed before. In Namburete [11] a supervised multi-task approach was presented, which employed prior knowledge of the orientation of the head in the volume, annotated slices, and manual segmentations of the head and eye. Spatial alignment and segmentation was achieved on fetal US scans acquired at 22 till 30 weeks gestational age. Atlas-based registration was proposed by Kuklisova-Murgasova [9] where a MRI atlas and block matching was used to register ultrasound images of fetuses of 23 till 28 week gestational age. Finally Schmidt [13] proposed a CNN and deformable shape models to segment the abdomen in 3D fetal ultrasound. All these works focus on ultrasound data acquired during the second trimester or later and rely on manual annotations. Ground truth segmentations for our application were not available and are laborious to obtain, which motivated our unsupervised approach.

Developing methods for processing of ultrasound data acquired during the first trimester is of great clinical relevance, since the periconception period (14 weeks before till 10 weeks after conception) is of crucial importance for future health [15]. Therefore our method is developed for first trimester ultrasound.

Recently there has been quite some attention for unsupervised deep learning approaches for image registration, since these methods circumvent the need for manual annotations. Several methods were developed to learn dense nonrigid deformations under the assumption that the data is affinely registered [2,17]. Employing multi-level or multi-stage methods, affine registration can also be included [6,7,16]. The framework presented here is based on the method presented in [2] and follows the idea of [6,7,16] to dedicate part of the network to learn the affine transformation.

To the best of our knowledge this is the first work that addresses the development of a framework for the alignment and segmentation of the embryonic brain, captured by ultrasound during the first trimester, applying unsupervised deep learning methods for atlas-based registration. Segmentation and alignment are important preprocessing steps for any image analysis task, hence this method contributes to our ultimate goal: further improve precision medicine of human brain disorders from the earliest moment in life.

2   Method

Let I and A be two images defined in the n-D spatial domains $(\Omega_I, \Omega_A) \in \mathbb{R}^n$, with I the target image and A the atlas. Both images contain single-channel grayscale data. Assume that A is in standard orientation and the segmentation S_A is available. Our aim is to find two deformations ϕ_a and ϕ_d such that:

$$A(x) \approx I\left(\phi_a \circ \phi_d(x)\right) \quad \forall x \in \Omega_A, \tag{1}$$

where ϕ_a is an affine transformation and ϕ_d a voxelwise nonrigid deformation.

To obtain ϕ_a and ϕ_d a convolutional neural network (CNN) is used to model the function $g_\theta \colon (\phi_a, \phi_d) = g_\theta(I, A)$, with θ the network parameters. The affine transformation $\phi_a := Tx$ is learned as a m-dimensional[1] vector containing the coefficients of the affine transformation matrix $T \in \mathbb{R}^{(n+1)\times(n+1)}$. The voxelwise nonrigid deformation is defined as a displacement field $u(x)$ with $\phi_d := x + u(x)$.

Figure 1 provides an overview of our method. The input of the network is an image pair consisting of the atlas A and target image I. The first part of the network outputs ϕ_a and the affine registered image $I(\phi_a(x))$. The input of the second part is the affinely registered image together with atlas A. The final output of the network consists of ϕ_a, ϕ_d, along with the registered and segmented target image $I_{S_A}(\phi_a \circ \phi_d(x)) = S_A(x) \cdot I(\phi_a \circ \phi_d(x))$ and the affinely registered image $I(\phi_a(x))^2$.

Since this is an unsupervised method no ground truth deformations are used for training. The parameters θ are found by optimizing the loss function on the training set. The proposed loss function is described in the next section. After training, a new image I can be given to the network together with the atlas to obtain the registration.

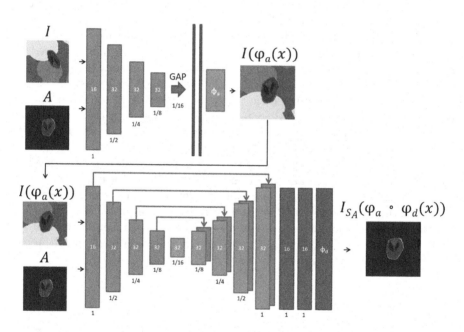

Fig. 1. Architecture of our network. Light blue: convolutional layers with a stride of 2 (encoder). Green: convolutional layers with stride of 1, skip-connection, up-sampling layer (decoder). Purple: fully connected layers with 500 neurons and ReLU activation. Dark blue: convolutional layers at full resolution. Orange: ϕ_a, red: ϕ_d. All convolutional layers have a kernel size of 3 and have a LeakyReLU with parameter 0.2. (Color figure online)

---

[1] For $n = 2$, $m = 6$ and for $n = 3$, $m = 12$.
[2] Note that $I(\phi_a(x))$ is not segmented, since this is an intermediate result.

2.1   Network Architecture

The target image I and atlas A are fed to the network as a two-channel image. The first part of the network consists of an encoder where the images are down-sampled, followed by a global average pooling layer. The global average pooling layer outputs one feature per feature map, which forces the network to encode position and orientation globally, and is followed by fully connected layers. The output layer consists of the entries of the affine transformation matrix T. The architecture of the second part of the network is the same as Voxelmorph [2] and consists of an encoder and decoder and convolutional layers at full resolution. The output layer contains the dense displacement field $u(x)$.

The method is implemented using Keras [3] with Tensorflow backend [1]. The ADAM optimizer is used with a learning rate of 10^{-4}. Each training batch consist of one pair of volumes and by default we use 500 epochs.

2.2   The Loss Function

The loss function is defined as follows:

$$\mathcal{L}(A, I, \phi_d, \phi_a) = \mathcal{L}_{\text{sim}}\left[A, I\left(\phi_a \circ \phi_d(x)\right)\right] + \lambda_{\text{diffusion}}\mathcal{L}_{\text{diffusion}}\left[\phi_d\right] \\ + \lambda_{\text{scaling}}\mathcal{L}_{\text{scaling}}\left[\phi_a\right]. \tag{2}$$

The first term promote intensity based similarity between the atlas and the deformed image, the second and third therm regularize ϕ_d and respectively ϕ_a. Each term is discussed in detail below.

Since in 3D first trimester ultrasound there are other objects in the volumes besides the brain, the similarity terms are only calculated within the region of interest defined by segmentation of the atlas S_A. $\mathcal{L}_{\text{sim}}$ is chosen as either the mean squared error (MSE) or cross-correlation (CC). They are defined as follows:

$$\text{MSE}(A, Y) = \frac{1}{M}\sum_{p\in\Omega} W(p) \cdot (A(p) - Y(p))^2 \tag{3}$$

$$\text{CC}(A, Y) =$$

$$\frac{1}{M}\sum_{p\in\Omega} W(p) \cdot \frac{\left(\sum_{p_i}[A(p_i) - \bar{A}(p)][Y_{S_A}(p_i) - \bar{Y}_{S_A}(p)]\right)^2}{\left(\sum_{p_i}[A(p_i) - \bar{A}(p)]^2\right)\left(\sum_{p_i}[Y_{S_A}(p_i) - \bar{Y}_{S_A}(p)]^2\right)}, \tag{4}$$

where M is the number of nonzero elements in W, unless stated otherwise $W = S_A$, the subscript S_A indicates segmented, $\bar{A}$ and $\bar{Y}$ denote: $\bar{A}(p) = A(p) - \frac{1}{j^3}\sum_{p_i} A(p_i)$, where p_i iterates over a j^3 volume around $p \in \Omega$ with $j = 9$ as in [2].

Image registration is an ill-posed problem; therefore regularization is needed. ϕ_d is regularized by:

$$\mathcal{L}_{\text{diffusion}}(u) = \frac{1}{M}\sum_{p\in\Omega} \|\nabla u(p)\|^2, \tag{5}$$

which penalizes local spatial variations in ϕ_d to promote smooth local deformations [4].

Initial experiments revealed that, when objects in the background of the target image are present, the affine transformation degenerate towards extreme compression or expansion. To prevent this, extreme zooming is penalized as regularization for ϕ_a. The zooming factors must be extracted for $T(x)$. This is done using the Singular Value Decomposition (SVD) [5], which states that any square matrix $T \in \mathbb{R}^{n \times n}$ can be decomposed in the following way:

$$T = U \Sigma V^*, \tag{6}$$

where the diagonal matrix Σ contains non-negative real singular values representing the zooming factors. The scaling loss is defined as:

$$\mathcal{L}_{\text{scaling}} = \|\text{Diag}(\Sigma) - S\|_1. \tag{7}$$

with S an n-dimensional vector containing ones.

For $\lambda_{\text{diffusion}}$ and λ_{scaling} the optimal values must be chosen. This is addressed in the experiments.

3   Data

The following three datasets were used in the experiments.

3.1   Synthetic 2D Dataset 1

To develop and validate our method against a ground truth, we created two synthetic 2D datasets. These synthetic datasets were created by affinely transforming and nonrigidly deforming the synthetic atlas. As synthetic atlas the Shepp-Logan phantom [14] is used, which was nonrigidly deformed. The first dataset was created by first applying a random affine transformation $\bar{\phi}_a^{-1}$ on the atlas, followed by a nonrigid deformation $\bar{\phi}_d^{-1}$.

The coefficients for the affine transformation matrix $\bar{\phi}_a^{-1}(x) := T_{gt}^{-1}x$ were drawn as follows: translation coefficients t_x, $t_y \in [0, 40]$ pixels, rotation angle $\theta \in [0, 360]$ degrees, anisotropic zooming factors z_x, $z_y \in [0.5, 1.5]$, and shear stress in the x direction $\theta_s \in [0, 30]$ degrees. The nonrigid deformation $\bar{\phi}_d^{-1}(x) := x + \alpha u_{gt}^{-1}(x)$ was generated using a normalized random displacement field $u_{gt}^{-1}(x)$, were α defines the magnitude of the displacement. The smoothness of $u_{gt}^{-1}(x)$ is controlled using σ, representing the standard deviation of the Gaussian, which was convolved with $u(x)$. We used $\alpha = 40$, and $\sigma \in [3, 7]$.

3.2   Synthetic 2D Dataset 2

The second synthetic dataset was created in the same manner as the first, with additionally a background consisting of ellipses which have a random size and orientation. The ellipses are around, behind and adjacent to the synthetic atlas, to mimic the presence of the uterine wall around the embryo, and the body of the embryo attached to the head. Both datasets contain 3000 training, 100 validation and 100 test images.

3.3 3D Ultrasound Data: Rotterdam Periconceptional Cohort

The Rotterdam Periconceptional Cohort (Predict study) is a large hospital-based cohort study embedded in tertiary patient care of the department of Obstetrics and Gynaecology, at the Erasmus MC, University Medical Center Rotterdam, the Netherlands. This prospective cohort focuses on the relationships between periconceptional maternal and paternal health and fetal growth development, and underlying (epi)genetics [15].

Scans collected at 9 weeks gestational age were used as proof of concept for our method. The image chosen as atlas was put in standard orientation and had sufficient quality to segment the embryo and brain semi-automatically using Virtual Reality [12]. There were 170 3D ultrasound scans available with sufficient quality, 140 are used for training and 30 for testing. All scans were padded with zeros and re-scaled to $64 \times 64 \times 64$ voxels to speed up training.

Since 140 scans is not sufficient for training, data augmentation was applied. When considering a 2D slice, the embryo is either visible in the coronal, saggital, or axial view. To keep this property during augmentation, first an axis was selected at random and a rotation was applied of either 90, 180 or 270 degrees. Subsequently a random rotation on this axis was applied between 0 and 30 degrees followed by a translation $t_x, t_y, t_z \in [-15, 15]$ and anisotropic zooming $z_x, z_y, z_z \in [0.9, 1.3]$. Each volume was augmented 30 times and this resulted in 4340 images for training.

4 Experiments

To validate our method three experiments are performed.

1. Comparison with Voxelmorph [2] on synthetic dataset 1 and $\mathcal{L}_{\text{sim}} = \text{MSE}$. Goal: evaluate influence of adding a dedicated part of the network for affine registration on images where the object of interest has a wide variation in position and orientation.
2. Evaluation of hyperparameters in loss function Eq. (2) on synthetic dataset 2 and $\mathcal{L}_{\text{sim}} = \text{MSE}$. Goal: set $\lambda_{\text{diffusion}}$ and λ_{scaling} in the presence of objects in the background.
3. Testing method on 3D ultrasound data acquired at 9 weeks gestational age with $\mathcal{L}_{\text{sim}} = \text{CC}$ and different types of atlases as input for the network. $\mathcal{L}_{\text{sim}} = CC$ is used, since it is well known that the cross-correlation is more robust to intensity variations and noise.

The main difference between the synthetic data and ultrasound data is that for the synthetic data the atlas is the only object with a clear structure, while the ultrasound data is noisy and more structures similar to the embryonic brain are present, for example the body of the embryo. The body of the embryo is also a prominent round structured shape. To address this, in the third experiment the influence of using an atlas containing the whole embryo versus only the brain is evaluated. Using the atlas containing the whole embryo as input gives more information for alignment. However we aim at registering only the brain, since this is our region of interest and registering the whole embryo introduces new challenges due to movement and wide variation in position of the limbs. To focus on registration of the brain, $W(x)$ in Eq. 4 is adjusted by assigning twice as much weight to the loss calculated in voxels that are part of the brain.

4.1   Evaluation

In the synthetic case the Target Registration Error (TRE) was calculated, which was defined as the mean Euclidean distance between $x_i \in \mathbb{R}^2$ for i in the set of evaluation points:

$$TRE\left[\bar{\phi}_a^{-1}, \bar{\phi}_d^{-1}, \phi_a, \phi_d\right] = \frac{1}{n}\sum_{i=1}^{n} \|\bar{\phi}_a^{-1} \circ \bar{\phi}_d^{-1} \circ \phi_a \circ \phi_d(x_i) - x_i\|, \qquad (8)$$

where the evaluation points mark the boundary of the shape and important internal structures. The TRE is given in pixels.

In the case of real ultrasound data we visually asses the quality of alignment in the 30 test images. The following scoring is used: 0: fail, 1: correct orthogonal directions, 2: brain and atlas overlap, 3: alignment. Where score 1 indicates the network was able to detect the correct plane, score 2 indicates the network was able to map the brain to the atlas and 3 indicates successful alignment.

5   Results

In the first experiment we compared our method with Voxelmorph [2] on the first synthetic dataset. The experiment was done for different values of $\lambda_{\text{diffusion}}$ with $\lambda_{\text{scaling}} = 0$. Table 1 shows that with the architecture of Voxelmorph it was not possible to capture the global transformation needed. This is also illustrated by row one in Fig. 2. Using our method a small TRE was achieved for both the train and validation set, see row 2 of Fig. 2 for an example. Setting $\lambda_{\text{diffusion}} = 0.8$ gave a TRE of 2.71 ± 1.67 pixels on the test set, which is comparable to the result on the train and validation set.

Table 1. Performance on first synthetic dataset using Voxelmorph [2] and our method for different values of $\lambda_{\text{diffusion}}$. TRE is expressed in pixels, standard deviation between brackets.

$\lambda_{\text{diffusion}}$	Voxelmorph		Our method		
	Train	Validation	Train	Validation	Test
0.05	34.27 (12.10)	34.87 (11.35)	3.46 (6.86)	4.25 (8.35)	-
0.2	34.15 (12.85)	35.23 (12.24)	2.71 (5.80)	3.63 (7.25)	-
0.8	40.40 (12.67)	42.12 (11.80)	2.20 (0.77)	3.10 (1.78)	2.71 (1.67)
3.2	-	-	32.61 (34.07)	35.60 (33.25)	-

Table 2. Target registration error for different hyperparameter settings of the loss function. TRE is expressed in pixels. The standard deviation is given between brackets.

$\lambda_{\text{diffusion}}$	λ_{scaling}	Train	Validation	Test
0.2	0	4.02 (8.26)	5.43 (11.17)	-
0.8	0	2.17 (3.64)	2.74 (2.30)	-
0.2	0.004	3.17 (3.08)	3.26 (1.46)	-
0.8	0.004	2.36 (3.53)	2.45 (3.53)	2.90 (1.97)
0.2	0.008	6.99 (10.26)	6.25 (7.52)	-
0.8	0.008	2.47 (3.35)	2.53 (1.10)	-

In the second experiment we evaluated how to deal with objects in the background by penalizing extreme zooming. In Table 2 one can find the results for $\lambda_{\text{diffusion}} = 0.2$ and $\lambda_{\text{diffusion}} = 0.8$ and for different values of λ_{scaling}. Setting λ_{scaling} too high restricts the network to much, setting this value too low causes extreme scaling. The best result on the validation set was found for $\lambda_{\text{diffusion}} = 0.8$ and $\lambda_{\text{scaling}} = 0.004$, using this model to register the test set gave a TRE of 2.90 ± 1.97 pixels, which is again comparable to the result for the training and validation set. An example can be found in row three of Fig. 2.

In the third experiment we evaluated our method on real ultrasound data, for different combinations of atlases as input to the two parts of the network. The results are shown in Table 3. Using the atlas of the whole embryo gives the best results, since the network has more information for alignment. Figure 3 gives an impression of the resulting registrations. Note that the images that are marked as aligned are not perfectly registered, this is caused by the fact that the

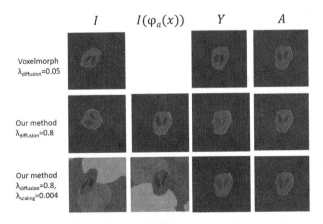

Fig. 2. Visual result for experiment 1 and 2, $Y = I(\phi(x))$ in case of Voxelmorph architecture, $Y = I(\phi_a \circ \phi_d(x))$ for our method and A the atlas.

Table 3. Performance on ultrasound data for different type of atlas. Scoring: 0: fail, 1: correct orthogonal directions, 2: brain and atlas overlap, 3: alignment.

Part 1	Part 2	0	1	2	3
Brain	Brain	21	7	2	0
Embryo	Brain	10	14	5	1
Embryo	Embryo	8	14	5	3

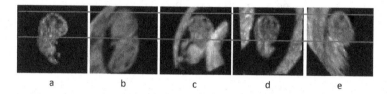

a   b   c   d   e

Fig. 3. Same slice for: a) ultrasound atlas, b) example of image after alignment with score 1, c) example of image after alignment with score 2, d, e): example of successfully affine aligned images with score 3. Red line indicates correct boundaries of the brain after alignment. (Color figure online)

network still roughly misaligned most images and therefore voxelwise alignment is not learned.

6   Conclusion

In this work we extended existing deep learning methods for image registration to developed an atlas-based registration method to align and segment the embryonic brain. Main extensions are the dedicated part of the network for affine registration and the loss function (2). For validation, synthetic 2D datasets containing a ground truth were used. These experiments showed that our method can deal with the wide variation in position and orientation and with simple objects in the background.

The final experiment using real 3D ultrasound data acquired during the first trimester showed that our method is not robust enough to align and segment the embryonic brain. The importance of the atlas was evaluated and it turns out that using an atlas of the whole embryo improves results slightly, since it gives more information. This information is needed since the images are noisy, have artefacts and the embryonic brain is small (on average only 1% of the volume). Another drawback is that the ultrasound images were rescaled to one-fourth of the original size and during registration the image is resampled twice which makes the deformed image blurry and this has influence on the calculated loss function. The rescaling was done to speed up training.

Another way to speed up training, is to train in two stages. The second part of the network learning the voxelwise registration, can only learn useful features when the images are already roughly aligned. So training first the affine part of the network is more efficient, since from the start the second part can then learn useful features for voxelwise alignment. This will be explored in the future.

Finally, we aim to extend our method to be applicable to the entire first trimester, to enable spatio-temporal modeling of the embryonic brain. This extension can be made by training different networks for each period. Another natural extension is multi-atlas image segmentation [8], both for networks trained within a certain period to get more robust results, or with a set of atlases covering the whole first trimester.

References

1. Abadi, M., et al.: TensorFlow: large-scale machine learning on heterogeneous distributed systems (2016)
2. Balakrishnan, G., Zhao, A., Sabuncu, M.R., Guttag, J., Dalca, A.V.: VoxelMorph: a learning framework for deformable medical image registration. IEEE Trans. Med. Imaging **38**, 1788–1800 (2019)
3. Chollet F., et al.: (2015). https://github.com/keras-team/keras
4. Fischer, B., Modersitzki, J.: Fast diffusion registration. In: AMS Contemporary Mathematics, Inverse Problems, Image Analysis and Medical Imaging, vol. 313, pp. 117–129 (2002)
5. Golub, G.H., Reinsch, C.: Singular value decomposition and least squares solutions. In: Bauer, F.L. (ed.) Linear Algebra. HDBKAUCO, vol. 2, pp. 134–151. Springer, Heidelberg (1971). https://doi.org/10.1007/978-3-662-39778-7_10
6. Hering, A., van Ginneken, B., Heldmann, S.: mlVIRNET: Multilevel Variational Image Registration Network (2019). http://arxiv.org/abs/1909.10084
7. Hu, Y., et al.: Weakly-supervised convolutional neural networks for multimodal image registration. Med. Image Anal. **49**, 1–13 (2018)
8. Iglesias, J.E., Sabuncu, M.R.: Multi-atlas segmentation of biomedical images: a survey. Med. Image Anal. **24**(1), 205–219 (2015)
9. Kuklisova-Murgasova, M., et al.: Registration of 3D fetal neurosonography and MRI. Med. Image Anal. **17**(8), 1137–1150 (2013)
10. Liu, S., et al.: Deep learning in medical ultrasound analysis: a review. Engineering **5**(2), 261–275 (2019)
11. Namburete, A.I., et al.: Fully-automated alignment of 3D fetal brain ultrasound to a canonical reference space using multi-task learning. Med. Image Anal. **46**, 1–14 (2018)
12. Rousian, M., et al.: Virtual reality imaging techniques in the study of embryonic and early placental health. Placenta **64**, S29–S35 (2018)
13. Schmidt-Richberg, A., et al.: Abdomen segmentation in 3D fetal ultrasound using CNN-powered deformable models. In: Cardoso, M.J., et al. (eds.) FIFI/OMIA - 2017. LNCS, vol. 10554, pp. 52–61. Springer, Cham (2017). https://doi.org/10.1007/978-3-319-67561-9_6
14. Shepp, L.A., Logan, B.F.: The fourier reconstruction of a head section. IEEE Trans. Nucl. Sci. **21**(3), 21–43 (1974)
15. Steegers-Theunissen, R.P., et al.: Cohort profile: the Rotterdam periconceptional cohort (predict study). Int. J. Epidemiol. **45**, 374–381 (2016)
16. de Vos, B.D., et al.: A deep learning framework for unsupervised affine and deformable image registration. Med. Image Anal. **52**, 128–143 (2019)
17. Yang, X., Kwitt, R., Styner, M., Niethammer, M.: Quicksilver: fast predictive image registration - a deep learning approach. NeuroImage **158**, 378–396 (2017)

Learning Deformable Image Registration with Structure Guidance Constraints for Adaptive Radiotherapy

Sven Kuckertz[1]([✉]), Nils Papenberg[1], Jonas Honegger[2], Tomasz Morgas[2], Benjamin Haas[2], and Stefan Heldmann[1]

[1] Fraunhofer Institute for Digital Medicine MEVIS, Lübeck, Germany
sven.kuckertz@mevis.fraunhofer.de
[2] Varian Medical Systems, Baden-Dättwil, Switzerland

Abstract. Accurate registration of CT and CBCT images is key for adaptive radiotherapy. A particular challenge is the alignment of flexible organs, such as bladder or rectum, that often yield extreme deformations. In this work we analyze the impact of so-called structure guidance for learning based registration when additional segmentation information is provided to a neural network. We present a novel weakly supervised deep learning based method for multi-modal 3D deformable CT-CBCT registration with structure guidance constraints. Our method is not supervised by ground-truth deformations and we use the energy functional of a variational registration approach as loss for training. Incorporating structure guidance constraints in our learning based approach results in an average Dice score of 0.91 ± 0.08 compared to a score of 0.76 ± 0.15 for the same method without constraints. An iterative registration approach with structure guidance results in a comparable average Dice score of 0.91 ± 0.09. However, learning based registration requires only a single pass through the network, yielding computation of a deformation fields in less than $0.1\,\mathrm{s}$ which is more than 100 times faster than the runtime of iterative registration.

Keywords: Image registration · Deep learning · Radiotherapy

1 Introduction

Deformable image registration (DIR) is an important tool in radiotherapy for cancer treatment. It is used for the alignment of a baseline CT and daily low-radiation cone beam CT (CBCT) images, allowing for motion correction, propagation of Hounsfield units and applied doses. Furthermore, organ segmentations, that are typically created by clinical experts during planning phase from the baseline CT, can be propagated to daily CBCT images. DIR has become a method of choice in image-guided radiotherapy and treatment planning over the last decades [2]. However, it is a demanding task that holds several challenges such as meaningful measurement of multi-modal similarity of CT and CBCT

© Springer Nature Switzerland AG 2020
Ž. Špiclin et al. (Eds.): WBIR 2020, LNCS 12120, pp. 44–53, 2020.
https://doi.org/10.1007/978-3-030-50120-4_5

images, having low contrast and containing artifacts. Aside from that, flexible organs, such as bladder or rectum, can introduce extreme deformations, complicating an accurate registration. Conventional DIR algorithms such as [11] tend to underestimate large deformations, which is why extended DIR approaches were presented [9,14]. These so-called *structure guided* approaches include information about corresponding anatomical delineations on the images in order to guide the registration. While the required delineations are usually available on the planning CT due to the workflow of radiotherapy, they need to be generated on CBCT scans before registration. As the advancements of machine learning algorithms proceed, fast and accurate generation of organ segmentations becomes easier, enabling structure guided DIR and making adaptive radiotherapy more feasible. However, DIR in radiotherapy remains a challenging task.

In the last few years, novel deep learning based registration methods have been proposed [12], showing potential of being superior to state-of-the-art iterative algorithms both in terms of accuracy and execution time. However, in the field of DIR in radiotherapy rather little work on deep learning based approaches has been done. In [3] for example a patch-based learning method for mono-modal CT-CT image registration has been proposed. Moreover, deep learning is used to overcome multi-modality by estimation of synthetic CT images from other modalities which then are used for registration [6]. As ground-truth deformations between images are hard to obtain, mostly unsupervised learning methods for DIR have been proposed in the past. Therefore a deep network is trained by minimization of a loss function inspired by the cost function of iterative registration methods [7,15]. To include additional available information, such as organ delineations during training, so-called *weakly supervised* methods have been proposed and showed improved registration accuracy [1,8]. Also in the context of radiotherapy these methods show promising results [10].

In this work we aim to combine the strengths of learning DIR with weak supervision and conventional registration using structure guidance. To this end we present a novel weakly supervised deep learning based method for multimodal 3D deformable CT-CBCT registration with structure guidance constraints. Our method is not supervised by hard to obtain ground-truth deformation vector fields. The minimized loss is inspired by variational structure guided DIR algorithms, including an image similarity measure suitable for multimodal CT-CBCT alignment and an additional term rating the alignment of given segmentation masks. Furthermore, we penalize deformation Jacobians to avoid local changes of topology and foldings. In contrast to existing learning based approaches, here we directly incorporate information on guidance structures as additional input to the networks. We evaluate our method on follow-up image pairs of the female pelvis and compare our results to conventional iterative registration algorithms.

2   Method

The goal of DIR is the generation of dense correspondences between a reference image $\mathcal{R}$ and a template image $\mathcal{T}$ with $\mathcal{R}, \mathcal{T} : \mathbb{R}^3 \rightarrow \mathbb{R}$. This is achieved by

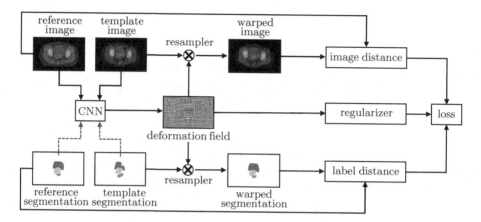

Fig. 1. Overview on our network training process. We train 3 different types of networks which all require the input of a reference and a template image. Additionally they can receive segmentations on the reference image or corresponding segmentations on both images as input (indicated by red dotted lines). The output is a deformation vector field that is applied to the template image and segmentations. The network parameters are updated using backpropagation based on the loss function presented in Sect. 2.2. (Color figure online)

estimating a reasonable deformation vector field $y : \Omega \to \mathbb{R}^3$ on the field of view $\Omega \subseteq \mathbb{R}^3$ of $\mathcal{R}$, such that the warped template image $\mathcal{T}(y)$ and $\mathcal{R}$ are similar. In a variational approach y is computed by minimizing a suitable cost function, usually consisting of an image similarity measure and a regularization term. In iterative registration this is typically done by a time-consuming gradient or Newton-type optimization scheme. However, in a deep learning based registration, the deformation is modeled by a convolutional neural network (CNN), that directly maps given input images to a vector field and that is parameterized with learnable parameters θ, i.e. $y \equiv y_\theta(\mathcal{R}, \mathcal{T})$. Due to the lack of ground-truth deformations, we adapt the variational approach and minimize the variational costs in average over all given training samples. In the context of learning, the cost function is the so-called loss function. An overview on the training process of our networks is given in Fig. 1.

2.1 Registration Types by Input

The networks require the input of a reference and a template image which need to be registered. Furthermore, we allow that available segmentations are provided as additional inputs. In this work, we distinguish between no additional input, a set $\Sigma_\mathcal{R} = \{\Sigma_\mathcal{R}^\ell \subset \mathbb{R}^3, \ell = 1, \ldots, L\}$ of segmentations $\Sigma_\mathcal{R}^\ell$ on the reference image, or two sets $\Sigma_\mathcal{R}, \Sigma_\mathcal{T}$ with corresponding segmentations $\Sigma_\mathcal{R}^\ell$ and $\Sigma_\mathcal{T}^\ell$ on reference and template image, respectively. On that account, we consider following three types of CNNs that predict a deformation field y depending on the given inputs:

Type I: $y \equiv y_\theta(\mathcal{R}, \mathcal{T})$ (images only)

Type II: $y \equiv y_\theta(\mathcal{R}, \mathcal{T}, \Sigma_\mathcal{R})$ (images + reference segmentations)
Type III: $y \equiv y_\theta(\mathcal{R}, \mathcal{T}, \Sigma_\mathcal{R}, \Sigma_\mathcal{T})$ (images + corresponding segmentations)

Note that all three CNN registration types use information about anatomical structures during training for weak supervision. For inference, only the respective network inputs are required. Once the training process is finished, only a single pass though the network is needed for registration of unseen image pairs.

Above classification is clearly not limited to deep learning based registration as the registration types just describe the given inputs. In our experiments we will also refer to iterative registration of type I and III in analogues manner indicating the provided inputs per registration.

2.2 Loss Function

The loss function our networks minimize is similar to cost functions in iterative registration schemes [14]. It is composed of four parts, weighted by factors $\alpha, \beta, \gamma > 0$:

$$\mathcal{L}(y) = \mathrm{NGF}(\mathcal{R}, \mathcal{T}(y)) + \frac{\alpha}{2}\|\mathcal{M}_\mathcal{R} - \mathcal{M}_\mathcal{T}(y)\|_{L_2}^2 + \frac{\beta}{2}\|\Delta y\|_{L_2}^2 + \gamma \int_\Omega \psi(\det \nabla y(x))\,\mathrm{d}x \tag{1}$$

with the edge-based normalized gradient fields (NGF) [5] distance measure

$$\mathrm{NGF}(\mathcal{R}, \mathcal{T}) = \frac{1}{2}\int_\Omega 1 - \frac{\langle \nabla \mathcal{R}(x), \nabla \mathcal{T}(x)\rangle_{\varepsilon_\mathcal{R}\varepsilon_\mathcal{T}}^2}{\|\nabla \mathcal{R}(x)\|_{\varepsilon_\mathcal{R}}^2 \|\nabla \mathcal{T}(x)\|_{\varepsilon_\mathcal{T}}^2}\,\mathrm{d}x, \tag{2}$$

where $\langle x, y\rangle_\varepsilon := x^\top y + \varepsilon$, $\|x\|_\varepsilon := \sqrt{\langle x, x\rangle_{\varepsilon^2}}$. Additionally, a L_2-penalty for weakly supervised structure guidance constraints is applied to segmentation masks hat are handled as multi-channel binary images $\mathcal{M}_\mathcal{R}, \mathcal{M}_\mathcal{T} : \mathbb{R}^3 \to \{0,1\}^L$, such that $\mathcal{M}_\mathcal{R}(x)_\ell = 1$ iff $x \in \Sigma_\mathcal{R}^\ell$ and $\mathcal{M}_\mathcal{T}(x)_\ell = 1$ iff $x \in \Sigma_\mathcal{T}^\ell$. A spatial second order curvature regularization [4], where $\Delta y \equiv (\Delta y_1, \Delta y_2, \Delta y_3)$ is the vector Laplacian, i.e. the Laplacian is applied component-wise, and a change of volume penalty with $\psi(t) := (t - 1)^2/t$ if $t > 0$ and $\psi(t) = \infty$ otherwise are utilized to force physically reasonable deformations. The latter term penalizes Jacobians that indicate high volume growth ($\det \nabla y > 1$), shrinkage ($0 < \det \nabla y < 1$) and especially unwanted grid foldings ($\det \nabla y \leq 0$).

2.3 Network Architecture

Our proposed CNN architecture is based on a U-Net [13] with four stages. Inputs are two 3D images $\mathcal{R}$ and $\mathcal{T}$ and, depending on the registration type (c.f. Sect. 2.1), additional reference segmentations $\Sigma_\mathcal{R}$ or corresponding segmentations $\Sigma_\mathcal{R}$ and $\Sigma_\mathcal{T}$. Note that for each type a separate network has to be trained. First, individual convolution kernels are applied to each input. The results are combined by concatenation and afterwards convolution blocks and $2 \times 2 \times 2$

max-pooling layers alternate. An convolution block consists of two convolutions with a kernel size of $3 \times 3 \times 3$, each followed by a ReLU and a batch normalization layer. In each stage the number of feature channels gets doubled. In the decoder path, we alternate between transposed convolutions, convolution blocks and concatenating skip connections. Finally, we apply a $1 \times 1 \times 1$ convolution, yielding the 3-channel deformation field with the same resolution as the inputs.

3   Experiments

We evaluate our proposed deep learning based method on image data of 31 female patients from multiple clinical sites. The dataset includes one planning CT and up to 26 follow-up CBCT scans of the pelvis for each patient, yielding 256 intra-patiental CT-CBCT image pairs in total. In order to focus on deformable parts of the registration, the images were affinely registered beforehand. Additionally the images were cropped to the same field of view and resampled to a size of $160 \times 160 \times 80$ voxels, each with a size of approximately $3 \, \text{mm} \times 3 \, \text{mm} \times 2 \, \text{mm}$ in a preprocessing step. Available delineations of bladder, rectum and uterus were generated by clinical experts.

We evaluate the performance of three network types, differing in their number of required inputs and guidance through delineated structures. First, we only input two images that need to be registered. Second, we additionally include available segmentations on the reference CT image that are usually available after treatment planning phase. Third, we also include corresponding segmentations on the daily CBCT image for structure guidance. For comparison of our method with classical variational approaches we perform an iterative registration of all test image pairs, both with and without the guidance of given structures. We therefore minimize the same loss function without a volume change control term using an iterative L-BFGS optimizer. The weights in our loss and objective function (1), respectively, have been chosen manually as $\alpha = 30$, $\beta = 3$, $\gamma = 0.3$.

Each network type is evaluated performing a $k-$fold cross-validation with $k = 4$, splitting the dataset patient-wise into four subsets, training on three of them and testing on the left out subset. As evaluation measures we use the Dice similarity coefficient and the average surface distance (ASD) for estimation of segmentation overlap and registration accuracy. We check the plausibility of the deformation fields using their Jacobians as an indicator of volume changes and undesired grid foldings. The implementation of our deep learning framework is done using PyTorch and processed on a NVIDIA GeForce RTX 2070 with 8 GB memory and an Intel Core i7-9700K with 8 cores.

4   Results

The outcome of our experiments is summarized in Table 1. As expected, the registration quality improves with providing further input. We found that solely forwarding the reference and template image to our weakly supervised trained CNN for registration of type I yields an average Dice score of 0.76 (Dice after

Table 1. Quantitative results of our experiments (c.f. Sect. 3). Mean and standard deviation of Dice scores and average surface distances (ASD) over all test images and average runtime for a single registration are shown. Furthermore, Jacobians and average percentage of voxels in which foldings occur (det(∇y) $\leq$ 0) are listed for the body region and the union of the guiding structures (bladder, rectum, uterus).

Method	Dice score	ASD [mm]	Body region		Guiding structures		Time
			Jacobians	Foldings	Jacobians	Foldings	
Preregist.	0.64 ± 0.15	5.49 ± 2.87	–	–	–	–	–
Iterative I	0.72 ± 0.13	4.13 ± 2.50	1.02 ± 0.28	0.02%	0.96 ± 0.47	0.14%	15 s
Iterative III	0.91 ± 0.09	1.07 ± 0.96	1.02 ± 0.34	0.17%	1.00 ± 0.97	2.58%	20 s
Learning I	0.76 ± 0.15	3.34 ± 2.40	1.01 ± 0.24	0.00%	0.97 ± 0.68	0.06%	<0.1 s
Learning II	0.80 ± 0.15	2.79 ± 2.42	1.01 ± 0.24	0.00%	0.95 ± 0.75	0.08%	<0.1 s
Learning III	0.91 ± 0.08	1.28 ± 1.16	1.01 ± 0.18	0.01%	0.99 ± 0.69	0.16%	<0.1 s

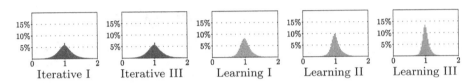

Fig. 2. Histrogram visualizations of the Jacobians (det ∇y) representing the voxel-wise volume change inside the body region on the x-axis for each registration type. The y-axis shows the relative number of voxels. The values are based on all test images.

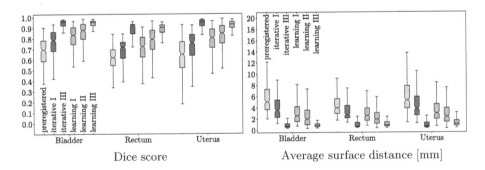

Fig. 3. Comparison of Dice scores and average surface distances for all test images and annotated labels (bladder, rectum and uterus). For each label the distributions after the affine preregistration (▨), a conventional iterative (▨) and our proposed deep learning based registration (▨) are illustrated (c.f. Sect. 3). (Color figure online)

affine preregistration was 0.64). The result is superior to iterative registration of type I with an average Dice of 0.72. This is not surprising, as a particular advantage of learning based DIR algorithms is to build in anatomical knowledge and guidance, respectively, by weakly supervised training. Learning based registration of type II with additionally passing reference segmentations to the

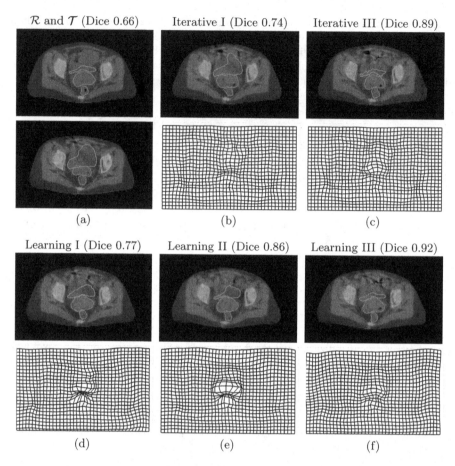

$\mathcal{R}$ and $\mathcal{T}$ (Dice 0.66)   Iterative I (Dice 0.74)   Iterative III (Dice 0.89)

(a)   (b)   (c)

Learning I (Dice 0.77)   Learning II (Dice 0.86)   Learning III (Dice 0.92)

(d)   (e)   (f)

Fig. 4. Qualitative comparison of registration results. (a) Reference and template with initial Dice score (average of the three scores for bladder, rectum, uterus). (b)-(f) Deformed template images $\mathcal{T}(y)$ and deformations y for iterative (type I+III) and learning based DIR (type I-III). Additionally, we show segmentations of the bladder (■), rectum (■) and uterus (■). (Color figure online)

network slightly improves the registration accuracy (Dice 0.80), while providing corresponding segmentations on the CT and CBCT yields best results. In fact, structure guided iterative and learning based registration of type III both lead to an average Dice score of 0.91. Looking at the average surface distance shows a comparable tendency, where the iterative and learning based structure guided approaches both achieve values lower than the spatial resolution. The distributions of Dice scores and average surface distances are visualized in Fig. 3, showing a systematic improvement of registration results from type I to III.

A visual comparison of registration results of all types for one case is given in Fig. 4. Additionally, the results of structure guided iterative and learning based registrations of type III for three different patients are shown in Fig. 5.

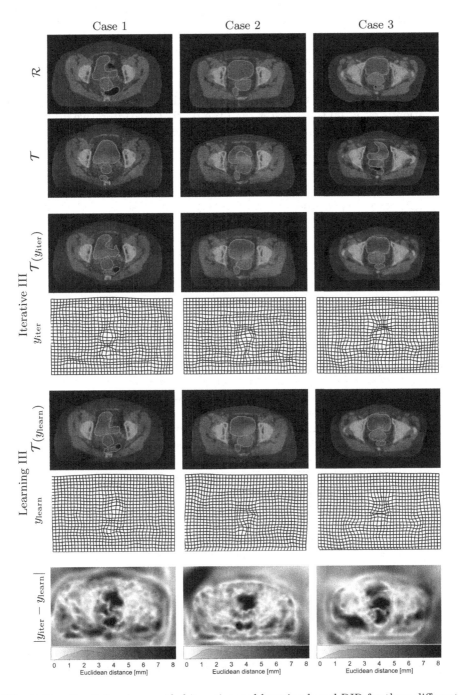

Fig. 5. Results of structure guided iterative and learning based DIR for three different cases. Additionally, Euclidean distances of the corresponding deformation vector fields are shown together with color scales including a histogram of the respective distances.

We observe that large deformations, especially of the bladder, are compensated due to the guidance of these structures. The plausibility of the underlying deformations can be checked with the help of the illustrated transformed grids. Furthermore, Fig. 2 displays the distributions of Jacobians for all approaches. As expected, Jacobians are centered around 1.0 with small standard deviations.

As specified in Table 1, the computational runtime of our deep learning based registration is over 100 times faster than the (CPU based) iterative approaches due to the fact that registration only needs a single pass through the CNN.

5 Conclusion

We presented a deep learning based method for multi-modal 3D deformable image registration with structure guidance constraints for adaptive radiotherapy. In our experiments we observed a significant improvement of learning based DIR by incorporation of structure guidance constraints, realized by providing organ segmentations as network input. More precisely, we showed that providing segmentations at first on the reference CT image improves registration results. These segmentations are typically generated and checked by clinical experts during the treatment planning phase and therefore available for all subsequent CT-CBCT registrations. Furthermore, corresponding segmentations on daily CBCT scans become available more easily as learning based segmentation algorithms advance. Incorporation of corresponding segmentations into our deep learning based method yields best results which are comparable to the output of state-of-the-art iterative approaches for structure guided image registration. However, generating deformations over 100 times faster, our learning based approach is capable of application nearly in real-time. Due to its short runtimes and accurate results, our method for structure guided image registration makes adaptive radiotherapy more feasible. It accelerates the clinical workflow and enables a more precise application of radiation doses, so target volumes get irradiated more effectively, while the harm of organs at risk is reduced.

Furthermore, we showed that the ability to build in anatomical knowledge by weakly supervised training of our network improves registration results even when this additional information is not provided during registration of unseen image pairs. Our learning based method does not rely on supervision by hard to obtain ground-truth deformations, but minimizes a suited loss function inspired by variational structure guided registration approaches.

For each registration type, differing in their number of provided inputs, we trained an independent neural network. In future work, we will investigate the implementation of a more flexible approach, handling a variable number of inputs. Additionally, we want to evaluate the integration of supplemental knowledge, especially from segmentations of target volumes that typically do not follow anatomical boundaries.

References

1. Balakrishnan, G., Zhao, A., Sabuncu, M.R., Guttag, J., Dalca, A.V.: VoxelMorph: a learning framework for deformable medical image registration. IEEE Trans. Med. Imaging **38**, 1788–1800 (2019)
2. Brock, K.K., Mutic, S., McNutt, T.R., Li, H., Kessler, M.L.: Use of image registration and fusion algorithms and techniques in radiotherapy: report of the AAPM radiation therapy committee task group no. 132. Med. Phys. **44**(7), e43–e76 (2017)
3. Elmahdy, M.S., Wolterink, J.M., Sokooti, H., Išgum, I., Staring, M.: Adversarial optimization for joint registration and segmentation in prostate CT radiotherapy. arXiv preprint arXiv:1906.12223 (2019)
4. Fischer, B., Modersitzki, J.: Curvature based image registration. J. Math. Imaging Vis. **18**(1), 81–85 (2003)
5. Haber, E., Modersitzki, J.: Intensity gradient based registration and fusion of multi-modal images. In: Larsen, R., Nielsen, M., Sporring, J. (eds.) MICCAI 2006. LNCS, vol. 4191, pp. 726–733. Springer, Heidelberg (2006). https://doi.org/10.1007/11866763_89
6. Han, X.: MR-based synthetic CT generation using a deep convolutional neural network method. Med. Phys. **44**(4), 1408–1419 (2017)
7. Hering, A., Heldmann, S.: Unsupervised learning for large motion thoracic CT follow-up registration. In: Medical Imaging 2019: Image Processing. International Society for Optics and Photonics (2019)
8. Hering, A., Kuckertz, S., Heldmann, S., Heinrich, M.P.: Enhancing label-driven deep deformable image registration with local distance metrics for state-of-the-art cardiac motion tracking. Bildverarbeitung für die Medizin 2019. I, pp. 309–314. Springer, Wiesbaden (2019). https://doi.org/10.1007/978-3-658-25326-4_69
9. Himstedt, M., et al.: Deformable image registration using structure guidance for dose accumulation. In: Proceedings of the International Conference on the Use of Computers in Radiation Therapy (ICCR) (2019)
10. Kuckertz, S., Papenberg, N., Honegger, J., Morgas, T., Haas, B., Heldmann, S.: Deep learning based CT-CBCT image registration for adaptive radio therapy. In: Medical Imaging 2020: Image Processing, vol. 11313, pp. 149–154. International Society for Optics and Photonics, SPIE (2020)
11. König, L., Rühaak, J., Derksen, A., Lellmann, J.: A matrix-free approach to parallel and memory-efficient deformable image registration. SIAM J. Sci. Comput. **40**(3), B858–B888 (2018)
12. Litjens, G., et al.: A survey on deep learning in medical image analysis. Med. Image Anal. **42**, 60–88 (2017)
13. Ronneberger, O., Fischer, P., Brox, T.: U-Net: convolutional networks for biomedical image segmentation. In: Navab, N., Hornegger, J., Wells, W.M., Frangi, A.F. (eds.) MICCAI 2015. LNCS, vol. 9351, pp. 234–241. Springer, Cham (2015). https://doi.org/10.1007/978-3-319-24574-4_28
14. Rühaak, J., Heldmann, S., Kipshagen, T., Fischer, B.: Highly accurate fast lung CT registration. In: Medical Imaging 2013: Image Processing, vol. 8669, p. 86690Y. International Society for Optics and Photonics (2013)
15. de Vos, B.D., Berendsen, F.F., Viergever, M.A., Staring, M., Išgum, I.: End-to-end unsupervised deformable image registration with a convolutional neural network. In: Cardoso, M.J., et al. (eds.) DLMIA/ML-CDS-2017. LNCS, vol. 10553, pp. 204–212. Springer, Cham (2017). https://doi.org/10.1007/978-3-319-67558-9_24

Interventional Registration

Multilevel 2D-3D Intensity-Based Image Registration

Annkristin Lange[(✉)] and Stefan Heldmann

Fraunhofer MEVIS, Lübeck, Germany
annkristin.lange@mevis.fraunhofer.de

Abstract. 2D-3D image registration is an important task for computer-aided minimally invasive vascular therapies. A crucial component for practical image registration is the use of multilevel strategies to avoid local optima and to speed-up runtime. However, due to the different dimensionalities of the 2D fixed and 3D moving image, the setup of multilevel strategies is not straightforward.

In this work, we propose an intensity-driven 2D-3D multiresolution registration approach using the normalized gradient fields (NGF) distance measure. We discuss and empirically analyze the impact on the choice of 2D and 3D image resolutions. Furthermore, we show that our approach produces results that are comparable or superior to other state-of-the-art methods.

Keywords: 2D-3D registration · Multilevel · Multiresolution · Normalized gradient fields · Vascular images

1 Introduction

Minimally invasive endovascular therapies are nowadays part of standard routine for many diseases of the vascular system. Before an intervention usually a planning CT with contrast agent is done. The navigation of the catheter through the vascular system during the intervention can be quite challenging, even if fluoroscopy images are obtained. Registration of 2D projection images to a 3D planning CT image provides more information and allows to reduce intervention time, radiation exposure and amount of contrast agent [1].

A nice overview about the topic of 2D-3D registration and classification of the different strategies developed over the years can be found in [6]. The strategies can roughly be divided into feature- and intensity-based methods. Intensity-based approaches rely on synthetic projections from the 3D planning volume that mimic the real projection process, so-called digitally reconstructed radiographs (DRRs). The registration is then based on the comparison between the DRRs and the measured projections. In contrast, feature-based methods attempt to align features computed from, e.g. gradients [7,8], surface/contour points [12] or directly from the images.

© Springer Nature Switzerland AG 2020
Ž. Špiclin et al. (Eds.): WBIR 2020, LNCS 12120, pp. 57–66, 2020.
https://doi.org/10.1007/978-3-030-50120-4_6

An important component for any practical image registration scheme is the use of multilevel strategies to avoid local optima and speed-up the registration [5]. The general idea behind multilevel strategies is, that coarser resolution mainly carry global image information and features, and local details gradually become present with finer resolutions, i.e. more details are added. On that account, registration is performed level-wise from coarse-to-fine and solutions from one level are used as initial guess for finding the solution at the next finer level.

However, in 2D-3D registration the application of multilevel strategies is not as straightforward as for the registration of images with same dimensionality. Here we compare given 2D projection images with DRRs created from 3D volume data. Clearly, coarsening and projecting do not commute, i.e. creating a coarse resolution 2D image from a given 2D projection image, e.g., by downsampling, is different from projecting a 3D coarse resolution image.

Nevertheless multilevel strategies are successfully employed in many 2D-3D registration methods (see [6] for a list of publications). To best of our knowledge, no work has been done on the relation of the resolutions between 2D images and 3D volumes. In [3] few experiments regarding the choice of resolutions are performed and [9] presents a general discussion motivating the use of multilevel strategies in 2D-3D registration. However, the relationship between the resolutions of the volumes and projections is not discussed.

In this work we present a multilevel 2D-3D registration with the so-called normalized gradient field distance measure (NGF) [2]. The focus of the paper is on the relation and the choice of resolutions for 2D and 3D image data.

2   Methods

In the following we describe our multilevel 2D-3D registration method. We start with the description of computing 2D projection images in Sect. 2.1. Subsequent we present our intensity-based 2D-3D image registration with the NGF distance measure in Sect. 2.2 and finally, we discuss our multilevel strategy in Sect. 2.3.

2.1   Digitally Reconstructed Radiographs (DRRs)

We consider X-ray imaging as the process of measuring the attenuation of radiation, that is emitted from a radiation point source located at position q with the initial energy I_0. Mathematically, this can be modeled by a projection operator $\mathcal{P}$ that maps a 3D attenuation map $\mu : \mathbb{R}^3 \to \mathbb{R}$ to a 2D image. Therefore, let $x \in \mathbb{R}^2$ be a location in the 2D projection image and let $d(x) \in \mathbb{R}^3$ be the location of the corresponding detector element in 3D-space. Then the projection is given by

$$\mathcal{P}[\mu](x) := I_0 \exp\left(-\int_{L(q,d(x))} \mu \, ds\right) \tag{1}$$

where $L(q, d(x)) := \{q + t(d(x) - q) \mid t \in [0,1]\}$ is the line from the radiation source q to the detector element $d(x)$. Theoretically, there exists an affine relationship between the attenuation map μ and the CT image, so we can estimate

μ from the CT intensity values. Furthermore, to accelerate the computationally expensive calculation of these synthetic projections, the so-called digitally reconstructed radiographs (DRR), we have implemented a GPU version.

2.2 Intensity-Based 2D-3D Image Registration

A common approach is to model d-dimensional images as intensity mappings, i.e. an image $I : \mathbb{R}^d \to \mathbb{R}$ that maps a position $x \in \mathbb{R}^d$ to an intensity $I(x)$. Image registration can then be described as the process of finding a plausible spatial transformation y such that the transformation applied to a given template image $T(y)$ is similar to a given reference image R, i.e. $T(y(x)) \approx R(x)$. To describe the similarity between the images, a suitable cost-function the so-called distance measure $\mathcal{D}$ is used. Then, the registration problem can be defined as a minimization problem $\mathcal{D}(R, T(y)) = \min$.

Unlike classical image registration, where reference and template image have same dimensionality, in 2D-3D registration the reference image $R : \mathbb{R}^2 \to \mathbb{R}$ is a 2D measured projection image while the template image $T : \mathbb{R}^3 \to \mathbb{R}$ still is a 3D image. Accordingly, the desired transformation is also a 3D mapping $y : \mathbb{R}^3 \to \mathbb{R}^3$. The similarity is then measured between the 2D reference image and a 2D DRR $\mathcal{P}[T(y)]$ of the deformed 3D template image $T(y) := T \circ y$ and the minimization problem for image registration becomes $\mathcal{D}(R, \mathcal{P}[T(y)]) = \min$. In this work we used the normalized gradient field (NGF) distance measure [2,10]. For two 2D images $R, \widetilde{T} : \mathbb{R}^2 \to \mathbb{R}$, it is given by

$$\text{NGF}(R, \widetilde{T}) = \int_{\Omega} 1 - \left(\frac{\langle \nabla R(x), \nabla \widetilde{T}(x) \rangle_{\varepsilon_R \varepsilon_T}}{\|\nabla R(x)\|_{\varepsilon_R} \|\nabla \widetilde{T}(x)\|_{\varepsilon_T}} \right)^2 dx \qquad (2)$$

with $\langle x, y \rangle_{\varepsilon} := x^\top y + \varepsilon$, $\|x\|_{\varepsilon} = \sqrt{\langle x, x \rangle_{\varepsilon^2}}$, domain $\Omega \subset \mathbb{R}^2$, that models the 2D field-of-view of the detector and so-called edge parameters $\varepsilon_R, \varepsilon_T > 0$.

In order to find plausible deformations, the search space of admissible transformations can be restricted. Here, we only allow for translations and rotations, i.e. rigid transformations $y(x) = Qx + b$ with 3-by-3 rotation matrix $Q \in SO(3)$ and translation vector $b \in \mathbb{R}^3$. As the rotation matrix can be parameterized by three rotation angles, we obtain a six-parameter deformation model $y \equiv y_\theta$ with the parameters $\theta \in \mathbb{R}^6$. Summarizing, our intensity-based rigid 2D-3D registration approach is

$$\min_{\theta \in \mathbb{R}^6} \text{NGF}\left(R, \mathcal{P}[T(y_\theta)]\right) \qquad (3)$$

To solve the optimization problem numerically, a Gauss-Newton optimization scheme with backtracking Armijo linesearch and analytically computed gradients is used. In the DRR computation a radial sampling with uniform step length is used.

2.3 Multilevel Strategy

The idea of any multilevel strategy is to represent a given problem on coarse resolutions with less detail, which allows for efficient solving and, above all, adds to finding solutions close to a global optimum of the original problem. Starting from a coarsest level, a solution for the coarse problem is computed and subsequently prolongated to the next finer level, where it serves as an initial guess for the optimization. The process is then continued until the finest level is reached.

The common approach in intensity-based image registration to represent the problem at coarse resolutions is to create low resolution versions of the given input image data, e.g. by downsampling or averaging pixels. We also follow this approach here. To this end, let R be the given 2D image, I_ℓ^{2D} be an operator that maps a 2D image to the resolution at ℓ-th level and let $R_\ell := I_\ell^{2D}[R]$. In the same way let T be the given 3D volume and $T_\ell := I_\ell^{3D}[T]$ with an operator I_ℓ^{3D} which maps a 3D image to a 3D image with the resolution for the ℓ layer. Now, we have two generic options to setup the registration problem at the ℓ-th level. First, we could search for a transformation y such that $\text{NGF}(R_\ell, I_\ell^{2D}[\mathcal{P}[T(y)]]) = \min$. Another option is to look for minimizers of $\text{NGF}(R_\ell, \mathcal{P}[T_\ell(y)])$. Clearly, projection and coarsening do not commute in general, i.e. $I_\ell^{2D}[\mathcal{P}[T]] \neq \mathcal{P}[I_\ell^{3D}[T]] = \mathcal{P}[T_\ell(y)]$ and we cannot expect that solutions for both problems coincide. Although the first approach seems more natural from a conceptual point of view, it is computationally demanding as it requires the computation of high quality projections at the original (finest) image resolution regardless of the resolution of the problem. Furthermore, we need to incorporate the projection operator I_ℓ^{2D} into our numerics, e.g., for computing derivatives. For this reason, we stick to the second approach.

Accordingly, we create image pyramids for the given input images by averaging neighboring pixels and voxels, respectively, so that the resolutions double from a coarse to the next finer level. Then, starting at coarsest level, we compute solutions to (2.3) using the data of the current level and the solution from the previous level as an initial guess. Our overall scheme can be summarized as follows:

1. Create R_ℓ, T_ℓ for $\ell = 1, \ldots, L$ from coarsest $(\ell = 1)$ to finest $(\ell = L)$ level
2. Choose initial guess y_0 for coarsest level
3. for level $\ell = 1, .., L$ do
   Use $y_{\ell-1}$ as initial guess for finding y_ℓ such that

$$\text{NGF}\left(R_\ell, \mathcal{P}[T_\ell(y_\ell)]\right) \overset{!}{=} \min$$

end

An important point with substantial impact on registration results, is the choice and alignment of the resolutions of 2D image and 3D projection data. The issue is illustrated in Fig. 1 showing 2D-DSA reference images R_ℓ and DRRs, i.e. projected 3D volumes $\mathcal{P}[T_\ell]$, for different resolutions. There is no obvious answer to the question what combination of resolutions to pick for optimal registration results. Besides evaluating and comparing our method with others, we focus on the analysis of this question with our experiments presented in the next section.

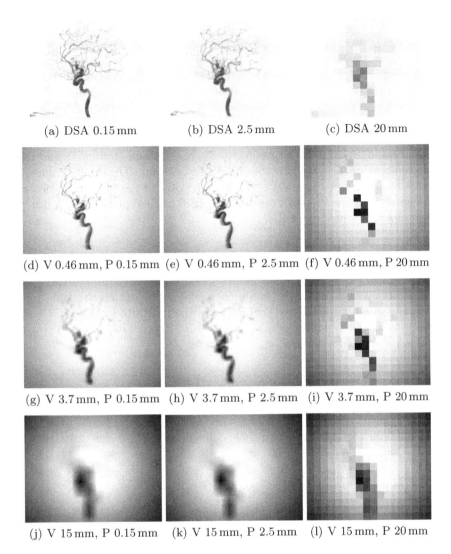

Fig. 1. Calculated DRRs from lateral view with different resolutions of the volume (changing from fine to coarse from top to bottom) and the projections (changing from fine to coarse from left to right). The 2D-DSAs with the same projection resolutions are given for comparison.

3   Experiments and Evaluation

In the following we will experimentally analyze how image resolutions for our 2D-3D multilevel registration can be selected and related. We will also investigate the choice of the finest resolution. Furthermore, we will compare our proposed 2D-3D multilevel registration method using the NGF distance measure with various state-of-the-art methods.

3.1   Clinical Database

Our evaluation is based on the public available clinical data presented in [7]. The data consists of images from 10 patients with cerebral vascular diseases such as aneurysms. Each data set contains a 3D digitally subtracted rotational angiogram (3D-DSA) volume, 2D digitally subtracted angiograms (2D-DSA) from lateral (LAT) and anterior-posterior (AP) views and a rigid gold standard transformation for the 3D volume. The gold standard transformations were derived from fiducial markers and have predicted mean target registration errors (mTRE) ranging from 0.033 to 0.056 mm [7]. In addition, landmarks and initial transformations are provided for comparative evaluation. The original image size of the 3D-DSA is $512 \times 512 \times 391$ voxel with an isotropic resolution of 0.4646 mm. The image size for the 2D-DSA ranges from 1920 to 2480 pixel with an isotropic resolution of 0.154 mm.

3.2   Evaluation Parameters

Error measures based on landmarks are often used to determine the quality of a registration. Two measures commonly used in 2D-3D registration are the mean Target Registration Error (mTRE) and the mean Re-Projection Distance (mRPD) [4]. Given N landmarks $x_1, ..., x_N \in \mathbb{R}^3$, the mTRE between transformation y_{reg} and gold standard y_{gold} is given by

$$\text{mTRE} = \frac{1}{N} \sum_{i=1}^{N} \| y_{\text{reg}}(x_i) - y_{\text{gold}}(x_i) \|. \tag{4}$$

The mRPD measures the distance of the ray passing through source q and transformed landmark to gold standard. It is defined as

$$\text{mRPD} = \frac{1}{N} \sum_{i=1}^{N} \min_{z \in L(q, y_{\text{reg}}(x_i))} \| z - y_{\text{gold}}(x_i) \| \tag{5}$$

where $L(q, y_{\text{reg}}(x_i))$ is the line passing through the source q and the registered landmark $y_{\text{reg}}(x_i)$.

3.3   Experiments

For almost all experiments we used the set of 400 initial displacements that was specified for each dataset. The mTRE of the displacements ranges from 0 mm to 20 mm, so that each interval of 1 mm contains 20 displacements. The displacements were generated by randomly translating about $(-20\,\text{mm}, 20\,\text{mm})$ and rotating around $(-10°, 10°)$ all three axes. Similar to [7] the validation criteria are the percentage of successful registration (SR), the mean and standard deviation of all successful registrations and the capture range (CR). A registration is viewed as successful, if the mTRE is less then 2 mm, which is approximately the radius of the larger cerebral vessels. The capture range is defined as the first interval in which less than 95% of the registrations are successful.

Registration with Original Resolution. Initially, we started our analysis with an experiment in which we perturbed a given gold standard transformation with a shift of 5 mm each along the in-plane axes x and y, resulting in an mTRE before registration of 7.1 mm. For this and the following experiments results were best, if on the coarsest level the resolution of the volume was around 15 mm. Using coarser levels did not achieve improvements, whereas using less levels led to a smaller capture range. The registration was then done for different combinations of finest resolutions. The number of levels depend on that choice as the coarser resolutions are computed from there. If, for example, a fine resolution of 0.93 mm for the volume and 0.31 mm for the projection is selected, the registration is performed on five levels, starting with the coarsest volume resolution of 15 mm and projection resolution of 5 mm (i.e. along the diagonal in Fig. 2(a): (5, 15), (2.5, 7.5), (1.2, 3.7), (0.62, 1.86), (0.31, 0.93)).

Our results show, that we obtain best results when the resolution of the projection is similar or slightly coarser than the resolution of the volume, see Fig. 2(a). It is noticeable that the registration with finest available but also quite different resolutions of 2D projection and 3D volume basically fails. In a next step we reviewed the result based on the set of given initial displacements (cf. Table 1). When using the original resolution of 2D-DSA and 3D-DSA as finest level, the results are not convincing, especially the capture range of only 3 mm is small. Much better results are obtained when not the finest resolution of the projection but the second or even third finest was used. In this case the capture

mTRE		Volume					
	Res (mm)	0.46	0.93	1.86	3.7	7.5	15
	0.15	44.6	138.2	418.4	515.9	985.0	450.0
	0.31	2.7	45.4	137.7	421.3	469.0	430.9
	0.62	1.2	2.7	44.4	138.1	403.9	339.8
Projection	1.2	1.1	1.1	2.8	47.5	157.8	260.6
	2.5	1.6	1.3	1.0	6.3	72.5	102.8
	5	7.1	2.1	1.5	2.7	24.6	54.4
	10	12.4	11.7	7.7	3.5	12.1	41.3
	20	15.8	11.8	12.7	21.1	17.1	36.7

(a) Original resolution

mTRE		Volume					
	Res (mm)	0.46	0.93	1.86	3.7	7.5	15
	0.46	1.1	5.9	74.3	230.3	86241.3	463.9
	0.93	1.1	1.0	6.6	81.1	231.1	277.2
Projection	1.86	1.3	1.3	0.9	11.7	100.2	152.5
	3.7	3.5	1.9	1.4	2.6	27.1	98.5
	7.5	9.4	7.2	4.1	3.0	9.4	47.7
	15	12.1	12.9	14.1	21.6	12.3	16.3

(b) Resampled projections

Fig. 2. mTRE (in mm) values for a registration of a 2D-DSA to a 3D-DSA averaged over all 10 datasets with an initial translation along the in-plane axes $(x, y) = (5\,\text{mm}, 5\,\text{mm})$ with different resolutions of the projection and the volume.

range is 12 and 16 mm, respectively and the success rate is around 96% instead of 68% with no loss of accuracy. The mTRE is in all three cases around 1.1 mm and the mRPD is 0.17 mm.

Summarizing, the results of this experiment led to the assumption that the best registration results are achieved when the resolution of the projection and the volume are comparable, as it is more or less the case for the second and third finest resolution of the projection compared to the finest resolution of the volume.

Table 1. Results for the registration of a 3D-DSA to a 2D-DSA from LAT view averaged over all 10 datasets for different finest resolutions of the 2D-DSA.

Resolution finest level		SR (%)	mTRE (mm)	mRPD (mm)	CR (mm)	Time (s)
2D-DSA	3D-DSA					
0.15	0.46	68.4	1.12 ± 0.12	0.17 ± 0.02	3	23.1
0.31	0.46	95.4	1.10 ± 0.12	0.17 ± 0.003	12	8.0
0.62	0.46	96.4	1.13 ± 0.15	0.17 ± 0.004	16	3.7
1.23	0.46	74.9	1.13 ± 0.14	0.17 ± 0.004	0	4.4

Registration with Same Resolution. Based on the previous results, we resampled the 2D projection images to the original resolution of the 3D volume data and repeated previous registration experiments. Both, the results for the initial translation (Fig. 2(b)) and the results for the given initial displacements (Table 2) confirm our assumption. For the latter, a success rate of 98.3% and 99.5% was achieved with the LAT and AP images, respectively, and a capture range of 20 mm. In addition, a mean value and a standard deviation of the mRPD of 0.17 mm ± 0.004 mm for the LAT images and 0.12 mm ± 0.003 mm for the AP images as well as an mTRE of 1.06 mm ± 0.15 mm and 0.55 mm ± 0.14 mm for the LAT and AP images were achieved. Since we use a publicly accessible database, we can directly compare the results with other results found in the literature for this database. The results achieved with our proposed method are comparable to the results from [12] and much better than the reported results in [7,11]. Except for the mean value and standard deviation of the mTRE for the LAT images, our results are the best results for all compared methods. The runtime for a single registration is not directly comparable as it is not always reported and even if, different hardware is used. The extensive DRR generation is done on a graphics card, but other than that no further runtime optimization was done. Still, registration is fast on of-the-shelf hardware.

Experiment Finest Resolution. As Table 1 already indicates, the registration on fine level is time consuming. This rises the question how the accuracy behaves if fine levels are omitted. We have also looked into this. Table 3 shows the results

Table 2. Results for the registration of a 3D-DSA to a 2D-DSA from LAT or AP view averaged over all 10 datasets of the proposed *DRR-NGF-ML* method compared to the results of other state-of-the-art methods reported in [7,11,12]. Given are the Success Rate (SR), the mean and standard deviation of the mTRE and mRPD, the capture range (CR) and the mean amount of time for one registration. Missing values are marked with a " - ".

View	Method	SR (%)	mTRE (mm)	mRPD (mm)	CR (mm)	Time (s)
LAT	MGP+BGB [7]	79.5	-	0.28 ± 0.21	6	15.3
	PB-BGC [11]	82.2	-	0.51 ± 0.29	9	**1.8**
	PPC-LADR [12]	95.6	0.91 ± 0.50	0.22 ± 0.08	16	-
	PPC-MCCR [12]	98.3	**0.64 ± 0.31**	0.23 ± 0.08	18	-
	DRR-NGF-ML	***99.3***	*1.06 ± 0.15*	***0.17 ± 0.004***	*20*	*4.7*
AP	MGP+BGB [7]	95.5	-	0.28 ± 0.19	12	11.5
	PPC-LADR [12]	97.3	0.57 ± 0.38	0.15 ± 0.08	16	-
	PPC-MCCR [12]	99.4	0.59 ± 0.27	0.16 ± 0.08	**20**	-
	DRR-NGF-ML	***99.5***	***0.55 ± 0.14***	***0.12 ± 0.003***	*20*	*3.6*

Table 3. Results for the registration of a 3D-DSA to a 2D-DSA from LAT view averaged over all 10 datasets with different resolutions of the finest level of both volume and projection.

Resolution finest level (mm)	SR (%)	mTRE (mm)	mRPD (mm)	CR (mm)	Time (s)
0.46	99.3	1.06 ± 0.15	0.17 ± 0.004	20	4.7
0.93	99.2	0.96 ± 0.20	0.17 ± 0.005	20	3.2
1.9	95.1	0.74 ± 0.29	0.18 ± 0.006	14	2.6

for the case of adjusted resolutions and for omitting the first and second finest levels. The success rate, accuracy and capture range are almost identical if the finest level is omitted, only the average registration time decreases significantly. If the two finest levels are omitted, the runtime further decreases, but also success rate and the detection range decreases significantly, too. Thus omitting the finest level seems to achieve the best trade-off between accuracy and speed.

4   Discussion

In this paper we discussed the relation between projection resolution and volume resolution. The main conclusion is that the resolutions should be comparable. One observation that may be surprising is that the use of finer resolutions does not bring any advantage, and may even bring disadvantages if the resolutions are not comparable. Another observation is that for reasons of acceleration, the finest level can be omitted and the accuracy for this particular database is not lost. Besides the investigations about the multilevel strategies, we proposed an efficient multilevel 2D-3D registration method using the NGF distance measure yielding results that are comparable and even superior to the state-of-the-art.

Acknowledgement. This work was funded by the German Federal Ministry of Education and Research (BMBF, project NavEVAR, funding code: 13GW0228C).

References

1. Goudeketting, S.R., Heinen, S.G., Ünlü, Ç., et al.: Pros and cons of 3D image fusion in endovascular aortic repair: a systematic review and meta-analysis. J. Endovasc. Therapy **24**(4), 595–603 (2017). https://doi.org/10.1177/1526602817708196
2. Haber, E., Modersitzki, J.: Intensity gradient based registration and fusion of multi-modal images. In: Larsen, R., Nielsen, M., Sporring, J. (eds.) MICCAI 2006. LNCS, vol. 4191, pp. 726–733. Springer, Heidelberg (2006). https://doi.org/10.1007/11866763_89
3. Jonic, S., Thévenaz, P., Unser, M.A.: Multiresolution-based registration of a volume to a set of its projections. In: Medical Imaging 2003: Image Processing, vol. 5032, pp. 1049–1052. International Society for Optics and Photonics (2003). https://doi.org/10.1117/12.480241
4. Van de Kraats, E.B., Penney, G.P., Tomazevic, D., Van Walsum, T., Niessen, W.J.: Standardized evaluation methodology for 2-D-3-D registration. IEEE Trans. Med. Imaging **24**(9), 1177–1189 (2005). https://doi.org/10.1109/TMI.2005.853240
5. Maes, F., Vandermeulen, D., Suetens, P.: Comparative evaluation of multiresolution optimization strategies for multimodality image registration by maximization of mutual information. Med. Image Anal. **3**(4), 373–386 (1999). https://doi.org/10.1016/s1361-8415(99)80030-9
6. Markelj, P., Tomaževič, D., Likar, B., Pernuš, F.: A review of 3D/2D registration methods for image-guided interventions. Med. Image Anal. **16**(3), 642–61 (2012). https://doi.org/10.1016/j.media.2010.03.005
7. Mitrović, U., Špiclin, Ž., Likar, B., Pernuš, F.: 3D–2D registration of cerebral angiograms: a method and evaluation on clinical images. IEEE Trans. Med. Imaging **32**(8), 1550 (2013). https://doi.org/10.1109/TMI.2013.2259844
8. Mitrović, U., Likar, B., Pernuš, F., Špiclin, Ž.: 3D–2D registration in endovascular image-guided surgery: evaluation of state-of-the-art methods on cerebral angiograms. Int. J. Comput. Assist. Radiol. Surg. **13**(2), 193–202 (2017). https://doi.org/10.1007/s11548-017-1678-2
9. Munbodh, R., et al.: Automated 2D–3D registration of a radiograph and a cone beam CT using line-segment enhancement. Med. Phys. **33**(5), 1398–1411 (2006). https://doi.org/10.1118/1.2192621
10. Rühaak, J., Heldmann, S., Kipshagen, T., Fischer, B.: Highly accurate fast lung CT registration. In: SPIE Medical Imaging 2013: Image Processing, February 2013. https://doi.org/10.1117/12.2006035
11. Špiclin, Ž., Likar, B., Pernuš, F.: Fast and robust 3D to 2D image registration by backprojection of gradient covariances. In: Ourselin, S., Modat, M. (eds.) WBIR 2014. LNCS, vol. 8545, pp. 124–133. Springer, Cham (2014). https://doi.org/10.1007/978-3-319-08554-8_13
12. Wang, J., et al.: Dynamic 2-D/3-D rigid registration framework using point-to-plane correspondence model. IEEE Trans. Med. imaging **36**(9), 1939–1954 (2017). https://doi.org/10.1109/TMI.2017.2702100

Towards Automated Spine Mobility Quantification: A Locally Rigid CT to X-ray Registration Framework

David Drobny[1,2]($\boxtimes$), Marta Ranzini[2], Amanda Isaac[2],
Tom Vercauteren[2], Sébastien Ourselin[2], David Choi[3],
and Marc Modat[2]

[1] Wellcome/EPSRC Centre for Interventional and Surgical Sciences,
University College London, Gower Street, London WC1E 6BT, UK
d.drobny.17@ucl.ac.uk
[2] School of Biomedical Engineering & Imaging Sciences, King's College London,
King's Health Partners, St Thomas' Hospital, London SE1 7EH, UK
{marta.ranzini,a.isaac,tom.vercauteren,
sebastien.ourselin,marc.modat}@kcl.ac.uk
[3] University College Hospital, London NW1 2BU, UK
d.choi@ucl.ac.uk

Abstract. Different pathologies of the vertebral column, such as scoliosis, require quantification of the mobility of individual vertebrae or of curves of the spine for treatment planning. Without the necessary mobility, vertebrae can not be safely re-positioned and fused. The current clinical workflow consists of radiologists or surgeons estimating angular differences of neighbouring vertebrae from different x-ray images. This procedure is time consuming and prone to inaccuracy. The proposed method automates this quantification by deforming a CT image in a physiologically reasonable way and matching it to the x-ray images of interest. We propose a proof of concept evaluation on synthetic data. The automatic and quantitative analysis enables reproducible results independent of the investigator.

Keywords: Spine · Vertebra · Mobility quantification · 3D-2D registration · Volume-projection registration

1 Introduction

Spine mobility quantification (SMQ) describes the measurement of angles between vertebrae and their change between different positions, in order to evaluate the mobility of individual vertebrae. It is, for example, performed for scoliosis patients to determine whether vertebrae have the required mobility to be

Electronic supplementary material The online version of this chapter (https://doi.org/10.1007/978-3-030-50120-4_7) contains supplementary material, which is available to authorized users.

© Springer Nature Switzerland AG 2020
Ž. Špiclin et al. (Eds.): WBIR 2020, LNCS 12120, pp. 67–77, 2020.
https://doi.org/10.1007/978-3-030-50120-4_7

realigned and fused to improve the curvature of the spine. SMQ is typically evaluated manually based on x-ray images. The clinician measures the angles between neighbouring vertebrae in x-ray images acquired in two opposite and extreme positions, for example flexion and extension. The change of the angular difference from one position to the other informs about the mobility of those vertebrae. Manual measurements are subjective and prone to errors, especially when a 3D movement is assessed by rotations within one plane only.

In many clinical cases a CT image is available which could be used for 3D-2D registration. This could help automating SMQ by aligning the CT image to the X-ray target pose and deriving the SMQ values from the applied deformation.

Registration of CT volumetric images to x-ray projection images is a relevant task also for several other clinical applications, such as the automated localisation of an interventional image with respect to the pre-operative CT data. Specifically, this approach can be used in image-guided spine surgery where the target vertebra has to be identified reliably [3]. According to Mody et al. more than 0.3% of spine surgery procedures have been affected by wrong-level errors which can have a severe negative impact on the patient [5]. This demonstrates the difficulty of vertebra identification even for experienced surgeons. After robust identification, a precise registration further enables navigated surgery which typically makes use of intra-operative CT (iCT) imaging. A reliable and accurate 3D-2D registration for interventional x-ray images could thus decrease errors in surgical procedures, improve accuracy of image-guided interventions or otherwise maintain accuracy while decreasing radiation exposure to patients and clinicians, compared to using iCT imaging.

Previous work in volume-projection registration (of the spine) predominantly considers rigid registration frameworks [3,4,8,9,11]. This reduces the complexity of this ill-posed problem but limits the potential accuracy and applications, as it cannot capture local deformations of soft tissue related to different positions of the subject. Non-rigid advances have been mostly focused on other body parts, for example, on lung movement [12], and might be unrealistic in rigid anatomical structures such as bones.

To overcome the limitations of existing methods used for spine applications, we suggest a locally rigid registration framework based on the works of Arsigny et al. [1]. The proposed framework extends the poly-rigid transformation model to ensure the preservation of local rigidity during articulated movement and relies on a novel regulariser to enforce physiologically reasonable transformations. It enables better matching of images acquired with different patient position, e.g. flexion and extension, or pre-operative supine and intra-operative prone. Furthermore, the parametrisation of our model can be directly used to quantify relative positions of the vertebrae, for example for SMQ.

We demonstrate a proof of concept for spine mobility quantification based on simulated data using our registration framework. Rotation angles can be determined with high precision which motivates further development of this approach.

2   Methods

The proposed registration framework enables the recovery of spine movement via 3D-2D registration and the quantification of differential movement between neighbouring vertebrae. The underlying transformation model uses the poly-rigid approach which combines n local sets of rigid parameters $l = \{l_1, .., l_n\}$ into a single smooth deformation field [1]. It requires a set of non-overlapping regions R_i which, in our case, are given by a binary mask for each vertebra i. Based on the regions, individual weight maps w_i are computed that define the local influence of each rigid transformation T_i.

2.1   Registration Framework

The registration algorithm finds an optimal choice of parameters $p = (g, l)$, with global affine transformation parameters g and local rigid transformation parameters l, that describes the relationship between the reference x-ray image $\mathcal{X}$ and the CT volume $\mathcal{V}$ via the transformation $\mathcal{T}$. The transformation $\mathcal{T}$ combines the poly-rigid transformation $\mathcal{T}_{pr}(x, l)$ with a global affine transformation $\mathcal{A}(x, g)$:

$$\mathcal{T}(x, p) = \mathcal{A}(x, g) \circ \mathcal{T}_{pr}(x, l). \tag{1}$$

To enable the comparison of 3D and 2D images, a projection $\mathcal{P}$ is used:

$$\mathcal{P} : \mathbb{R}^3 \mapsto \mathbb{R}^2. \tag{2}$$

The distance measure $\mathcal{D}$ describes the dissimilarity of the images and is combined with a regulariser $\mathcal{R}$ to form the objective function $\mathcal{F}$:

$$\mathcal{F}[\mathcal{X}, \mathcal{V}, p] = \mathcal{D}\Big[\mathcal{X}, \mathcal{P}\big[\mathcal{T}(\mathcal{V}, p)\big]\Big] + \alpha\, \mathcal{R}(p). \tag{3}$$

The parameter α controls the ratio between both terms and thus adjusts the influence of the regularisation. Minimisation of $\mathcal{D}$ makes the appearance of the images more similar while $\mathcal{R}$ promotes a anatomically realistic transformation.

The numerical optimisation of $\mathcal{F}$ is performed iteratively via a gradient descent solver. In each step a subset of transformation parameters is evaluated, global rigid followed by local rigid parameters for each region, one at a time. Optimising only a subset of parameters reduces the complexity of the partial derivatives and empirically leads to a more stable behaviour of the model.

For increased robustness to local minima and to increase the capture range, a multi-resolution approach is applied that performs the optimisation on multiple levels – from coarse to fine. The framework also enables 3D-3D registration of a volume $\mathcal{V}$ to a reference volume $\mathcal{V}_{ref}$. In this case the projection step is omitted and the objective function is therefore:

$$\mathcal{F}_{3D-3D}[\mathcal{V}_{ref}, \mathcal{V}, p] = \mathcal{D}\big[\mathcal{V}_{ref}, \mathcal{T}(\mathcal{V}, p)\big] + \alpha\, \mathcal{R}(p). \tag{4}$$

2.2 Poly-rigid Transformation Model

The poly-rigid transformation model is based on a set of local rigid transformation parameters l_i with associated weight maps w_i defining its local influence for each region i. To combine the different local rigid transformations T_i into a single one, an ad hoc solution is the weighted average of the transformations' displacement fields. This does not preserve local behaviours and can lead to folding, i.e. breaking of the topology, which is to be avoided in most medical image processing.

Arsigny et al. proposed a method that provides a combined transformation that is invertible and thus does not lead to folding [1]. The local rigid transformations T_i are by definition homomorphisms, i.e. invertible. The average of infinitesimal small downscaled homomorphisms is also invertible as the displacement gets close to zero. The composition of homomorphisms is also a homomorphism so that the full scale transformation recovered by composition of the infinitesimal transformations is a homomorphism as well. The transformation $T(t, x)$ is parametrised as a velocity field and integrated over time $t \in [0, 1]$. At time $t = 0$ the transformation is the identity and at $t = 1$ it is T_{pr}.

The weighted average of the downscaled transformations is computed as

$$T\left(\frac{1}{m}, x\right) = \sum_{i=1}^{n} w_i(x) T_i(x)^{\frac{1}{m}}, \tag{5}$$

where $T^{\frac{1}{m}}$ describes the m-th matrix square root of the rigid transformation matrix T. m has to be chosen such that the downscaled velocity field is close enough to zero [1]. This average function needs to be upscaled to get the wanted poly-rigid transformation T_{pr}:

$$T_{pr}(x) = T(1, x) = T\left(\frac{1}{m}, x\right)^{m}. \tag{6}$$

Arsigny et al. use an efficient scaling-and-squaring scheme to integrate the final transformation [1]. However, to maintain the desired rigid properties for each region, the weights need to be updated after each integration step as suggested by Porras et al. [6]. Therefore we use the following Euler integration scheme:

For $j = 2, .., m$

$$w_i^{(j)}(x) = w_i\left(T^{(j-1)}\left(\frac{1}{m}, x\right)\right)$$
$$T^{(j)}\left(\frac{1}{m}, x\right) = \sum_{i=1}^{n} w_i^{(j)}(x) T_i^{\frac{1}{m}}(x) \tag{7}$$
$$T\left(\frac{j}{m}, x\right) = T\left(\frac{j-1}{m}, x\right) \circ T^{(j)}\left(\frac{1}{m}, x\right)$$

The superscript $\cdot^{(j)}$ indicates that the corresponding term is updated in step j.

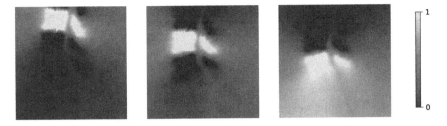

Fig. 1. Weight maps of the three lowest lumbar vertebrae. A vertebra in between other vertebrae has mostly influence perpendicular to the spine. The bottom vertebra (in this experiment the sacrum is not modelled as a rigid region) dominates the weights in the lower part of the image as the other vertebrae are further away and affect it less.

2.3   Weight Map Computation

Poly-rigid transformation models require weight maps w_i which define the spatial influence of multiple transformations T_i. Our model's weight computation is based on non-overlapping regions R_i, that represent a spine segmentation.

In the region based weight computation of Porras *et al.* [6], each weight w approximates the following values: $w(x) = 1$ if x is within the region, $0 < w(x) < 1$ otherwise. This implies that each region has a global influence and the rigid properties of a region are not preserved anywhere. To guarantee the rigid transformation of a region, weights with following properties are required.

$$
w_i(x) = \begin{cases} 1, & \text{if } x \in R_i \\ 0, & \text{if } x \in R_k, \ k \in \{1, .., n\} \setminus i \\ v, v \in \mathbb{R}, \ 0 < v < 1, & \text{elsewhere} \end{cases} \tag{8}
$$

The computation of the weight map can be split into three steps. First, creating a smooth weight map that is 1 within a region and decreases outside:

$$
w_i^a(x) = \frac{1}{\exp\left(s * EDT_i(x)\right)}, \tag{9}
$$

where EDT denotes the Euclidean Distance Transform of the binary mask of region R_i in mm (i.e. the distance to the nearest voxel of this region). The slope constant s controls how quickly the weight decays and is fixed for all regions throughout the computations.

To set the influence of all other regions R_k to 0 within region R_i, we multiply each region's weight by the complementary weight of all other regions:

$$
w_i^b(x) = w_i^a(x) \prod_{\substack{k=1 \\ k \neq i}}^{n} \left(1 - w_k^a(x)\right). \tag{10}
$$

Normalising the weights w_i^b to recover the maximal value of 1 within each region yields the final weight maps w_i that fulfil Eq. (8):

$$w_i(x) = \frac{w_i^b(x)}{\sum\limits_{k=1}^{n} w_k^b(x)}. \tag{11}$$

Figure 1 shows example weight maps computed for a CT slice containing the lowest lumbar vertebrae. This example visualises that within a region (i.e. a vertebra) the weight is one, smoothly decaying when moving away from it, and zero in each other region.

2.4 Regularisation

In order to guide the behaviour of the transformation model in a way that is closer to anatomical spine movement, we introduce a set of regularisation terms. These soft constraints penalise parameters that are in unexpected value ranges. The regulariser must have little influence while the parameters are within the expected value range and steeply increase when outside. Therefore the general form of each soft constraint C used is:

$$C(q) = \gamma \, |q - b|^c, \tag{12}$$

where b is the absolute upper bound for the value q and the exponent c controls how steep the penalty term increases.

Firstly, the parameters of the global affine registration g are limited as we assume the general direction of x-ray acquisition is known and thus, the volume should not translate or rotate too much away from the expected view.

$$\mathcal{R}^g(g) = C(|g^{trans}|) + C(|g^{rot}|) \tag{13}$$

Secondly, the local rigid parameters l are constrained via the parameter difference of pairs of neighbouring vertebrae, separate for rotation and translation:

$$\mathcal{R}^l(l) = \sum_{i=2}^{n} C(|l_i^{trans} - l_{i-1}^{trans}|) + C(|l_i^{rot} - l_{i-1}^{rot}|) \tag{14}$$

This way neighbouring vertebrae cannot translate or rotate too far from their initial relative position. This constraint guarantees that the spine moves consistently and retains its integrity.

An unregularised optimisation step might lead to local rigid parameters that would move regions into another. The overall poly-rigid transformation avoids this kind of folding but compromises the rigidity of the underlying transformations to achieve this. The third regulariser $\mathcal{R}^o$ is used to discourage such optimisation steps by penalising transformations that cause voxel overlap in order to achieve diffeomorphic transformations while preserving the local rigidity.

$$\mathcal{R}^o(p) = C\left(\left|\{x | x \in R_u \cap R_v, u, v \in \{1, .., n\}, u \neq v\}\right|\right) \tag{15}$$

The sum of all individual terms leads to the overall regulariser $\mathcal{R}$ as in Eq. (3):

$$\mathcal{R}(p) = \mathcal{R}^g(g) + \mathcal{R}^l(l) + \mathcal{R}^o(p) \tag{16}$$

3   Experiments

Data from the Spineweb database which consist of CT images and corresponding vertebra segmentation have been used for the experiments described in this work [13]. A CT image is cropped to the lumbar area including six vertebrae above the sacrum and resampled to a 1 mm isotropic image of $162 \times 162 \times 312$ voxel. The rigid parameters of the vertebrae are user-defined to simulate two movements: flexion and extension. The original CT image is considered as the starting position and angles are interpreted as differential angles to this position. The image axes x, y, and z correspond to the lateral, anterior-posterior, and superior-inferior patient axis, respectively. X-ray projections are simulated from the deformed CT images in lateral direction (along the x-axis) and are used as the reference images $\mathcal{X}$ while the initial CT volume is then used as moving image $\mathcal{V}$. The projection method $\mathcal{P}$ used for the synthetic experiments is a basic averaging of intensity values along a given direction, which can be easily replaced by other approaches to account for more clinically realistic scenarios, like those presented by Unberath et al. [7].

Table 1 shows the rotation angles chosen for each vertebra in the flexion and extension simulation. For this experiment only rotations around the x- and y-axis are considered, as those are the angles clinically measured for SMQ and rotations around z-axis are minor in the lumbar spine. The values are in the typical range observed in clinical practice, for example as reported by Wilke et al. [10]. Figure 2 shows the flexion, extension and initial position of the synthetic data as 3D rendered visualisations. The vertebrae are deformed rigidly while the surrounding soft tissue, like the arteries, are non-linearly deformable.

In our experiment, images in two different poses are target of the registration: flexion and extension. This resembles the application of SMQ where usually two opposite extremal positions are compared. For each pose, two experiments are evaluated: (1) 3D-3D registration—matching the original CT $\mathcal{V}$ to the synthetic CT image $\mathcal{V}_{ref}$ and (2) 3D-2D registration—matching the CT image $\mathcal{V}$ to the synthetic x-ray image $\mathcal{X}$. Two metrics are used to evaluate the registration results: the error of the estimated angle difference and the average error of the recovered displacement field at the location of the vertebrae. The displacement field error gives information about whether the vertebrae are in the right position while the angle errors describe how well the orientation of the vertebrae was recovered, which is the focus of SMQ.

For performance reasons, the poly-rigid transformation computed by Eq. (7) is used only as a post processing step and we use the direct weighted average during the optimisation, as was suggested by Commowick et al. [2]. We used the mean of squared difference as similarity measure $\mathcal{D}$ during our experiments. The parameters are either motivated by clinical movement ranges or chosen empirically: four levels of multi-resolution approach, with the finest resolution of 1 mm, the weight constant $s = 0.05$, the constraint scaling parameter $\alpha = 100$. Referring to Eqs. 12 and 16, the first two constraint functions have the exponent $c = 6$, scaling $\gamma = 1$ and the boundaries b of 20 mm, 30° for the global rigid

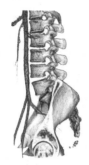 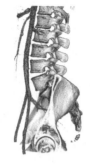 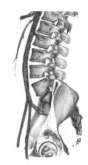

Fig. 2. 3D render of the original CT scan (centre), the synthetic CT scan in flexion (left) and extension (right) (see Supplementary material for animated figure).

Table 1. Rotation angles in degree per vertebra used to generate the synthetic images.

vertebra	flexion			extension		
	x	y	z	x	y	z
L1	− 11.00	−5.00	0.00	+10.00	+5.00	0.00
L2	− 8.50	−4.00	0.00	+7.50	+4.00	0.00
L3	− 5.00	−2.00	0.00	+4.00	+2.00	0.00
L4	0.00	0.00	0.00	0.00	0.00	0.00
L5	+ 4.00	+1.00	0.00	−3.50	−1.00	0.00

parameters and 8 mm, 7° for the local differences, the overlap constraint has $b = c = 1$ and $\gamma = 0.001$.

4   Results

Our experiments show that with both 3D-3D as well as 3D-2D registration, the parameters of the synthetic images can be recovered. In Table 2 the quantitative results of all experiments are summarised. Using the 3D-3D registration higher accuracy was achieved compared to the 3D-2D cases which is due to the higher information retained in a volume compared to its projection. In the 3D-3D experiments, the average of the mean absolute angle error was reduced from the initial 2.47° to 0.12° and from 2.70° to 0.16° for extension and flexion respectively. In the 3D-2D case, the respective average errors are 0.59° and 0.42°. The deformation field error (DFE) is also reported as a measure of registration accuracy in Table 2. The DFE confirms the higher accuracy of the 3D-3D approach compared to the 3D-2D registration.

For the spine mobility quantification the angular difference between the two positions for each vertebra is of interest. This can be directly derived from the individual registration results as the difference of the respective angles.

Table 2. For each experiment, this table shows the mean absolute angle error [in degrees] per rotation axis, averaged over all vertebrae, as well as combined into a single average error, the mean and maximum displacement field errors (DFE) [in mm] before and after registration. The DFEs are evaluated within the spine mask only.

	flexion			extension		
	initial	3D-3D	3D-2D	initial	3D-3D	3D-2D
error x	5.70	0.11	0.45	5.00	0.06	0.37
error y	2.40	0.06	0.55	2.40	0.07	0.99
error z	0.00	0.31	0.30	0.00	0.23	0.41
average error	2.70	0.16	0.43	2.47	0.12	0.59
average DFE	4.37	0.05	0.52	3.11	0.10	1.71
max DFE	24.32	0.50	2.06	16.13	2.49	11.31

5   Discussion

The non-rigid alignment of a volumetric to a projection image is challenging because several degrees of freedom affecting the 3D volume have to be recovered by only comparing 2D images. We presented a framework based on a locally rigid transformation model that enables 3D-3D and 3D-2D registration of spine images. These synthetic experiments show that both 3D-3D and 3D-2D registration can be recovered, demonstrating that the registration with our transformation model can lead to clinically useful results for spine mobility quantification.

This framework offers the full processing pipeline needed for different applications and is flexible to adaptations required by the use of real clinical data. We also introduced simple constraints to guide a consistent movement of the spine while optimising individual vertebrae parameters iteratively. Our experiments are limited by only considering synthetic x-ray images generated from deformed CT scans. Clinical x-ray images are more challenging to register and thus need specialised image similarity measures. Future work will thus focus on the identification of a measure suitable for clinical data, and on the benchmarking of the proposed approach against the current clinical practice on real patient data. Furthermore we will use a higher level parametrisation of the spine shape, e.g. using principal components of a spine shape model, to optimise the position of multiple vertebrae simultaneously in a consistent way. This will be helpful to capture larger deformations especially in an extended field of view. Such a model could also be used to extract population statistics like the principal modes of spine variability and movement patterns. As the proposed framework proved effective also for 3D-3D registration, it will be tested on further clinical applications, such as spine CT-MRI registration. Finally, as this pipeline requires vertebra segmentations, automated segmentation techniques (*e.g.* using deep learning approaches) will be explored to complete the registration framework.

Acknowledgments. This work is supported by the UCL EPSRC Centre for Doctoral Training in Medical Imaging [EP/L016478/1], the Wellcome/EPSRC Centre for Interventional and Surgical Sciences [NS/A000050/1], the Wellcome/EPSRC Centre for Medical Engineering [WT 203148/Z/16/Z] and EPSRC [NS/A000027/1]. TV is supported by a Medtronic/Royal Academy of Engineering Research Chair [RCSRF1819/7/34]. This research was supported by the NIHR BRC based at GSTT and KCL.

References

1. Arsigny, V., Commowick, O., Ayache, N., Pennec, X.: A fast and log-euclidean polyaffine framework for locally linear registration. J. Math. Imag. Vis. **33**(2), 222–238 (2009)
2. Commowick, O., et al.: An efficient locally affine framework for the smooth registration of anatomical structures. Med. Image Anal. **12**(4), 427–441 (2008)
3. De Silva, T., et al.: 3D–2D image registration for target localization in spine surgery: investigation of similarity metrics providing robustness to content mismatch. Phys. Med. Biol. **61**(8), 3009–3025 (2016)
4. Duménil, A., Kaladji, A., Castro, M., Göksu, C., Lucas, A., Haigron, P.: A versatile intensity-based 3D/2D rigid registration compatible with mobile C-arm for endovascular treatment of abdominal aortic aneurysm. Int. J. Comput. Assisted Radiol. Surg. **11**(9), 1713–1729 (2016)
5. Mody, M.G., Nourbakhsh, A., Stahl, D.L., Gibbs, M., Alfawareh, M., Garges, K.J.: The prevalence of wrong level surgery among spine surgeons. Spine **33**(2), 194–198 (2008)
6. Porras, A.R., et al.: Locally affine diffeomorphic surface registration and its application to surgical planning of fronto-orbital advancement. IEEE Trans. Med. Imag. **37**(7), 1690–1700 (2018)
7. Unberath, M., et al.: DeepDRR – a catalyst for machine learning in fluoroscopy-guided procedures. In: Frangi, A.F., Schnabel, J.A., Davatzikos, C., Alberola-López, C., Fichtinger, G. (eds.) MICCAI 2018. LNCS, vol. 11073, pp. 98–106. Springer, Cham (2018). https://doi.org/10.1007/978-3-030-00937-3_12
8. Varnavas, A., Carrell, T., Penney, G.: Fully automated 2D–3D registration and verification. Med. Image Anal. **26**(1), 108–119 (2015)
9. Wang, L., Gao, X., Zhang, R., Xia, W.: A comparison of two novel similarity measures based on mutual information in 2D/3D image registration. In: ICMIPE 2013 - Proceedings of 2013 IEEE International Conference on Medical Imaging Physics and Engineering, pp. 215–218. IEEE, October 2013
10. Wilke, H.J., Schmidt, R., Richter, M., Schmoelz, W., Reichel, H., Cakir, B.: The role of prosthesis design on segmental biomechanics semi-constrained versus unconstrained prostheses and anterior versus posterior centre of rotation. Eur. Spine J. **21**(SUPPL. 5), 577–584 (2012)
11. Wu, J., Kim, M., Peters, J., Chung, H., Samant, S.S.: Evaluation of similarity measures for use in the intensity-based rigid 2D–3D registration for patient positioning in radiotherapy. Med. Phys. **36**(12), 5391–5403 (2009)

12. Xia, W., Jin, Q., Ni, C., Wang, Y., Gao, X.: Thorax x-ray and CT interventional dataset for nonrigid 2D/3D image registration evaluation. Med. Phys. **45**(11), 5343–5351 (2018)
13. Yao, J., Burns, J.E., Munoz, H., Summers, R.M.: Detection of vertebral body fractures based on cortical shell unwrapping. In: Ayache, N., Delingette, H., Golland, P., Mori, K. (eds.) MICCAI 2012. LNCS, vol. 7512, pp. 509–516. Springer, Heidelberg (2012). https://doi.org/10.1007/978-3-642-33454-2_63

Landmark Based Registration

Reinforced Redetection of Landmark in Pre- and Post-operative Brain Scan Using Anatomical Guidance for Image Alignment

Diana Waldmannstetter[1,2(✉)], Fernando Navarro[1,4], Benedikt Wiestler[3],
Jan S. Kirschke[3], Anjany Sekuboyina[1,3,4], Ester Molero[1],
and Bjoern H. Menze[1,2,4]

[1] Department of Informatics, Technical University of Munich, Munich, Germany
diana.waldmannstetter@tum.de
[2] Munich School of BioEngineering, Munich, Germany
[3] Department of Neuroradiology, Klinikum rechts der Isar, Munich, Germany
[4] TranslaTUM - Central Institute for Translational Cancer Research,
Munich, Germany

Abstract. Re-identifying locations of interest in pre- and post-operative images is a hard identification problem, as the anatomical landscape changes dramatically due to tumor resection and tissue displacement. Classical image registration techniques oftentimes fail in vicinity of the tumor, where the enclosing structures are massively altered from one scan to another. Still, locations nearby the tumor or the resection cavity are the most relevant for evaluating tumor progression patterns and for comparing pre- and post-operative radiomic signatures. We address this issue by exploring a Reinforcement Learning (RL) approach. An artificial agent is self-taught to find the optimal path towards a target driven by a feedback signal from the environment. Incorporating anatomical guidance, we restrict the agent's search space to surgery-unaffected structures only. By defining landmarks for each patient individually, we aim to obtain a patient-specific representation of its differential radiomic features across different time points for enhancing image alignment. Estimated landmarks reach a remarkable mean distance error around 3 mm. In addition, they show a high agreement with expert annotations on a challenging dataset of MR scans from the brain before and after tumor resection.

Keywords: Reinforcement Learning · Image registration · Image alignment · Differential radiomics · Brain tumor

1 Introduction

The most effective treatment for progression delay in aggressive primary brain tumors is tumor resection, usually followed by radiation therapy or chemotherapy [4]. When evaluating the post-operative scans, the areas that show signs of

Ž. Špiclin et al. (Eds.): WBIR 2020, LNCS 12120, pp. 81–90, 2020.
https://doi.org/10.1007/978-3-030-50120-4_8

tumor re-growth are compared to the same areas in the pre-operative scans. As there is almost always a shift in brain tissue as well as tumor- and resection-induced intensity changes, conventional image registration techniques oftentimes fail when it comes to map the differing structures, see Fig. 1. We aim to evaluate local patterns with anatomical guidance for a better adaption in this task. We perform re-identification of landmarks for making use of quantitative radiomic approaches, since radiomics intend to improve image analysis by extracting large amounts of quantitative features [8]. In order to detect reference points before and after tumor resection, we use individual landmarks for each patient, representing locations prone to progression. Redetecting these landmarks automatically in follow-up scans may simplify future image alignment for the same patient. Therefore, we define multiple patient-specific landmarks around the tumor and take a first step towards differential radiomic feature extraction and therefore, a more precise alignment of the resection-affected regions.

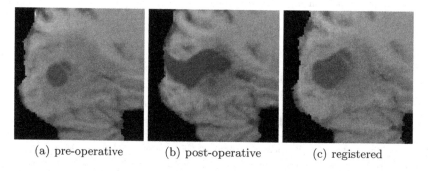

(a) pre-operative   (b) post-operative   (c) registered

Fig. 1. 2D zoom into tumor-/resection-affected regions in (a) a pre-operative scan, (b) the corresponding post-operative scan and (c) the result of a standard image registration

Recent literature shows a variety of approaches towards localization of anatomical landmarks in medical images. Li *et al.* [9] developed a patch-based CNN for landmark localization combining regression and classification for the detection of both single and multiple landmarks simultaneously by involving Principle Component Analysis (PCA). Zheng *et al.* [19] evolved a two-step approach combining a shallow network with a deep network for efficient landmark detection. Another two-stage approach was proposed by Zhang *et al.* [18] comprising a patch-based CNN regression model followed by another CNN for predicting landmarks in an end-to-end manner. For the first time, Ghesu *et al.* [6] introduced Deep RL for localizing anatomical landmarks using Q-learning. Their method is further developed by exploring multiple scales in [5,7]. In [11], Maicas *et al.* adopt this method and extend it to the more complex detection of breast lesions. There, adaptive bounding boxes are leveraged to train the agent. Alansary *et al.* [2] presented a multi-scale strategy by iteratively training their agent using action steps with different sizes on multiple scales. Additionally, they evaluate several Q-Learning approaches as there are Double, Dueling and Dueling Double Q-Learning. A variant of their approach towards automatic view planning is shown in [1] and an extension towards the detection of multiple landmarks simultaneously in [15].

The recent success of RL in the field of landmark localization [2,5–7,15] in combination with the ability of RL agents to adapt to a specific environment, encouraged us to transfer this approach for landmark redetection to pre- and post-operative brain images. Furthermore, RL has the benefit of being able to perform on limited training data, which is crucial for our task. Based on the approach in [2], we further develop the method to consider anatomical guidance and propose the following contributions: First, we present two RL-based agents. A baseline agent and an extended version of it under anatomical guidance, improving the agent's ability to adapt to the issue of altering tissue structures by integrating patient-specific anatomy into our model. Second, we evaluate our approach on a challenging dataset of MR scans before and after tumor resection, provided by the BraTS challenge [12] and TCIA [3], achieving results comparable to an expert performance. Additionally, we provide annotations for this data.

In the following, we present how we utilize Q-Learning in RL (Sect. 2) and introduce our extension (Sect. 3), before demonstrating the performance of our approach on a complex data set.

2   Deep Reinforcement Learning Using Q-Learning

In RL, an artificial agent is self-taught by interacting with an environment. In every step, the agent retrieves a reward from its environment after executing an action. The final goal of the agent is to find an optimal policy, guiding the agent from any given state to the target by maximizing future rewards. This can be formulated as a sequential decision process. RL then is modeled as a *Markov Decision Process* (MDP), which defines the interaction between the agent and its environment. The agent executes an action $a \in A$ at state $s \in S$, returning a reward signal $r \in R$ at each time step t [14].

Finding the optimal policy is described by the action-value function $Q(s, a)$, which is optimized during training and gives the maximum expected discounted future reward, where the accumulated discounted reward after τ time steps is defined as

$$R_\tau = \sum_{\tau=0}^{\infty} \gamma^\tau r_{t+\tau+1}, \tag{1}$$

with the discount rate $\gamma \in [0, 1]$ for weighting immediate and future rewards [17]. Using the Bellman optimality equation, the action-value function can be solved recursively [14]:

$$Q(s, a) = \mathbb{E}\left[r + \gamma \max_{a'} Q(s', a') \right], \tag{2}$$

where s' and a' are the possible subsequent state and action.

Mnih *et al.* [13] developed the Deep Q-Network (DQN), which approximates

$$Q(s,a) \approx Q(s,a;\theta), \tag{3}$$

using a CNN with the network parameters θ. For stability reasons, a target network $Q(\theta^-)$ is introduced. It estimates the actual Q-network iteratively by updating the parameters of the target network only every nth iteration with the steadily updated Q-network parameters. The loss function reads:

$$L_n(\theta_n) = E_{s,a,r,s'} \left[\left(r + \gamma \max_{a'} Q(s',a';\theta_n^-) - Q(s,a;\theta_n) \right)^2 \right] \tag{4}$$

Experience replay technique [10] is added, training the network using randomly sampled minibatches from experiences the agent has already gained. This is stored in an experience replay memory.

The DQN was further improved by Wang *et al.* [16], separating the network into two partitions. One handles the state-value function $V(s)$ and the other one deals with the advantage function $A(s,a)$, see Fig. 2. Both are then combined by an aggregation layer to provide a single Q-function

$$Q(s,a) = V(s) + A(s,a). \tag{5}$$

Here, estimating the state-value function is essential in every time step, while this is not necessary for the advantage function. Consequently, the dueling network learns the state-value function more accurately, thus improving the network performance with increasing number of actions.

3   Anatomically Guided RL Agent

Similar to [2], we make use of a Deep Q-Network with dueling architecture, shown in Fig. 2. Each state in our image environment is modeled as a 3D patch centered around the current location of the agent, see Fig. 3(a). Hence, the agent sees a different part of its environment in every time step. Due to the experience replay technique, we define an experience buffer storing the last four patches, which the network can see in one iteration, enhancing the agent's robustness.

We define the action space with the six actions *right, left, forward, backward, up, down*. This results in two actions along each axis in positive and negative direction, $a \in A = \{+x, -x, +y, -y, +z, -z\}$, thus moving the agent by one voxel. The reward is defined similar to [6], calculating the relative change in the distance to the position of the target landmark. Furthermore, we make use of a search strategy operating on multiple scales [2,5,7] for more robustness and efficiency.

A key feature of our approach is the anatomical guidance. We return a negative reward $r = -1$ when the agent steps inside the surgery-affected regions. Therefore, we provide the segmentation mask to the agent, so the agent learns to stay in unaffected structures only, see Fig. 3(b). Since this guides the agent to move towards the target without touching the immense tissue changes inside the most affected regions, this leads to a policy that is more generalizable to altering brain tissue.

4   Experimental Setup

We evaluate our approach on a challenging dataset provided by the BraTS challenge [12] and TCIA [3]. We use MR image data from 10 patients with brain tumors, with one scan before and one scan after tumor resection, comprising 20 image volumes in total. All images are skull-stripped, rigidly co-registered and interpolated to a common resolution of $1\,mm^3$, while the initial resolution is in the range of 3–$8\,mm$ for most sequences. The dataset includes the image volumes and their corresponding segmentation masks of the tumor- and resection-affected regions in the pre- and post-operative scans, respectively. For each patient, 3 landmarks in the post-operative scan are annotated by a clinical expert, in varying distances up to 4 cm around the resection-affected region. The same expert redetected the landmarks in the corresponding pre-operative scan for generating ground truth annotations.

Training and Testing. Before training, we crop an initialization box of size $50 \times 50 \times 50$ voxels around the target in the training image, see Fig. 3(a). When training under anatomical guidance, we exclude the resection mask, see Fig. 3(b). Then, we randomly initialize the agent inside this region and sample a patch of size $15 \times 15 \times 15$ voxels, which follows the agent in every step. For every patient and landmark individually, we train on the respective post-operative scan and test on the corresponding pre-operative scan, generating patient-specific models. Similar to [2], we define the terminal state in training as the point, when the distance between the agent and the target landmark is less or equal to 1 mm. During testing, the agent is stopped, when it is oscillating around the same location.

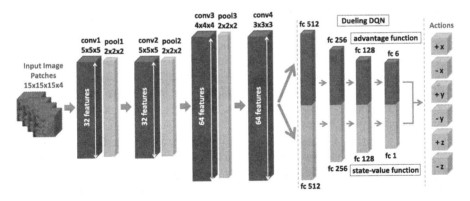

Fig. 2. Our network architecture with a dueling DQN. A 3D patch is sampled around the current position of the agent and fed to the network, consisting of convolutional (conv) layers alternating with pooling (pool) layers, followed by a dueling DQN with fully connected (fc) layers. The network outputs the Q-value for the six possible actions, whereof the agent selects the one with the highest value.

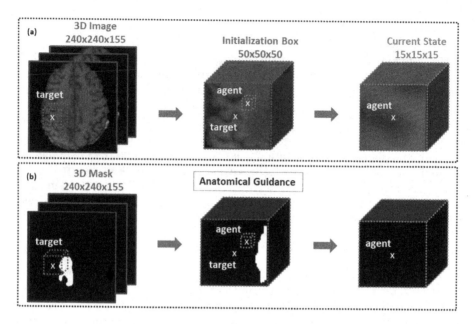

Fig. 3. (a) Patch generation. A box of size $50 \times 50 \times 50$ is sampled around the target for initialization reasons. Then, a patch of size $15 \times 15 \times 15$ is extracted around the current position of the agent, representing the current state. (b) Anatomical Guidance. We provide the segmentation mask to the agent for excluding this region during training. When stepping inside the masked region, a negative reward is returned, so that the agent is guided to avoiding affected structures.

Experiments. We use two different agents for each experiment. One is trained on the baseline method without anatomical guidance, whereas the other one is anatomically guided. Due to the lack of a validation set, we tune the model on the respective training image. For each experiment, we then choose the model that is performing best on the corresponding test image. Although this might lead to some underestimation regarding the distance error measurements, it makes sure that we provide the same conditions for the two agents in the different experiments, leading to comparable results. During evaluation, we define 20 fixed starting points, typically converging to slightly different final endpoints. Since we initialize the training agent inside the initialization box, we use the same box for testing and select the starting points from there. For each of the 20 evaluation runs per experiment, we calculate the Euclidean distance in mm between the final location of the agent and the true landmark, which gives us the distance error, and calculate the mean, for producing comparable results. Subsequently, for the sake of simplicity, we refer to this mean distance error simply as distance error.

5   Results

Quantitative results can be observed from Fig. 4(a) and (b), showing the distance errors in mm for the baseline method (BM), the extended method using anatomical guidance (AM), as well as another expert's annotation for comparison. Therefore, we take the landmark annotations of a second expert, when performing the redetection task manually, and calculate the Euclidean distance to the ground truth annotations, giving us the distance errors of an expert. For further comparisons, we calculate additional measurements on the distance errors, the mean and the median distance as well as the normalized mean and median, respectively, see Table 1. All measurements are calculated on landmark level. Qualitative results are presented in Fig. 5, showing a sample redetection for two different landmarks, where both methods achieve high precision with a distance error of 0 mm.

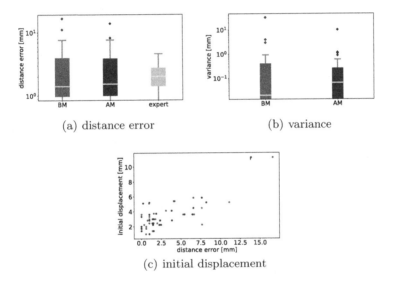

(a) distance error   (b) variance

(c) initial displacement

Fig. 4. Results for the baseline method (BM, green), the extended method with anatomical guidance (AM, dark blue) and an expert annotation for comparison (light blue). (a) shows the distance mean errors in mm and (b) the variances in the distance errors due to the multiple starting points. (c) shows the relation between the initial expert annotation displacements and the distance errors. The dots represent the respective offsets of the initial expert annotation for the training and test images in relation to the corresponding distance errors of BM and AM. (Color figure online)

RL vs Expert. The lowest distance errors for both methods are close to 0 mm, representing a perfect redetection. The highest lie above 1 cm. Due to the 20 starting points, we achieve variances in the distance errors, tending to increase with growing errors, see Fig. 4(a) and (b). High variances are caused by some

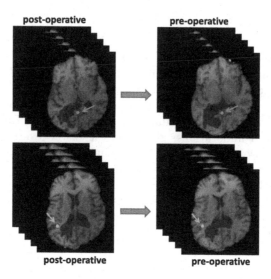

Fig. 5. Sample redetection for two different landmarks (top, bottom) in the same patient. The masked region is marked in red. The landmarks in blue and green, respectively. (Color figure online)

outliers, where the agent gets lost in the environment. However, it is remarkable that we achieve a variance of 0 in some experiments, which means that the agent navigates towards the same target from every starting point, demonstrating high robustness. As Fig. 4(c) shows, the distance errors from BM and AM both scale with the initial displacements between the ground truth annotations in the training and test images, when annotated by an expert. That means, a larger offset between the initial expert landmark annotation in the training and the test image results in larger distance errors. This makes sense, since larger initial annotation displacements are linked to larger tissue changes. Nevertheless, the majority ranges within smaller errors from 0–4 mm. From Table 1, we observe that the mean of all distance errors is lowest for the comparison expert, while both BM and AM show high agreement with it. Still, the median of all distance errors is smaller for BM and AM. A normalization with the initial displacements leads to similar mean errors of both RL methods and the comparison expert, see Table 1.

Benefits of Anatomical Guidance. Figure 4(a) and (b) as well as Table 1 show that AM performs more robust than BM, since the outliers have slightly smaller mean distance errors and variances. Hence, incorporating anatomical guidance outperforms the baseline agent in average, while showing high agreement with the comparison expert's annotations. Our approach achieves noticeable performance with an average distance error below 3 mm. Moreover, anatomical guidance provides potential to incorporate additional anatomical information.

Table 1. Calculations on the distance errors for BM, AM and an expert annotation.

	Mean distance [mm]	Median distance [mm]	Normalized mean	Normalized median
BM	3.05	1.41	0.79	0.57
AM	2.82	1.53	0.74	0.64
Expert	2.18	2.0	0.75	0.72

6   Conclusion

In this work, we presented a RL framework for landmark redetection in a challenging dataset of pre- and post-operative brain scans. We evaluated two RL agents: a basic one exploring the full environment and an extended one guided by the resection anatomy for finding the optimal path towards the target landmark. Overall, both approaches showed good results in terms of speed and accuracy, while the agent under anatomical guidance performs better in average. Therefore, this approach allows to further develop the guidance by anatomical structures, especially in analyzing the connection between different time points before and after tumor resection, for generating a more representative and efficient model of the anatomical changes. For further automatization, the segmentation masks can be produced using some segmentation framework, which would be of minimal additional effort here and would be needed to be done once for training only. Additionally, we will invest in finetuning our approach towards a more robust redetection for eliminating outliers. Moreover, we will further investigate in generating a dense representation of patient-specific differential radiomics by localizing multiple landmarks simultaneously, ideally incorporating the spatial relationships between tumor structures, resection region and landmarks.

Acknowledgements. Supported by Deutsche Forschungsgemeinschaft (DFG) through TUM International Graduate School of Science and Engineering (IGSSE), GSC 81.

References

1. Alansary, A., et al.: Automatic view planning with multi-scale deep reinforcement learning agents. In: Frangi, A.F., Schnabel, J.A., Davatzikos, C., Alberola-López, C., Fichtinger, G. (eds.) MICCAI 2018. LNCS, vol. 11070, pp. 277–285. Springer, Cham (2018). https://doi.org/10.1007/978-3-030-00928-1_32
2. Alansary, A., Oktay, O., Li, Y., et al.: Evaluating reinforcement learning agents for anatomical landmark detection. Med. Image Anal. **53**, 156–164 (2019)
3. Clark, K., Vendt, B., Smith, K., et al.: The cancer imaging archive (TCIA): maintaining and operating a public information repository. J. Digit. Imag. **26**(6), 1045–1057 (2013)
4. DeAngelis, L.: Brain tumors. New Engl. J. Med. **344**(2), 114–123 (2001)

5. Ghesu, F.C., Georgescu, B., Grbic, S., Maier, A.K., Hornegger, J., Comaniciu, D.: Robust multi-scale anatomical landmark detection in incomplete 3D-CT data. In: Descoteaux, M., Maier-Hein, L., Franz, A., Jannin, P., Collins, D.L., Duchesne, S. (eds.) MICCAI 2017. LNCS, vol. 10433, pp. 194–202. Springer, Cham (2017). https://doi.org/10.1007/978-3-319-66182-7_23

6. Ghesu, F.C., Georgescu, B., Mansi, T., Neumann, D., Hornegger, J., Comaniciu, D.: An artificial agent for anatomical landmark detection in medical images. In: Ourselin, S., Joskowicz, L., Sabuncu, M.R., Unal, G., Wells, W. (eds.) MICCAI 2016. LNCS, vol. 9902, pp. 229–237. Springer, Cham (2016). https://doi.org/10.1007/978-3-319-46726-9_27

7. Ghesu, F., et al.: Multi-scale deep reinforcement learning for real-time 3D-landmark detection in CT scans. IEEE TPAMI 41(1), 176–189 (2017)

8. Lambin, P., Rios-Velazquez, E., Leijenaar, R., et al.: Radiomics: extracting more information from medical images using advanced feature analysis. Eur. J. Cancer 48(4), 441–446 (2012)

9. Li, Y., et al.: Fast multiple landmark localisation using a patch-based iterative network. In: Frangi, A.F., Schnabel, J.A., Davatzikos, C., Alberola-López, C., Fichtinger, G. (eds.) MICCAI 2018. LNCS, vol. 11070, pp. 563–571. Springer, Cham (2018). https://doi.org/10.1007/978-3-030-00928-1_64

10. Lin, L.J.: Self-improving reactive agents based on reinforcement learning, planning and teaching. Mach. Learn. 8(3–4), 293–321 (1992)

11. Maicas, G., Carneiro, G., Bradley, A.P., Nascimento, J.C., Reid, I.: Deep reinforcement learning for active breast lesion detection from DCE-MRI. In: Descoteaux, M., Maier-Hein, L., Franz, A., Jannin, P., Collins, D.L., Duchesne, S. (eds.) MICCAI 2017. LNCS, vol. 10435, pp. 665–673. Springer, Cham (2017). https://doi.org/10.1007/978-3-319-66179-7_76

12. Menze, B., Jakab, A., Bauer, S., et al.: The multimodal brain tumor image segmentation benchmark (BRATS). IEEE Trans. Med. Imag. 34(10), 1993–2024 (2015)

13. Mnih, V., Kavukcuoglu, K., Silver, D., et al.: Human-level control through deep reinforcement learning. Nature 518(7540), 529 (2015)

14. Sutton, R., Barto, A.: Introduction to Reinforcement Learning, 1st edn. MIT Press, Cambridge (1998)

15. Vlontzos, A., Alansary, A., Kamnitsas, K., Rueckert, D., Kainz, B.: Multiple landmark detection using multi-agent reinforcement learning. In: Shen, D., et al. (eds.) MICCAI 2019. LNCS, vol. 11767, pp. 262–270. Springer, Cham (2019). https://doi.org/10.1007/978-3-030-32251-9_29

16. Wang, Z., Schaul, T., Hessel, M., Van Hasselt, H., Lanctot, M., De Freitas, N.: Dueling network architectures for deep reinforcement learning. In: International Conference on Machine Learning, pp. 1995–2003 (2016)

17. Watkins, C., Dayan, P.: Q-learning. Mach. Learn. 8(3–4), 279–292 (1992)

18. Zhang, J., Liu, M., Shen, D.: Detecting anatomical landmarks from limited medical imaging data using two-stage task-oriented deep neural networks. IEEE Trans. Image Process. 26(10), 4753–4764 (2017)

19. Zheng, Y., Liu, D., Georgescu, B., Nguyen, H., Comaniciu, D.: 3D deep learning for efficient and robust landmark detection in volumetric data. In: Navab, N., Hornegger, J., Wells, W.M., Frangi, A.F. (eds.) MICCAI 2015. LNCS, vol. 9349, pp. 565–572. Springer, Cham (2015). https://doi.org/10.1007/978-3-319-24553-9_69

Deep Volumetric Feature Encoding
for Biomedical Images

Brian Avants[1,2(✉)], Elliot Greenblatt[2], Jacob Hesterman[2],
and Nicholas Tustison[1]

[1] Department of Radiology and Medical Imaging, University of Virginia,
Charlottesville, VA, USA
stnava@gmail.com
[2] Invicro, LLC, Boston, MA, USA

Abstract. Deep learning research has demonstrated the effectiveness of using pre-trained networks as feature encoders. The large majority of these networks are trained on 2D datasets with millions of samples and diverse classes of information. We demonstrate and evaluate approaches to transferring deep 2D feature spaces to 3D in order to take advantage of these and related resources in the biomedical domain. First, we show how VGG-19 activations can be mapped to a 3D variant of the network (VGG-19-3D). Second, using varied medical decathlon data, we provide a technique for training 3D networks to predict the encodings induced by 3D VGG-19. Lastly, we compare five different 3D networks (one of which is trained only on 3D MRI and another of which is not trained at all) across layers and patch sizes in terms of their ability to identify hippocampal landmark points in 3D MRI data that was not included in their training. We make observations about the performance, recommend different networks and layers and make them publicly available for further evaluation.

Keywords: Code: 3D VGG-19 · Landmarks · Key-point detection ·
Deep features

1 Introduction

Feature detection for pattern matching in images has a long history in computer vision, dating at least to the 1950s [11]. Perhaps the most well-known of these approaches is the scale invariant feature transform (SIFT) [5] which, as is typical of many of these methods, uses engineered features to localize salient features in images. These key-points are then filtered and matched in order to compute a geometric correspondence between image sets with little computational overhead. As such, SIFT is widely adopted as a core tool in industrial applications of computer vision.

While SIFT and related methods are powerful, their extension to 3D biomedical imaging has not, as yet, met with the same level of adoption and success.

© Springer Nature Switzerland AG 2020
Ž. Špiclin et al. (Eds.): WBIR 2020, LNCS 12120, pp. 91–100, 2020.
https://doi.org/10.1007/978-3-030-50120-4_9

Rister, et al. [10] extended SIFT to 3D but found that, although it performed well within-subject, it did not reach usability in inter-subject registration. This finding suggests that more general approaches – or different feature sets – may be of value.

New approaches to feature matching and registration of biomedical imaging data are also needed to handle its ever increasing diversity and magnitude. Furthermore, the desire to integrate imaging with other forms of data (e.g. genomics) leads to additional motivation to develop fast, general purpose search and matching based on biomedical (often volumetric) image features.

Feature-based matching, in this context, provides a powerful solution that, like SIFT, may be less sensitive than dense registration methods to occlusion, noise, resolution and modality. Furthermore, feature extraction methods may be more memory efficient which is of tremendous value when full datasets (e.g. CLARITY images) cannot be stored in memory without special handling [6].

Pre-trained convolutional networks, such as VGG-19 [14], have proven to be powerful feature encoders with applications in a variety of areas [4,16]. Distances between activation maps from intermediate layers of deep architectures (deep features) are effective metrics in domains beyond the original application area and have transformed practice in super-resolution, key point matching [8] and semantic segmentation. The use of these resources is relatively limited in the biomedical domain because these features are typically derived from 2D datasets.

The current paper is motivated by the desire to build a library of general purpose, pre-trained deep networks for volumetric feature encoding that may be used for transfer learning within the context of regression, classification, super-resolution and matching problems. ModelsGenesis [17] (Generic Autodidactic Models for 3D Medical Image Analysis) has similar goals to ours. However, in contrast to our focus on regression, Models Genesis leverages encoding/decoding (U-net like) architectures frequently used in segmentation tasks. Our contributions include: (1) an extension of the long-term proven 2D VGG-19 features to 3D, (2) approximation of these features with 3D regression networks and (3) comparison of the derived feature spaces to intrinsically 3D regression networks, including one that undergoes no training at all. The analysis contrasts the value of these networks' features at different layer depths – and with different input patch sizes – in terms of landmark matching in 3D MRI of the hippocampus [1].

2   Methods

We develop five different 3D networks based on established approaches. Two of these networks do not require additional training and extend 2D VGG 19 to 3D. Two others are based on regressing against VGG-19 activations. The final network is trained to solve a completely separate regression and classification problem and is treated as a fixed, intrinsically 3D pre-trained network space. Later, we compare the features generated by these networks in terms of their ability to perform a pure feature-based landmark matching problem. All of the work below is implemented with R [7] and `tensorflow` within `ANTsR`.

2.1   Network 1: 3D VGG-19 - No Training

There is a long line of research revolving around the use of randomly selected features in machine learning. Such features are unbiased and, at large scale and for general purpose application, provably good. Convolutional neural network architectures may encode valuable feature representations even without training [12]. While evidence of this has existed for some time, recent work has put the claims on more solid foundation [2]. Ramanujan et al., for instance, successfully "validate the unreasonable effectiveness of randomly weighted neural networks for image recognition" [9]. Following this work, we include an untrained 3D VGG-19 architecture among the networks we test. This network uses layers with randomly initialized weights for encoding. Its architecture is the same as the following two networks and includes groups of two (in shallower parts of the network) and four convolutional layers with filters of size $3 \times 3 \times 3$ followed by 3D max pooling. The number of filters increases dyadically with depth, except in the last block. See [14] for details. Our 3D variant is identical to an expanded 2D version with the exception that the input layer, for our 3D version, is single-channel and, of course, has more parameters (60,058,688) in line with its increased dimensionality.

2.2   Network 2: Transfer Learning from 2D VGG-19 to Pseudo-3D VGG-19

Both work in segmentation [13] and video has demonstrated the ability to transfer weights from multi-channel 2D convolutional filters into 3D. As in prior work, we adapt the *keras vgg19* imagenet weights from its canonical 2D implementation into a 3D single channel variant with all filter sizes, filter counts and biases the same. Two observations are key here. First, while acknowledging the limitations of this assumption, we treat the x-y spatial orientation of the original VGG-19 filters as rotatable into y-z and x-z planes where channel information occupies the orthogonal dimension. Second, this results in three variants of the network, one for each orientation. When applied to perform inference on new data, the outputs of each oriented network should be either concatenated or averaged. In the evaluation study described below, we concatenate features before use in landmark matching. See Fig. 1 for an overview of the approach to transferring 2D VGG to pseudo-3D space.

2.3   Network 3: Direct 3D VGG Learning of Pseudo-3D VGG-19 Activations

This network shares the same architecture as the prior two. Our task, here, is to train a 3D VGG-19 to approximate the sum of the oriented pseudo-3D VGG-19 outputs. By outputs, here, we mean the activations at the deepest layer of the VGG-19 architectures which is known as conv5_4, where 5 and 4 indicate

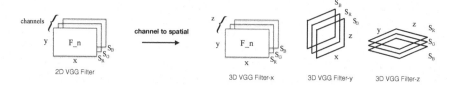

Fig. 1. Multi-channel VGG-19 (2D) to single-channel pseudo-3D VGG-19 filter transfer. The transfer operation results in 3 variants, one for each orientation, x, y, z. See the code for additional details.

its position is at the 4th convolutional layer of the 5th VGG block. The loss function, then, is:

$$\frac{1}{3}\sum_{i=1}^{3}\|\phi_{54}(X) - \phi_{54}^{i}(X)\|^2$$

where ϕ is the 3D-VGG-19 network, ϕ^i is the oriented pseudo-3D VGG-19 network, X denotes a tensor input and $\|\cdot\|$ is the Frobenius norm. The output layer is denoted by the *54* subscript.

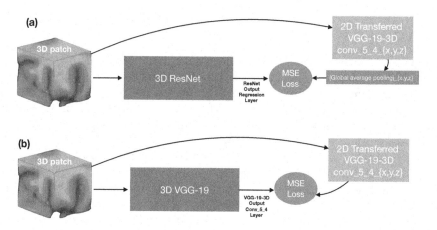

Fig. 2. Two approaches to learning the 3D distance space induced by the 2D to 3D VGG19. (a) 3D Resnet learning of 2D-to-3D VGG-19 activation maps. The loss function averages over the oriented outputs from the 2D to 3D transferred features. (b) 3D VGG-19 learning of 2D-to-3D VGG-19 activation maps. The loss function averages over the oriented outputs.

We train this network using a V100 NVIDIA GPU on tasks 1 through 10 of the medical decathlon dataset [15] which includes a variety of 3D CT and MRI images from the brain, heart, liver, prostate, lung, pancreas, spleen and colon. We use the `tensorflow` ADAM optimizer with learning rate 1e−4. Patch sizes of 32^3 are extracted from datasets that permit this dimensionality. Otherwise, patches of size 16^3 are used. Each patch is scaled to $[-127.5, 127.5]$. Batch sizes of 32 were employed. We trained on 64,000 patches and validated on patches extracted from left out images. Note that validation was used to guide the point at which we extracted the best weights from the training history. At convergence (67 epochs), the overall correlation (in validation data) between the real and predicted activation maps reached 0.792 with a training error reduction (from initialization) of a factor of 2.2. See Fig. 2 for an overview of this training paradigm.

2.4   Network 5: Direct 3D ResNet Learning of Pseudo-3D VGG-19 Activations

This comparison network is similar to the prior one but, here, we employ our 3D variant of the ResNet architecture [3]. ResNet is a classification or regression network and its output dimensions do not match that of 3D VGG19. To overcome this barrier – and still allow ResNet to predict pseudo-3D VGG encodings – we add a global average pooling layer to the output of each ϕ_{54}^i. This leads to a 512 vector regression target for each oriented network. The ResNet can directly learn this encoding using the loss function:

$$\frac{1}{3}\sum_{i=1}^{3} \|\psi(X) - \phi_{54g}^i(X)\|^2$$

where ψ is the ResNet and ϕ_{54g}^i is the ϕ_{54}^i output followed by global average pooling. The norm is Euclidean.

We train this ResNet (25,851,112 parameters) in the same manner as the prior network. We use the same patches, optimizer parameters and convergence criterion. At convergence (28 epochs), the overall correlation (in validation data) between the real and predicted activation maps reached 0.881 with a training error reduction (from initialization) of a factor of 1.7.

2.5   Network 5: Pre-trained ResNet Network

Our last comparison network is a ResNet with 25,851,112 parameters that predicts age, gender and data collection site based on T1-weighted neuroimaging (also known as brainAge). This network was trained on a dataset of control subjects where each image is bias corrected and affinely registered to a template image. Training data include:

- Dallas Lifespan Brain Study (DLBS): n = 275 (lifespan);
- Human Connectome Project (HCP): n = 1245 (young control);
- Information eXtraction from Images (IXI): n = 563 (lifespan);
- Nathan Kline Institute Rockland (NKI): n = 1260 (lifespan);
- Open Access Series of Imaging Studies (Oasis-2): n = 433 (lifespan, 18–93);
- Southwest University Adult Lifespan Dataset (SALD): n = 494 (young control).

As this network is not a primary topic of this work, we leave further details of training and performance to its online documentation (see ANTsR brain age network documentation and application). Nevertheless, the network achieves – in completely independent validation data from sites not included in training – an age prediction absolute error of 3.4 years over the lifespan and 88% accuracy for gender classification. This suggests that the network is encoding "real" information about shape and structure in human neuroimages and, as such, is sufficient to use as the source of deep features.

2.6   Evaluation Strategy in Terms of Landmark Matching in 7T Hippocampus Data

We obtained public 7T T2-weighted MRI of the human hippocampus ($n = 34$) [1] as a resource for anatomical labels and point-wise landmarks. Each image was labeled by a manual rater with two anatomically identified points at the head and tail of the hippocampus. We selected these two points for their relative saliency within the structure of these images. One subject (001) was arbitrarily selected as the template image. All other subjects serve as testing data where the task is for the underlying matching algorithm to use deep features to identify the anatomically homologous landmark points in the target image.

Figure 3 shows example activation maps from this network demonstrating that the ResNet layers capture shape variation associated with the example input patch. Such activation maps are the source of the feature distances that will drive the automated landmark matching. Similar maps are generated by each of the candidate networks.

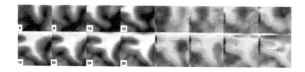

Fig. 3. 3D Activation maps for an example patch input for the brain-age network. The patch is shown at left and activation is at right. Slices within the 3D patch are indexed in the lower left of each image panel.

Each of the networks under study has five-dimensional weights per convolutional layer. The first three dimensions are spatial. The fourth is the channel dimension. The fifth is the number of filters. In general, the number of filters increases with depth. The VGG-19 architectures start with 64 filters and end with 512. The ResNet architectures range from 64 filters to 2048 at the deepest level. We select shallow, mid-range and deep layers for comparison of performance on automated landmark identification. For VGG, we select conv2_2, conv4_2 and conv5_4 layers. For ResNet architectures, we select layers 6, 140 and 1290 as the shallow, mid and deep feature layers to evaluate. For each of these variants, we also explore patch sizes of 12, 16, 20, 24, 28 and 32 voxels per patch axis. In total, this results in 90 different performance comparisons on the landmark matching task.

The evaluation metric is the mean Euclidean distance between the target ground truth landmark locations (in physical space) and the estimated landmark position. An overview of the paradigm is in Fig. 4. The features, for each run of the matching algorithm, are constant for the template image and are simply the deep features that arise from the patch centered at the landmark position. The best match in the target image is then identified by taking the voxel position in the target image whose feature map is closest under either the Frobenius or Euclidean norm, depending on the network. This amounts to a landmark matching process that evaluates the deep feature space as a strict similarity metric without further regularization.

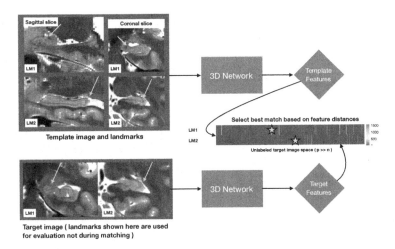

Fig. 4. Evaluation strategy for landmark localization accuracy based on deep feature matching with five different networks. In brief, the deep feature spaces are employed as similarity metrics. The matching is greedy and unconstrained. As such, this serves as a pure test of deep features' ability to match anatomy based on feature similarity.

3   Evaluation Results

Figure 5 provides an overview of results that visualizes the outcome of all 90 comparisons. Results are reported in the form of the t-statistic resulting from a pairwise t-test between the initial landmark distances and the final landmark distances after matching. We first provide general observations and then focus on the best performers.

In general, patch sizes significantly impact performance. The `ResNet` and `brainAge` networks, in particular, benefit from increasing patch sizes in the deeper and mid-range layers, respectively. This is verified by regressing patch size against the improvement in landmark distance and – despite a small sample of only 6 patch values against which to regress – p-values < 0.005 emerge. Conversely, the no Train, 3D VGG and pseudo 3D VGG networks show the opposite effect at the deep layers: decreasing patch size significantly improves performance. However, at shallow layers, the VGG architectures perform better with larger patch sizes.

The best networks succeed, with some configurations, at performing substantially better than chance with the lowest p-value being well below an aggressive Bonferroni correction level of $0.05/90 = 0.00056$ where we correct for all 90 test comparisons (a t-statistic of 5 with 33 degrees of freedom results in a p-value of $1.772e{-}05$). The best result is gained by the brainAge ResNet with results of patch size 32 and the middle and deep layer being nearly equivalent with t-statistics of 5.86 and 5.85 respectively. The second best result is gained from the brain age network shallow layer with patch size 20. Interestingly, the third best result is gained by the no training 3D VGG19 network with a t-statistic of 5.01 at the mid-layer and with patch size 32.

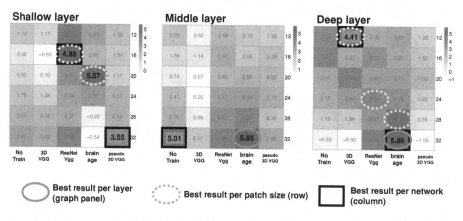

Fig. 5. Landmark localization accuracy results relative to initial distances (pairwise t-test, 33 degrees of freedom). The heatmap and entries in each panel correspond to the t-statistic from the pairwise test.

4   Discussion

This effort evaluated several deep 3D networks as feature encoders and their use and evaluation in landmark matching. These networks are publicly available at https://figshare.com/articles/pretrained_networks_for_deep_learning_applications/7246985 and may serve purposes beyond those exhibited here. Potential applications include disease classification, dimensionality reduction and use within loss functions for problems such as image translation or super-resolution.

Several interesting findings arose from the evaluation study. First, the performance of the **no training** 3D VGG network validates, in 3D, prior claims of the potentially good performance of 2D convolutional networks with random weights [9]. Second, pre-trained ResNet architectures are able to provide valuable 3D feature encodings for landmark matching even if they are trained on very different data and problem domains than which they are being applied. Third, complex effects of patch size are apparent in these results. These may be confounded by the way in which these networks were trained although further investigation of that question will be left to future work.

The findings in this work are insufficient to determine the extent to which network depth impacts performance in landmark matching. Additional tests across many more layers – and concomitant statistical modeling of depth × filter number effects – would be needed to understand these likely complex interactions. However, network depth (anecdotally speaking) does appear to impact performance, as has been shown previously in 2D. This impact, like that of patch size, will likely vary with network architecture and problem domain.

It is a substantial challenge to identify the optimal layers, patch sizes and training paradigms for generating repurposable deep feature networks. The number of evaluation runs is inevitably large and computationally demanding when exploring deep 3D networks. If we use the field of super-resolution as an example (see [16]), we must rely on the community to employ these networks in creative ways and arrive at consensus about their usefulness. Until we have larger 3D datasets, we may not achieve the generality of VGG-19. More work is also needed to establish a general similarity metric based on deep features.

In conclusion, we are releasing this work as public domain investigation into the questions posed here that are at the interface of deep learning, image registration and biomedical applications. We must also acknowledge that this work must continue with more sophisticated matching strategies that go beyond the greedy method used here. Furthermore, we hope that more detailed, landmark-based evaluations will be performed in the future. We believe that such studies may (relative to evaluations that fixate on segmentation overlap) provide greater insight and specificity during the evaluation of similarity metrics and transformation models for medical registration problems.

References

1. Berron, D., et al.: A protocol for manual segmentation of medial temporal lobe subregions in 7 Tesla MRI. NeuroImage Clin. (2017). https://doi.org/10.1016/j.nicl.2017.05.022
2. Gaier, A., Ha, D.: Weight Agnostic Neural Networks, June 2019. http://arxiv.org/abs/1906.04358
3. He, K., Zhang, X., Ren, S., Sun, J.: Deep residual learning for image recognition. In: Proceedings of the IEEE Computer Society Conference on Computer Vision and Pattern Recognition (2016). https://doi.org/10.1109/CVPR.2016.90

4. Kim, J., Lee, J.K., Lee, K.M.: Accurate image super-resolution using very deep convolutional networks. In: Proceedings of the IEEE Computer Society Conference on Computer Vision and Pattern Recognition (2016). https://doi.org/10.1109/CVPR.2016.182

5. Lowe, D.G.: Distinctive image features from scale-invariant keypoints. Int. J. Comput. Vis. (2004). https://doi.org/10.1023/B:VISI.0000029664.99615.94

6. Mang, A., Gholami, A., Biros, G.: Distributed-memory large deformation diffeomorphic 3D image registration. In: International Conference for High Performance Computing, Networking, Storage and Analysis, SC (2016). https://doi.org/10.1109/SC.2016.71

7. Muschelli, J., et al.: Neuroconductor: an R platform for medical imaging analysis. Biostatistics **20**(2), 218–239 (2018). https://doi.org/10.1093/biostatistics/kxx068. http://dx.doi.org/10.1093/biostatistics/kxx068

8. Neubert, T., Makrushin, A., Hildebrandt, M., Kraetzer, C., Dittmann, J.: Extended StirTrace benchmarking of biometric and forensic qualities of morphed face images. In: IET Biometrics (2018). https://doi.org/10.1049/iet-bmt.2017.0147

9. Ramanujan, V., Wortsman, M., Kembhavi, A., Farhadi, A., Rastegari, M.: What's Hidden in a Randomly Weighted Neural Network? November 2019. http://arxiv.org/abs/1911.13299

10. Rister, B., Horowitz, M.A., Rubin, D.L.: Volumetric image registration from invariant keypoints. IEEE Trans. Image Process. **26**(10), 4900–4910 (2017). https://doi.org/10.1109/TIP.2017.2722689

11. Rosenfeld, A.: Picture processing by computer. ACM Comput. Surv. (CSUR) (1969). https://doi.org/10.1145/356551.356554

12. Saxe, A.M., Koh, P.W., Chen, Z., Bhand, M., Suresh, B., Ng, A.Y.: On random weights and unsupervised feature learning. In: Proceedings of the 28th International Conference on Machine Learning, ICML 2011 (2011)

13. Shan, H., et al.: 3-D convolutional encoder-decoder network for low-dose CT via transfer learning from a 2-D trained network. IEEE Trans. Med. Imag. (2018). https://doi.org/10.1109/TMI.2018.2832217

14. Simonyan, K., Zisserman, A.: VGG-16. arXiv preprint (2014). https://doi.org/10.1016/j.infsof.2008.09.005

15. Simpson, A.L., et al.: A large annotated medical image dataset for the development and evaluation of segmentation algorithms, February 2019. http://arxiv.org/abs/1902.09063

16. Zhang, R., Isola, P., Efros, A.A., Shechtman, E., Wang, O.: The unreasonable effectiveness of deep features as a perceptual metric. In: Proceedings of the IEEE Computer Society Conference on Computer Vision and Pattern Recognition (2018). https://doi.org/10.1109/CVPR.2018.00068

17. Zhou, Z., et al.: Models genesis: generic autodidactic models for 3D medical image analysis. In: Shen, D., et al. (eds.) MICCAI 2019. LNCS, vol. 11767, pp. 384–393. Springer, Cham (2019). https://doi.org/10.1007/978-3-030-32251-9_42

Multi-channel Registration

Multi-channel Image Registration of Cardiac MR Using Supervised Feature Learning with Convolutional Encoder-Decoder Network

Xuesong Lu[1(✉)] and Yuchuan Qiao[2]

[1] College of Biomedical Engineering, South-Central University for Nationalities,
Wuhan 430074, China
xslu-scuec@hotmail.com
[2] Laboratory of Neuro Imaging, Keck School of Medicine of USC,
Los Angeles, CA 90033, USA

Abstract. It is difficult to register the images involving large deformation and intensity inhomogeneity. In this paper, a new multi-channel registration algorithm using modified multi-feature mutual information (α-MI) based on minimal spanning tree (MST) is presented. First, instead of relying on handcrafted features, a convolutional encoder-decoder network is employed to learn the latent feature representation from cardiac MR images. Second, forward computation and backward propagation are performed in a supervised fashion to make the learned features more discriminative. Finally, local features containing appearance information is extracted and integrated into α-MI for achieving multi-channel registration. The proposed method has been evaluated on cardiac cine-MRI data from 100 patients. The experimental results show that features learned from deep network are more effective than handcrafted features in guiding intra-subject registration of cardiac MR images.

Keywords: Multi-channel image registration · Multi-feature mutual information · Supervised feature learning · Convolutional encoder-decoder network

1 Introduction

Image registration is an important technique in medical image analysis [1]. Many clinical applications, such as multi-modal image fusion, radiotherapy, and computer-assisted surgery, can benefit from this technique. However, large deformation and intensity inhomogeneity bring great challenges into this procedure. To deal with these problems, the standard metrics like sum of squared difference (SSD), correlation coefficient (CC), and mutual information (MI) are not sufficient for intensity-based registration.

Recently, some studies have focused on multi-channel image registration for these issues. Legg et al. [2] extracted several feature images from the original images, and subsequently incorporated these feature images into a dissimilarity measure based on regional mutual information for multi-modal image registration. Staring et al. [3] adopted k-nearest neighbors graph (KNNG) to implement multi-feature mutual

© Springer Nature Switzerland AG 2020
Ž. Špiclin et al. (Eds.): WBIR 2020, LNCS 12120, pp. 103–110, 2020.
https://doi.org/10.1007/978-3-030-50120-4_10

information (α-MI) in order to register cervical MRI data. Rivaz et al. [4] introduced a self-similarity weighted α-MI using local structural information to register multiple feature images. Li et al. [5] developed an objective function that relies on the auto-correlation of local structure (ALOST) into registration of intra-image with signal fluctuations. Guyader et al. [6] proposed to formulate multi-channel registration as a group-wise image registration problem, in which the modality independent neighborhood descriptor (MIND) was used as the feature images.

It is critical for these methods to select discriminative features that can establish accurate anatomical correspondences between two images. Most of multi-channel image registrations utilized handcrafted features, such as multi-scale derivatives or descriptor engineering, to achieve good performance. In general, handcrafted features need manually intensive efforts to design the model for specific task. Learning-based methods have been developed to select the best feature set from a large feature pool, which can be adapted to the data at hand [7]. Moreover, deep learning can automatically and hierarchically learn effective feature representation from the data. Shin et al. [8] applied the stacked auto-encoders to organ identification in MR images. Chmelik et al. [9] classified lytic and sclerotic metastatic lesions in spinal 3D CT images by deep convolutional neural network (CNN). Wu et al. [10] employed a convolutional stacked auto-encoder to identify intrinsic deep feature representations for multi-channel image registration.

In contrast, we propose an end-to-end feature learning method to improve the performance of α-MI based on minimal spanning tree (MST). The convolutional encoder-decoder architecture that combines semantic information from a deep, coarse layer with appearance information from a shallow, fine layer is trained in a supervised fashion. Various latent features can be learned by forward computation and backward propagation. The local feature representation of testing image extracted from the first layer of encoder part is integrated into α-MI metric. The proposed method is evaluated on intra-subject registration of cardiac MR images.

2   Method

2.1 α-MI Implementation Using MST

In the previous work [11], multi-channel registration of two images $I_f(\boldsymbol{x})$ and $I_m(\boldsymbol{x})$ can be formulated as $\hat{\mu} = \arg\min_{\mu} \alpha MI\big(T_\mu; I_f(\boldsymbol{x}), I_m(\boldsymbol{x})\big)$, where T_μ is the free-form deformation (FFD) model based on B-spline. Assume that $\boldsymbol{z}(x_i) = [z_1(x_i) \cdots z_d(x_i)]$ denotes a vector of dimension d containing all feature values at point x_i. Let $\boldsymbol{z}^f(x_i)$ be the feature vector of the fixed image at point x_i, and $\boldsymbol{z}^m\big(T_\mu(x_i)\big)$ be that of the moving image at the transformed point $T_\mu(x_i)$. Let $\boldsymbol{z}^{fm}\big(x_i, T_\mu(x_i)\big)$ be the concatenation of the two feature vectors: $\big[\boldsymbol{z}^f(x_i), \boldsymbol{z}^m\big(T_\mu(x_i)\big)\big]$. Three MST graphs with N samples can be constructed by:

$$L_f = min \sum_{ij=1}^{N-1} \left\| z^f(x_i) - z^f(x_j) \right\|^{\gamma}, \tag{1}$$

$$L_m = min \sum_{ij=1}^{N-1} \left\| z^m(T_\mu(x_i)) - z^m(T_\mu(x_j)) \right\|^{\gamma}, \tag{2}$$

$$L_{fm} = min \sum_{ij=1}^{N-1} \left\| z^{fm}(x_i, T_\mu(x_i)) - z^{fm}(x_j, T_\mu(x_j)) \right\|^{2\gamma}, \tag{3}$$

where $\|\cdot\|$ is the Euclidean distance, and $\gamma \in (0,d)$. So α-MI based on MST can be expressed as:

$$\alpha MI = \frac{1}{1-\alpha} \left(\log \frac{L_f}{N^\alpha} + \log \frac{L_m}{N^\alpha} - \log \frac{L_{fm}}{N^\alpha} \right), \tag{4}$$

where $\alpha = (d - \gamma)/d$.

2.2   Network Architecture

The network architecture like 2D U-Net [12] for deep feature learning consists of encoding and decoding branches connected with skip connections. The encoding stage contains padded 3×3 convolutions followed by rectified linear unit (ReLU) activation functions. A 2×2 maxpooling operation with stride 2 is applied after every two convolutional layers. After each downsampling, the number of feature channels is doubled. In the decoding stage, a 2×2 upsampling operation is applied after every two convolutional layers. The resulting feature map is concatenated to the corresponding feature map from the encoding part. After each upsampling, the number of feature channels is halved.

The input size of the encoder-decoder architecture should be divisible by 16, and equal to the output size. At the final layer, a 1×1 convolution is used to generate the same depth of feature map as the desired number of classes.

2.3   Feature Representation with Supervised Learning

To train the encoder-decoder network, the input images and their labels are used to optimize the weights of convolutional layers through the softmax classifier. For the class imbalance between the foreground and background, we adopt weighted cross entropy as the loss function:

$$L = -\sum_{x \in \Omega} \omega(x) y(x) log(\hat{y}(x)), \tag{5}$$

where $y(x)$ is the true label, $\hat{y}(x)$ is the probability estimation by softmax, and $\omega(x)$ is the weight coefficient at the pixel x within domain Ω.

Due to supervised learning, global features containing semantic information are prone to be biased. Here local features containing appearance information are extracted from the first layer of our network for multi-channel registration. Figure 1 shows an example of 64 features from a 2D slice of cardiac MR image. Finally, we embed 65 features (original intensity image, 64 deep features) into α-MI based on MST metric.

Before performing registration, these features are normalized to have zero mean and unit variance. Note that feature extraction is executed in 2D manner, while registration is performed in 3D.

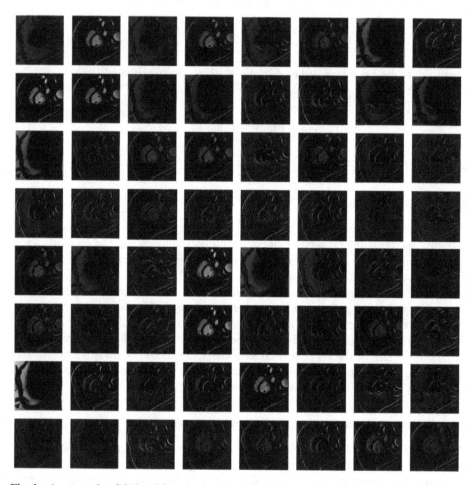

Fig. 1. An example of 64 local feature representations with supervised learning from a 2D slice of cardiac MR image.

3   Experiment and Result

The multi-feature mutual information using MST was implemented in the registration package *elastix* [13] with multi-threaded mode, which is mainly based on the Insight Toolkit. The registration experiments were run on a Windows platform with an Intel Dual Core 3.40 GHz CPU and 32.0 GB memory. A Tensorflow implementation of convolutional encoder-decoder network was trained on a Nvidia GeForce GTX 1070 GPU.

3.1   Dataset and Evaluation Method

To evaluate the performance of the proposed method, our experiments were on cardiac cine-MRI training data of the ACDC challenge [14], which consists of 100 patient scans. The image spacing varies from $0.70 \times 0.70 \times 5$ mm to $1.92 \times 1.92 \times 10$ mm. We resampled the data to an in-plane spacing of 1.37×1.37 mm, and then cropped all resampled images to an in-plane size of 224×224 pixels. The manual delineation of the left ventricle (LV), the left ventricle myocardium (LVM), and the right ventricle (RV) at the end-diastolic (ED) and end-systolic (ES) phases of each patient is provided as the ground truth for quantitative evaluation.

The data were divided into the training and validation set. The training set comprising 80 subjects was used to train the deep network in a slice-by-slice manner for feature extraction. The validation set with the remaining 20 subjects was performed registration between images at ED and ES. In total 40 different registration results were available for evaluation. The propagated segmentations can be generated by transforming the manual segmentation of the moving image to the fixed image domain, with obtained deformation field.

The Dice Similarity Coefficient (DSC) as a measure of overlap was calculated between propagated segmentation and ground truth of the fixed image. To compare two methods, a value of $p < 0.05$ in two-sided Wilcoxon tests is regarded as a statistically significant difference. The Hausdorff distance (HD) between the surface of propagated segmentation and the surface of ground truth was also used to measure the quality of registration.

3.2   Parameter Settings

The proposed α-MI based on MST using the deep feature representation (in total 65 features, called aMI+SDF) was compared to localized MI (called LMI) [15] and α-MI based on MST with the Cartesian feature set [3] (in total 15 features, called aMI+HCF). Since cardiac MR images only show local deformations between the time phases, initial rigid registration was not necessary.

For weighted cross entropy, we set a weight of 0.3 for the foreground class, and 0.1 for the background class. To train the encoder-decoder network, we used the Adam optimizer, where learning rate 1.0×10^{-3} and 60 epochs with batch size of 4 were set.

For all experiments on intra-subject registration, a multiresolution scheme using Gaussian smoothing was applied. Scales $\sigma = 4.0$, 2.0, and 1.0 voxels in the x and y directions were used. For the z direction, $\sigma = 2.0$, 1.0, and 0.5 voxel was used. As for transformation model, the parameterized B-splines with grid spacing of 20, 10, and 5 mm was employed for three resolution levels respectively.

For LMI, a local region of $50 \times 50 \times 25$ mm was randomly selected. About the parameter optimization, $A = 200$, $\tau = 0.6$, $a = 2000$, and 2000 iterations were set. The number of random samples was set to $N = 2000$. For aMI+HCF and aMI+SDF, $A = 50$, $\tau = 0.602$, $a = 2000$, and 600 iterations were set. The number of random samples was set to $N = 5000$.

In multi-feature mutual information, the kD trees, a standard splitting rule, a bucket size of 50, and an errorbound value of 10.0 were selected. The $k = 20$ nearest neighbors were set. In addition, α value was set to 0.99.

3.3   Registration Accuracy

The boxplot of overlap scores using the three methods is shown in Fig. 2. It is clear that registration quality of LMI is the worst. Compared to aMI+HCF, the median overlap of aMI+SDF increases significantly from 0.898 to 0.921 ($p = 2.70 \times 10^{-3}$) for the LV, from 0.781 to 0.822 ($p = 4.57 \times 10^{-6}$) for the LVM, and from 0.775 to 0.813 ($p = 1.92 \times 10^{-5}$). The overall mean and standard deviation of the measures are summarized in Table 1. The same trend can be found in the HD measure. The median HD of aMI+SDF for the LV is as low as 9.171 mm. Figure 3 displays a typical example of registration results. It can be observed that aMI+SDF performs much better than aMI+HCF for these anatomical structures.

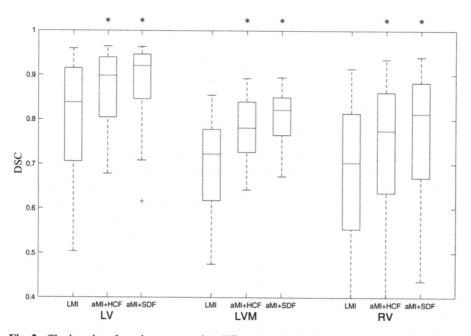

Fig. 2. The boxplot of overlap scores using different methods at different anatomical structures. A star indicates a statistical significant difference of the median overlap compared to the previous column.

Table 1. The mean and standard deviation of quantitative measures using the three methods for different anatomical structures.

Structures	Methods	DSC	HD (mm)
LV	LMI	0.797 ± 0.135	12.567 ± 4.111
	aMI+HCF	0.868 ± 0.085	10.072 ± 3.412
	aMI+SDF	**0.888 ± 0.080**	**9.614 ± 3.348**
LVM	LMI	0.696 ± 0.104	12.243 ± 3.804
	aMI+HCF	0.776 ± 0.069	10.481 ± 3.260
	aMI+SDF	**0.808 ± 0.055**	**10.009 ± 3.130**
RV	LMI	0.680 ± 0.168	19.065 ± 7.503
	aMI+HCF	0.732 ± 0.162	17.745 ± 8.095
	aMI+SDF	**0.765 ± 0.155**	**17.378 ± 7.513**

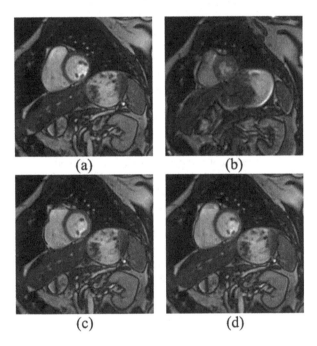

Fig. 3. (a) The fixed image. (b) The moving image. (c) The fusion result by aMI+HCF registration. (d) The fusion result by aMI+SDF registration. The fixed image is combined with the warped moving image, using a checkerboard pattern.

4 Conclusion

In this paper, we present a multi-channel registration algorithm for cardiac MR images. To make the feature representation more robust to large appearance variations of cardiac substructures, we propose to extract the features with convolutional encoder-decoder network. Afterwards, the learned features in a supervised fashion are incorporated into multi-feature mutual information framework. With experiments on cardiac cine-MRI data, the proposed method demonstrates the superior performance regarding to intra-subject registration accuracy.

References

1. Aristeidis, S., Christos, D., Nikos, P.: Deformable medical image registration: a survey. IEEE Trans. Med. Imag. **32**(7), 1153–1190 (2013)
2. Legg, P.A., Rosin, P.L., Marshall, D., Morgan, J.E.: A robust solution to multi-modal image registration by combining mutual information with multi-scale derivatives. In: Yang, G.-Z., Hawkes, D., Rueckert, D., Noble, A., Taylor, C. (eds.) MICCAI 2009. LNCS, vol. 5761, pp. 616–623. Springer, Heidelberg (2009). https://doi.org/10.1007/978-3-642-04268-3_76
3. Staring, M., Heide, U.A., Klein, S., Viergever, M.A., Pluim, J.P.W.: Registration of cervical MRI using multifeature mutual information. IEEE Trans. Med. Imag. **28**(9), 1412–1421 (2009)
4. Rivaz, H., Karimaghaloo, Z., Collins, D.L.: Self-similarity weighted mutual information: a new nonrigid image registration metric. Med. Image Anal. **18**, 343–358 (2014)
5. Li, Z., Mahapatra, D., Tielbeek, J.A.W., Stoker, J., Vliet, L.J., Vos, F.M.: Image registration based on autocorrelation of local structure. IEEE Trans. Med. Imag. **35**(1), 63–75 (2016)
6. Guyader, J.M., et al.: Groupwise multichannel image registration. IEEE J. Biomed. Health Inform. **23**(3), 1171–1180 (2019)
7. Bengio, Y., Courville, A., Vincent, P.: Representation learning: a review and new perspectives. IEEE Trans. Pattern Anal. Mach. Intell. **35**(8), 1798–1828 (2013)
8. Shin, H., Orton, M.R., Collins, D.J., Doran, S.J., Leach, M.O.: Stacked autoencoders for unsupervised feature learning and multiple organ detection in a pilot study using 4D patient data. IEEE Trans. Pattern Anal. Mach. Intell. **35**(8), 1930–1943 (2013)
9. Chmelik, J., et al.: Deep convolutional neural network-based segmentation and classification of difficult to define metastatic spinal lesions in 3D CT data. Med. Image Anal. **49**, 76–88 (2018)
10. Wu, G.R., Kim, M.J., Wang, Q., Munsell, B.C., Shen, D.G.: Scalable high-performance image registration framework by unsupervised deep feature representations learning. IEEE Trans. Biomed. Eng. **63**(7), 1505–1516 (2016)
11. Lu, X.S., Zha, Y.F., Qiao, Y.C., Wang, D.F.: Feature-based deformable registration using minimal spanning tree for prostate MR segmentation. IEEE Access **7**, 138645–138656 (2019)
12. Ronneberger, O., Fischer, P., Brox, T.: U-Net: convolutional networks for biomedical image segmentation. In: Navab, N., Hornegger, J., Wells, W.M., Frangi, A.F. (eds.) MICCAI 2015. LNCS, vol. 9351, pp. 234–241. Springer, Cham (2015). https://doi.org/10.1007/978-3-319-24574-4_28
13. Shamonin, D.P., Bron, E.E., Lelieveldt, B.P.F., Smits, M., Klein, S., Staring, M.: Fast parallel image registration on CPU and GPU for diagnostic classification of Alzheimer's disease. Front. Neuroinform. **7**(50), 1–15 (2014)
14. Bernard, O., et al.: Deep learning techniques for automatic MRI cardiac multi-structures segmentation and diagnosis: is the problem solved? IEEE Trans. Med. Imag. **37**(11), 2514–2525 (2018)
15. Klein, S., Heide, U.A., Lips, I.M., Vulpen, M., Staring, M., Pluim, J.P.: Automatic segmentation of the prostate in 3D MR images by atlas matching using localized mutual information. Med. Phys. **35**(4), 1407–1417 (2008)

Multi-channel Registration for Diffusion MRI: Longitudinal Analysis for the Neonatal Brain

Alena Uus[✉], Maximilian Pietsch, Irina Grigorescu, Daan Christiaens, Jacques-Donald Tournier, Lucilio Cordero Grande, Jana Hutter, David Edwards, Joseph Hajnal, and Maria Deprez

School of Imaging Sciences and Biomedical Engineering, King's College London, St. Thomas' Hospital, London, SE1 7EH, UK
alena.uus@kcl.ac.uk

Abstract. In multi-channel (MC) registration, fusion of structural and diffusion brain MRI provides information on both cortex and white matter (WM) structures thus decreasing the uncertainty of deformation fields. However, the existing solutions employ only diffusion tensor imaging (DTI) derived metrics which are limited by inconsistencies in fiber-crossing regions. In this work, we extend the pipeline for registration of multi-shell high angular resolution diffusion imaging (HARDI) [15] with a novel similarity metric based on angular correlation and an option for multi-channel registration that allows incorporation of structural MRI. The contributions of channels to the displacement field are weighted with spatially varying certainty maps. The implementation is based on MRtrix3 (MRtrix3: https://www.mrtrix.org) toolbox. The approach is quantitatively evaluated on intra-patient longitudinal registration of diffusion MRI datasets of 20 preterm neonates with 7–11 weeks gap between the scans. In addition, we present an example of an MC template generated using the proposed method.

Keywords: High angular resolution diffusion imaging · Multi-channel registration · Fibre orientation distribution registration · Certainty maps

1 Introduction

The combined analysis of diffusion and structural MRI is extensively used in adult and neonatal [20] brain studies. Structural MRI has the highest contrast for the cortex region, while dMRI primarily provides information about white matter (WM) structures.

The uncertainty of deformation fields in the regions characterised by low contrast or homogeneous intensities (e.g., low WM fibre density regions in dMRI) is one the primary challenges associated with both longitudinal and inter-subject registration. Multi-channel registration that includes both anatomical and

© Springer Nature Switzerland AG 2020
Ž. Špiclin et al. (Eds.): WBIR 2020, LNCS 12120, pp. 111–121, 2020.
https://doi.org/10.1007/978-3-030-50120-4_11

diffusion channels has been shown to improve registration and label-propagation results [2, 7, 19]. The reported MC registration solutions generally employ fractional anisotropy (FA) [7, 8, 14, 19] or DTI [2, 9, 13] as an additional channel. However, DTI-extracted metrics are characterised by inconsistencies in fibre-crossing regions. On the other hand, higher-order techniques such as constrained spherical deconvolution (CSD) [21] alleviate some of the limitations of the DTI model and allow extracting orientation-resolved microstructural information as so-called orientation distribution functions (ODFs) from HARDI data.

The classical approach for the fusion of information from different channels is based on simple averaging of individual channel updates [2]. More recently proposed solutions include scalar weighs for ROIs defined by thresholded FA maps [13] or local certainty maps based on normalised gradients correlated to structural content [7]. While the detailed overview of the choice of registration metrics is out-of-scope of this work, it can be summarised that the published works on intensity-based multi-channel registration primarily use the sum of squared differences (SSD) [2, 7, 8, 14] or local normalised cross-correlation (LNCC) [4] metrics. There is also a reported approach for T1-DTI atlas generation where datasets are spatially normalized only according to the structural channel [9].

Contributions. In this work we present a framework for multi-channel brain registration that allows local certainty-based fusion of dMRI-derived ODFs and structural MRI and is based on a novel similarity metric for dMRI. The solution is an extension of the multi-contrast ODF registration framework [15, 17]. The novel elements include implementation of local angular correlation (AC) as a metric for ODF channels, LNCC for structural channels and weighted fusion based on local certainty maps. The pipeline was implemented in MRtrix3 [22].

The method is evaluated on 20 longitudinal (intra-patient) neonatal MRI datasets from the developing Human Connectome Project (dHCP)[1] which constitutes a particularly challenging task for registration due to the rapid changes that occur in volume, structure and intensities during brain development. In addition, we demonstrate an example of a MC template of neonatal brain generated from 10 datasets (40–43 weeks PMA) using the proposed registration approach.

2   Method

2.1   Datasets, Acquisition and Pre-processing

The data used for evaluation of the proposed method include 20 longitudinal datasets of neonates scanned as a part of the dHCP project at St. Thomas Hospital, London. The gap between the scans is in the range of 7–11 weeks which is associated with significant changes in volume, myelination and cortical folding [16]. The postmenstrual age (PMA) at the first scan is within 30–35 weeks.

---

[1] dHCP project: http://www.developingconnectome.org.

Each dataset includes two scans with diffusion and structural MRI volumes acquired on a Philips 3T scanner. The multi-shell HARDI volumes were acquired with four phase-encode directions on four shells with b-values of 0, 400, 1000 and 2600 s/mm^2 with TE 90 ms, TR 3800 ms [10] with $1.5 \times 1.5 \times 3$ mm resolution and 1.5 mm slice overlap and reconstructed to 1.5 mm isotropic resolution using the SHARD pipeline [5]. The structural T2-weighted volumes were acquired using a TSE sequence with TR $= 12$ s, TE $= 156$ ms. The T1-weighted volumes were acquired using an IR TSE sequence with TR 4.8 s, TE 8.7 ms. The isotropic T2 and T1 volumes with 0.5 mm resolution were reconstructed using a combination of motion correction [6] and super-resolution reconstruction [11]. All volumes of the same modality were normalised to the same global intensity ranges. The tissue segmentations were generated by the Draw-EM pipeline [12].

The preprocessing of the datasets was performed in MRtrix3 including: (i) decomposition of WM ODF from HARDI data via constrained spherical deconvolution (CSD) [21] followed by intensity normalisation; (ii) extraction of FA and mean diffusivity (MD) DTI-metrics; (iii) alignment of the structural to dMRI volumes based on affine registration of T2 to MD volumes using global NCC metric; (iv) resampling of all channels to 1 mm isotropic resolution with B-Spline interpolation. In addition, we manually segmented internal capsules (IC) in FA volumes for all datasets.

2.2   Multi-channel Registration Pipeline

The proposed registration pipeline is an extension of the multi-contrast ODF registration framework [15,17]. The original method is based on SyN Demons [2] with an SSD metric and reorientation of ODF using apodized point spread functions [18]. In order to decrease the sensitivity to acquisition or physiology related changes in signal intensities, we replace SSD with a novel similarity metric based on angular correlation [1] and add certainty-maps weighting for fusion of structural and diffusion channels.

The input channels for each of the cases include: WM ODFs, structural MRI (T2-weighted and T1-weighted) volumes and FA maps. At first, the cases are globally aligned using affine registration of structural volumes using the global NCC metric. Next, we employ symmetric diffeomorphic LNCC demons [3] for structural and FA channels and local angular correlation metric [1] for ODF channels. In comparison to the classical ODF registration approach based on SSD metric in [15], using AC provides a more robust solution since it is less susceptible to the local changes in signal intensities while preserving directional information. However, unlike SSD, AC might be affected by the noise in the directional information.

Angular correlation r_A between two ODFs F^{ODF} and G^{ODF} represented with real valued spherical harmonic (SH) orthonormal basis functions $Y_{lm}(\theta, \phi)$

$$F^{ODF}(\theta, \phi) = \sum_{l=0}^{\infty} \sum_{m=-l}^{l} f_{lm} Y_{lm}(\theta, \phi), \quad G^{ODF}(\theta, \phi) = \sum_{l=0}^{\infty} \sum_{m=-l}^{l} g_{lm} Y_{lm}(\theta, \phi) \tag{1}$$

is computed as [1]:

$$r_A = \frac{\sum_{l=2}^{L}\sum_{m=-l}^{l}f_{lm}g_{lm}}{[\sum_{l=2}^{L}\sum_{m=-l}^{l}|f_{lm}|^2]^{\frac{1}{2}}[[\sum_{l=2}^{L}\sum_{m=-l}^{l}|g_{lm}|^2]^{\frac{1}{2}}}, \tag{2}$$

where g_{lm} and f_{lm} are the SH coefficients of $G^{ODF}(\theta, \phi)$ and $F^{ODF}(\theta, \phi)$ of order L with even $l = \{2, 4, ..., L\}$ harmonic degree terms, correspondingly. The $l = 0$ term does not contribute to AC values.

Since this is a correlation metric, the corresponding symmetric updates to the displacement fields Λ^F and Λ^G can be computed in a similar manner to LNCC demons [3] but with respect to the 4D ODFs rather than only the 3D local neighbourhood (Eq. 3).

$$\Lambda^F = \frac{2FG}{F^2G^2}\left(G - \frac{FG}{F^2}F\right)\nabla F, \quad \Lambda^G = \frac{2FG}{F^2G^2}\left(F - \frac{FG}{G^2}G\right)\nabla G, \tag{3}$$

where $G = \{g_{lm}^n\}_{l=2,...,l_{max},m=-l,...,l}$ and $F = \{f_{lm}^n\}_{l=2,...,l_{max},m=-l,...,l}$ are the vectors of SH coefficients at a given location in the 3D volume space with local neighbourhood $n = 1, ..., N$. We refer to this registration metric as local angular cross-correlation (LAC).

The updates from the structural channels are computed similarly to [3]. We also consider $Y_{00}(\theta, \phi)$ as a separate channel and use the LNCC metric for its contributions since it is excluded from the AC metric formalisation (Eq. 2).

The contributions from each of the channels i to the global symmetric displacement field update Λ^{global} are locally weighted with respect to the 3D certainty maps based on the approach proposed in [7]. At first, the certainty maps α_i^F and α_i^G are computed from the original volumes F and G for each of the channels (including structural and ODF volumes) and normalised as:

$$\alpha_i^F = \| \nabla F_i^T \nabla F_i \|, \quad \widehat{\alpha}_i^F = \frac{\alpha_i^F}{max(\alpha_i^F)} \tag{4}$$

Then, the global symmetric updates to the displacement fields are computed by weighted averaging of the channel-specific update fields with respect to the certainty maps:

$$\Lambda_{global}^F = \frac{\sum_i \widehat{\alpha}_i^F \Lambda_i^F}{\sum_i \widehat{\alpha}_i^F}, \quad \Lambda_{global}^G = \frac{\sum_i \widehat{\alpha}_i^G \Lambda_i^G}{\sum_i \widehat{\alpha}_i^G} \tag{5}$$

Figure 1 shows an example of the certainty gradient maps $\widehat{\alpha}_i$ for structural, FA and one of the ODF component channels and the $\sum_i \widehat{\alpha}_i$ of all channels. This approach ensures that the output deformation fields are defined by the contribution of the local channel regions with the highest structural content. This is relevant for the ROIs where one of the channels has low intensity contrast. In comparison, the multi-variate SyN (MVSyN) approach [2] is based on averaging of the individual channel updates.

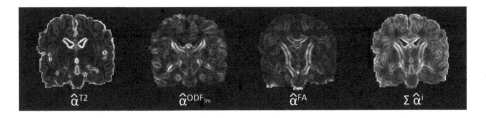

Fig. 1. An example of the certainty maps $\widehat{\alpha}_i$ for T2, one of the ODF component channels ($l_{max} = 2$), FA, and the sum of all channels ($\sum_i \widehat{\alpha}_i$).

2.3   Implementation Details

The method was implemented in MRtrix3 [22]. The new elements include: LAC metric for ODF registration and certainty-based weighting of the channels. In addition, we transferred ANTs[2] implementation of LNCC Demons metric [3] to MRtrix3 for registration of structural, $Y_{00}(\theta, \phi)$ ODF and FA channels.

It was experimentally identified that multi-resolution $\{0.5; 0.75; 1.0\}$ and SH order $l_{max} = \{0; 2; 4\}$ schemes and 3 voxel radius for the local neighbourhood for both structural and ODF channels are optimal for deformable registration of the investigated datasets. We used the standard MRtrix3 regularisation of gradient update and displacement fields based on Gaussian smoothing with 1 voxel standard deviation. The MRtrix3 parameter settings employed for generation of the multi-channel template are based on the pipeline formalised in [16].

3   Experiments and Results

3.1   Longitudinal Registration Study

For each of the investigated 20 cases, we performed a set of longitudinal (intra-patient) registrations with different settings including different combinations of channels {T2; FA; T2+FA; STR (structural: T1+T2); ODF; ODF+STR; ODF+STR+FA} and similarity metrics {SSD; LNCC; LAC}. The channel weighting options include average and weighted: {A-; W-}. The employed parameter settings are given in Sect. 2.3.

The MRtrix3-based implementation of LNCC Demons [3] is based on the ANTs toolbox and provides similar performance for structural registration. Therefore, we compare the proposed method directly to the existing MRtrix3 registration module. The main aim is an improvement of the combined quality of label propagation and image similarity for the structural and diffusion channels.

Table 1 presents the results of the comparison study. The quantitative evaluation is performed with respect to the quality of label propagation (Dice score) and similarity of the registered ODF volumes. The labels include: cortical grey

---

[2] ANTs: http://stnava.github.io/ANTs.

matter (C-GM), hippocampus (HIP) and internal capsule (IC). The intensity-based similarity is assessed in terms of ODF AC (Eq. 2) for $l_{max} = 4$. The best performance results are highlighted in blue.

Firstly we can observe that locally weighted fusion [7] of T2 and FA improves the combined results while slightly lowering the dice score for cortex compared to single channel T2.

Table 1. Quantitative evaluation of the proposed multi-channel registration approach on longitudinal dMRI datasets of 20 neonates: Dice coefficient for brain tissue labels and AC between ODF volumes.

Channels/metrics	IC	CGM	HIP	ODF AC
ANTs LNCC demons: single-channel registration [3]				
T2:LNCC	0.676 ± 0.021	$\mathbf{0.724 \pm 0.034}$	0.794 ± 0.027	0.427 ± 0.035
FA:LNCC	0.686 ± 0.021	0.569 ± 0.031	0.770 ± 0.025	0.348 ± 0.040
ANTs LNCC demons: MC registration with certainty map weighting [7]				
T2+FA:W-LNCC	0.686 ± 0.036	0.700 ± 0.034	0.800 ± 0.023	0.429 ± 0.037
MRtrix3 MC Syn demons (SSD): registration of ODFs [15,17]				
ODF:SSD	0.710 ± 0.019	0.619 ± 0.045	0.784 ± 0.026	0.422 ± 0.045
ODF+STR:A-SSD	0.667 ± 0.116	0.628 ± 0.047	0.768 ± 0.072	0.413 ± 0.054
MRtrix3 LAC/LNCC demons: MC registration of ODFs and structural volumes with certainty map weighting (proposed method)				
ODF:LAC	0.709 ± 0.022	0.661 ± 0.041	0.788 ± 0.032	0.448 ± 0.039
ODF+STR: A-LAC/LNCC	0.709 ± 0.020	0.678 ± 0.039	0.799 ± 0.028	0.451 ± 0.039
ODF+STR:W-LAC/LNCC	0.713 ± 0.023	0.689 ± 0.038	$\mathbf{0.803 \pm 0.027}$	$\mathbf{0.455 \pm 0.038}$
ODF+STR+FA:W-LAC/LNCC	$\mathbf{0.714 \pm 0.022}$	0.677 ± 0.039	0.800 ± 0.028	0.454 ± 0.039

In general, myelination and cortical folding occurring during 7–11 weeks period significantly change local intensities in both structural and diffusion MRI data [16]. Therefore, even though all input volumes were normalised, using SSD metric for ODF or structural MC registration leads to the lower quality results in comparison to the proposed LAC metric which produced statistically significant ($p < 0.05$) improvement for C-GM and HIP Dice scores and ODF AC, while there was not a significant difference in Dice scores of IC.

Figure 2 demonstrates an example of the original and transformed WM ODF SH coefficients ($l = 2, m = 0$) for longitudinal registration of 31 to 42 weeks PMA datasets. There is a clear difference in the magnitude of SH coefficients between the original scans. Using MC registration with LAC for ODF and LNCC for structural channels produces visually sharper results for the IC region in comparison to both classical SSD ODF registration [15,17] or fusion of T2 and FA [7]. This is in agreement with the higher AC values reported in Table 1.

Furthermore, there is a clear indication that additional structural channels (in this case T1+T2) and certainty-based weighting increase the quality of label propagation and AC similarity of ODF volumes. Adding the FA channel did not significantly affect the results since ODFs contain the WM structure information.

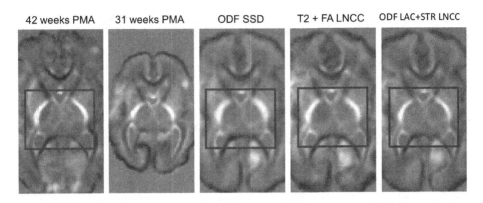

Fig. 2. An example of longitudinal intra-patient registration for 31 $\implies$ 42 weeks PMA datasets. Difference between the original and transformed WM ODF SH coefficients ($l = 2, m = 0$) for the classical ODF registration with SSD metric, weighted MC registration of T2+FA channels with LNCC metric and weighted MC registration of ODF+T1+T2 channels with LAC and LNCC metrics.

All ODF-based options resulted in approximately the same range for the IC Dice score values due to its high contrast and showed significant improvement (p < 0.05) in comparison to using the FA and T2 channels only. Apart from the IC values for ODF registration, the improvement in performance of the proposed method (ODF+STR: W-LAC/LNCC) in comparison to the baseline methods (structural LNCC Demons, ODF MRtrix registration as well as fused T2+FA) is statistically significant with p < 0.05.

An example of symmetric LAC+LNCC MC registration for 31 $\longleftrightarrow$ 42 weeks PMA at scan case is presented in Fig. 3. The registration of the structural and ODF channels was successful even though there are significant differences in contrast of both structural and ODF volumes, cortex folding surface and the global shape. Visualisation of the original and transformed normalised ODFs over the same padded T1 volume (third row) confirms that the global shape and features of the volumes are sufficiently well aligned. Label propagation for tissue and IC segmentations also resulted in relatively similar results. This, however, might also be affected by the quality of the original segmentations produced by the automated Draw-EM method [12].

3.2 Multi-channel Template Example

Figure 4 shows and example of a multi-channel template generated using MRtrix3 *population_template* tool with the proposed MC registration pipeline and LAC+LNCC metrics. The template with 1 mm resolution was generated from 10 neonatal MRI datasets from 40–43 weeks PMA. It includes T2, T1, normalised WM ODF and FA channels. The resulting volumes are characterised by well defined features of both cortex and WM structures.

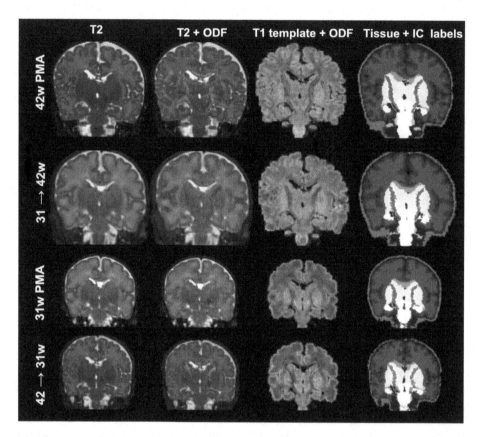

Fig. 3. An example of longitudinal symmetric MC registration for 31 $\Longleftrightarrow$ 42 weeks PMA at scan case including: original and transformed T2 volumes, original and transformed ODF over T2, original and transformed ODF over masked original T1 volume (used as a template), original and transformed labels.

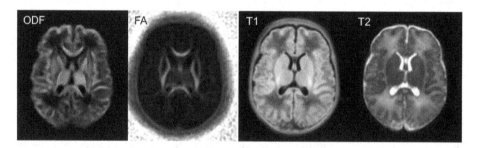

Fig. 4. An example of multi-channel template of neonatal brain generated from 40–43 PMA datasets including: WM ODF, FA, T1 and T2 channels.

4   Discussion and Conclusions

This paper presents a solution for multi-channel registration combining multi-shell HARDI and structural MRI data. It is based on a novel similarity metric for diffusion MRI and certainty-based weighting of the channels. The method was implemented in MRtrix3 and can be integrated into neuroimaging pipelines.

The quantitative evaluation was performed on 20 longitudinal neonatal datasets from the dHCP project. The results showed that fusion of structural and diffusion ODF channels improves overall results, compared to single-channel registrations. The weighting of channels based on certainty maps also improves the results thus potentially minimising the uncertainty of deformation fields. Furthermore, the proposed LAC metric outperforms the state-of-the-art ODF registration method for challenging cases.

An example of the generated multi-modal template shows that this tool has a potential application for generation of spatio-temporal multi-modal brain MRI templates that require robust similarity metrics. Simultaneous segmentation of WM and cortex structures could also potentially improve the accuracy of morphometry in structural MRI processing pipelines.

However, these results also emphasise the fact that accurate alignment of diffusion and structural volumes is a critical step for multi-channel registration since affine registration might not fully solve this due to distortions in dMRI data. Future work will focus on further optimisation of the MC ODF registration pipeline and extensive evaluation on adult and multi-site datasets.

Acknowledgments. This work was supported by the Academy of Medical Sciences Springboard Award (SBF004\1040), European Research Council under the EU's Seventh Framework Programme (FP7/ 20072013)/ERC grant agreement no. 319456 dHCP project, the Wellcome/EPSRC Centre for Medical Engineering at Kings College London (WT 203148/Z/16/Z), the NIHR Clinical Research Facility (CRF) at Guy's and St Thomas' and by the National Institute for Health Research Biomedical Research Centre based at Guy's and St Thomas' NHS Foundation Trust and King's College London. The views expressed are those of the authors and not necessarily those of the NHS, the NIHR or the Department of Health.

References

1. Anderson, A.W.: Measurement of fiber orientation distributions using high angular resolution diffusion imaging. MR in Med. **54**(5), 1194–1206 (2005)
2. Avants, B., Duda, J.T., Zhang, H., Gee, J.C.: Multivariate normalization with symmetric diffeomorphisms for multivariate studies. In: Ayache, N., Ourselin, S., Maeder, A. (eds.) MICCAI 2007. LNCS, vol. 4791, pp. 359–366. Springer, Heidelberg (2007). https://doi.org/10.1007/978-3-540-75757-3_44
3. Avants, B.B., Epstein, C.L., Grossman, M., Gee, J.C.: Symmetric diffeomorphic image registration with cross-correlation: evaluating automated labeling of elderly and neurodegenerative brain. Med. Image Anal. **12**(1), 26–41 (2008)

4. Cattell, L., Schnabel, J.A., Declerck, J., Hutton, C.: Combined PET-MR brain registration to discriminate between Alzheimer's disease and healthy controls. In: Ourselin, S., Modat, M. (eds.) WBIR 2014. LNCS, vol. 8545, pp. 134–143. Springer, Cham (2014). https://doi.org/10.1007/978-3-319-08554-8_14

5. Christiaens, D., et al.: Multi-shell SHARD reconstruction from scattered slice diffusion MRI data in the neonatal brain. In: ISMRM, p. 464 (2018)

6. Cordero-Grande, L., Hughes, E.J., Hutter, J., Price, A.N., Hajnal, J.V.: Three-dimensional motion corrected sensitivity encoding reconstruction for multi-shot multi-slice MRI: application to neonatal brain imaging. MR in Med. **79**(3), 1365–1376 (2018)

7. Forsberg, D., Rathi, Y., Bouix, S., Wassermann, D., Knutsson, H., Westin, C.-F.: Improving registration using multi-channel diffeomorphic demons combined with certainty maps. In: Liu, T., Shen, D., Ibanez, L., Tao, X. (eds.) MBIA 2011. LNCS, vol. 7012, pp. 19–26. Springer, Heidelberg (2011). https://doi.org/10.1007/978-3-642-24446-9_3

8. Geng, X., Styner, M., Gupta, A., Shen, D., HGilmore, J.: Multi-contrast diffusion tensor image registration with structural MRI. In: ISBI 2012, pp. 684–687 (2012)

9. Gupta, V., Malandain, G., Ayache, N., Pennec, X.: A framework for creating population specific multimodal brain atlas using clinical T1 and diffusion tensor images. In: Fuster, A., Ghosh, A., Kaden, E., Rathi, Y., Reisert, M. (eds.) Computational Diffusion MRI. MV, pp. 99–108. Springer, Cham (2016). https://doi.org/10.1007/978-3-319-28588-7_9

10. Hutter, J., et al.: Time-efficient and flexible design of optimized multishell HARDI diffusion. MR in Med. **79**(3), 1276–1292 (2018)

11. Kuklisova-Murgasova, M., Quaghebeur, G., Rutherford, M.A., Hajnal, J.V., Schnabel, J.A.: Reconstruction of fetal brain MRI with intensity matching and complete outlier removal. Med. Image Anal. **16**(8), 1550–1564 (2012)

12. Makropoulos, A., et al.: Automatic whole brain MRI segmentation of the developing neonatal brain. IEEE TMI **33**(9), 1818–1831 (2014)

13. Nadeau, H., Chai, Y., Thompson, P., Leporé, N.: Simultaneous registration of structural and diffusion weighed images using the full DTI information. In: SPIE, vol. 9287 (2015)

14. Park, H.J., et al.: Spatial normalization of diffusion tensor MRI using multiple channels. Neuroimage **20**(4), 1195–2009 (2003)

15. Pietsch, M., Raffelt, D., Dhollander, T., Tournier, J.D.: Multi-contrast diffeomorphic non-linear registration of orientation density functions. In: ISMRM (2017)

16. Pietsch, M., et al.: A framework for multi-component analysis of diffusion MRI data over the neonatal period. NeuroImage **186**(October 2017), 321–337 (2019)

17. Raffelt, D., Tournier, J.D., Fripp, J., Crozier, S., Connelly, A., Salvado, O.: Symmetric diffeomorphic registration of fibre orientation distributions. NeuroImage **56**(3), 1171–80 (2011)

18. Raffelt, D., et al.: Reorientation of fiber orientation distributions using apodized point spread functions. MR in Med. **67**(3), 844–855 (2012)

19. Roura, E., et al.: Multi-channel registration of fractional anisotropy and T1-weighted images in the presence of atrophy: application to multiple sclerosis. Funct. Neurol. **30**(4), 245–256 (2015)

20. Rutherford, M., Biarge, M.M., Allsop, J., Counsell, S., Cowan, F.: MRI of perinatal brain injury. Pediatr. Radiol. **40**(6), 819–833 (2010). https://doi.org/10.1007/s00247-010-1620-z

21. Tournier, J.D., Calamante, F., Connelly, A.: Robust determination of the fibre orientation distribution in diffusion MRI: non-negativity constrained super-resolved spherical deconvolution. NeuroImage **35**(4), 1459–1472 (2007)
22. Tournier, J.D., et al.: MRtrix3: a fast, flexible and open software framework for medical image processing and visualisation. NeuroImage **202**, 116–137 (2019)

An Image Registration-Based Method for EPI Distortion Correction Based on Opposite Phase Encoding (COPE)

Hester Breman[1,2(✉)], Joost Mulders[1], Levin Fritz[1], Judith Peters[2,3,4], John Pyles[5], Judith Eck[1,2], Matteo Bastiani[6,7,8], Alard Roebroeck[2], John Ashburner[9], and Rainer Goebel[1,2]

[1] Brain Innovation, Maastricht, The Netherlands
breman@brainvoyager.com
[2] Department of Cognitive Neuroscience, Faculty of Psychology and Neuroscience, Maastricht University, Maastricht, The Netherlands
[3] Maastricht Brain Imaging Center, Maastricht University, Maastricht, The Netherlands
[4] Department of Vision and Cognition, Netherlands Institute for Neuroscience, An Institute of the Royal Netherlands Academy of Arts and Sciences (KNAW), Amsterdam, The Netherlands
[5] Center for the Neural Basis of Cognition, Carnegie Mellon University, Pittsburgh, USA
[6] Sir Peter Mansfield Imaging Centre, School of Medicine, University of Nottingham, Nottingham, UK
[7] NIHR Biomedical Research Centre, University of Nottingham, Nottingham, UK
[8] Wellcome Centre for Integrative Neuroimaging, University of Oxford, Oxford, UK
[9] The Wellcome Centre for Human Neuroimaging, University College London, London, UK

Abstract. Surprisingly, estimated voxel displacement maps (VDMs), based on image registration, seem to work just as well to correct geometrical distortion in functional MRI data (EPI) as VDMs based on actual information about the magnetic field. In this article, we compare our new image registration-based distortion correction method 'COPE' to an implementation of the pixelshift method. Our approach builds on existing image registration-based techniques using opposite phase encoding, extending these by local cost aggregation. Comparison of these methods with 3T and 7T spin-echo (SE) and gradient-echo (GE) data show that the image registration-based method is a good alternative to the fieldmap-based EPI distortion correction method.

Keywords: Image registration · Susceptibility distortion correction

H. Breman, J. Mulders, L. Fritz—The three authors contributed equally to this paper.

1   Introduction and Background

In this article we introduce an image registration-based method for EPI distortion Correction based on Opposite Phase Encoding (COPE). To ensure its usefulness, we compare the new, image-registration-based approach with a fieldmap-based approach for reducing geometric distortion in EPI data due to the susceptibility artifact.

In the fieldmap-based geometric distortion correction method for EPI data based on the 'pixelshift method' by Jezzard and Balaban [6], a pixelshift map, also called voxel displacement map (VDM), is calculated from a T_2-weighted reference scan. The VDM indicates how far the voxels need to be translated back to their original locations.

In image registration-based distortion correction methods, the VDM is estimated by acquiring EPI data with two opposite phase encoding directions. In EPI, the frequency and phase are modulated such that the original location of each signal can be found; due to the susceptibility artifact, the field inhomogeneity 'disrupts' the phase encoding, but by acquiring data in the opposite phase encoding direction, pixel shifts occur in the same amount in opposite directions in the functional images. Image registration-based methods use a suitable cost function to minimise, which is a function that measures the dissimilarity between the opposite phase encoded images.

In the next section, we will explain our distortion correction method 'COPE' in more detail. In Sect. 3 we show the experiment we performed for testing the performance of our method. In the final section we will discuss the results (Fig. 1).

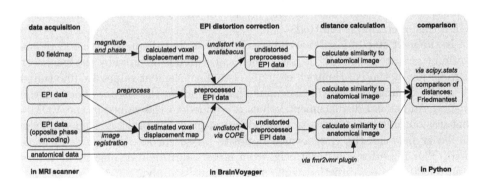

Fig. 1. Setup of the EPI distortion correction comparison

2   Methods

In our image-registration based distortion correction method 'COPE', opposite phase encoded echo planar images (EPI) are registered to each other. Acquiring an opposite phase encoded EPI volume requires a few seconds. We use one model for the forward and backward transformation, which estimates a voxel displacement map, so the forward and backward transformations are each others inverse.

First, the optimal transformations (scaling and translation) in the y-direction are estimated column-wise; for each iteration, the distance D^{SSD} between the images is established via sum of square differences (SSD) or normalised cross-correlation (NCC). Let $D^{SSD}[I_1, I_2; \mathbf{p}]$ be a function of parameters $\mathbf{p}$ using the 1D columns I_1 (from image in one phase encoding direction) and I_2 (from image in the opposite phase encoding direction), and where $f(\mathbf{p}) = \sum \mathbf{r}$ is the sum of the residuals, quantifying the difference between each voxel in one image and the opposite phase encoded image:

$$D^{SSD}(\mathbf{p}) = \frac{1}{2}(f(\mathbf{p}))^2 \quad \text{with} \quad f(\mathbf{p}) = I_2 \circ \phi_{\mathbf{p}} - I_1 \circ \phi_{\mathbf{p}}^{-1}, \tag{1}$$

$\phi : \mathbb{R}^2 \to \mathbb{R}^2$ and $x \mapsto p_s x + p_t$, where ϕ is the transformation for each coordinate, composed of p_s and p_t, the scaling resp. translation parameters. Gauss-Newton optimisation [7] involves approximating the function D^{SSD} with a second-degree Taylor expansion in order to iteratively minimise it. Like in Gauss-Newton optimisation methods, the Hessian $\mathbf{H}$ is approximated with the Jacobian $\mathbf{J}$ and the parameter change s is obtained using both $\mathbf{H}$ and $\mathbf{J}$ and differences between columns δ: $s = -\mathbf{H} \, \mathbf{J}^T \delta$. Instead of regularization, smoothing with a Gaussian kernel is applied to the scaling and translation matrices and the EPI volumes that are used to estimate the VDM. The algorithm is inspired by Andersson et al. [1] and Ruthotto et al. [9].

If the "spin echo" (SE) option has been selected, intensity correction is applied using the derivative of the inverse of the VDM; for "gradient echo" (GE), this operation is omitted.

In the next step, a local search is performed to find the most plausible deformation (measured via NCC or SSD); the local search is inspired by the local cost aggregation method of Heinrich et al. [5]. The displacement values are fine-tuned by locally finding the best displacement that minimizes the distance between the images. Additional displacement values are added to the values in the VDM - that was obtained via Gauss-Newton optimisation in the previous step - and the similarity between the transformed opposite phase encoded images is recalculated. This is performed iteratively, from larger additional displacement values from ±5.00 in the y-direction while simultaneously applying strong smoothing, to smaller displacements until ±0.75 with lighter smoothing; the image similarity is calculated accordingly and the displacement value for each voxel that results in the highest image similarity is kept (see also Fig. 2). The voxel displacement map can then be applied to distorted EPI data using cubic spline interpolation.

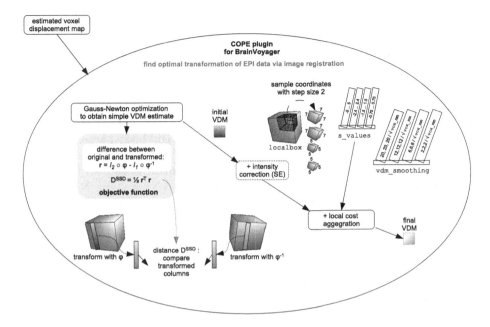

Fig. 2. Estimation of a voxel displacement map (VDM) via COPE

We compare fieldmap based-correction with image registration-based correction of SE-EPI and GE-EPI data on 3T and 7T. The distance of each EPI dataset to the anatomical image of the same subject is compared before and after distortion correction. To assess the generality of the performance of fieldmap-based vs image registration-based distortion, we use EPI data sets acquired with different field strengths (3T and 7T), multi-band factors and sequences (spin-echo (SE)-EPI, gradient echo (GE)-EPI), modality (BOLD and diffusion weighted) and different sites (Maastricht vs Carnegie-Mellon)(see Table 1) on Siemens scanners (Siemens Medical Systems, Erlangen, Germany).

2.1   Data Pre-processing

All processing was performed in native scanner space. Pre-processing steps specific for each modality are described below.

Anatomical Data. Anatomical data were corrected for B_1 inhomogeneity and skull-stripped in BrainVoyager (v20.6, Maastricht, The Netherlands) [4].

Fieldmaps. For datasets 6–10, the combined 32-channel fieldmaps, differential phase maps $\Delta\phi$ were calculated in Matlab (R2014a) via a custom script according to $-\arctan(\Im(z_1 z_2^*)/\Re(z_1 z_2^*))$, where z_1 is the first echo, z_2 the second echo, $\Im$ denotes the imaginary part, $\Re$ the real part and * the complex conjugate [2].

All following processing steps were performed on the fieldmaps using `anatabacus` plugin v1.1 for BrainVoyager. All phase maps were converted to radians using a linear transformation [8]. Unwrapping of the phase maps was calculated using 3D multigrid, the deviation from B_0 in Hz and pixel shifts calculated according to [6]. Undistortion was applied using linear 1D interpolation.

EPI Data. The functional (BOLD) EPI data were slice scan time corrected using cubic interpolation, corrected for motion using rigid body parameters estimated using trilinear interpolation and resliced with SINC interpolation; finally, a temporal high pass filter was applied in Fourier domain with 0.0078 Hz cutoff in BrainVoyager v20.6.

Concerning diffusion weighted data, unprocessed b_0 images were used for fieldmap-based and opposite phase encoding correction.

Table 1. Acquisition parameters of data used to compare fieldmap-based with image registration-based distortion correction. Sequence = sequence: field maps/EPI data, SE = spin echo, GE = gradient echo, MB = multiband factor: fieldmap/EPI data, Slices = number of slices in EPI data, iPAT = acceleration in EPI data, FOV = field of view (mm), TR = repetition time (ms), TE = echo time (ms) of EPI data, Echo sp = Echo spacing (ms), T = B_0 field strength in Tesla. All EPI data were scanned in anterior-posterior phase encoding direction. Sets 1–4 were acquired at a Siemens scanner in Pittsburgh, USA, and sets 5–10 at the University of Maastricht, The Netherlands. For the diffusion weighted data (set 5), opposite phase encoded b = 0 images were used to estimate the VDM.

Dataset	Sequence	MB	Slices	iPAT	Matrix size (y)	TR (ms)	TE (ms)	Echo sp.	T	BW_{pe}
1	SE/GE	1/3	72	1	212	2000	30.0	0.72	3	13.10
2	SE/GE	3/3	72	1	212	2000	30.0	0.72	3	13.10
3	SE/GE	1/3	72	1	212	2000	30.0	0.72	3	13.10
4	SE/GE	3/3	72	1	212	2000	30.0	0.72	3	13.10
5	SE b3000	1	52	1	220	6600	94.0	0.40	3	28.41
6	GE	3	99	3	160	2000	19.0	0.81	7	23.15
7	GE	2	82	3	220	2027	21.0	0.80	7	17.05
8	GE	2	58	2	136	2000	21.0	0.80	7	18.38
9	GE	3	99	3	182	2000	21.0	1.00	7	16.48
10	GE	2	64	2	100	2000	30.0	0.65	3	30.77

2.2   Data Comparison

The uncorrected, fieldmap-based corrected and image-registration-based corrected EPI data are mapped to anatomical space using the `fmr2vmrplugin` (v0.9.1) for BrainVoyager, after which the similarity is calculated via

$$D(I_1, I_2) = \frac{\sum_{i=1}^{n}(I_{1i} \cdot I_{2i})^2}{\sum_{i=1}^{n}(I_{1i}I_{1i}) \cdot \sum_{i=1}^{n}(I_{2i}I_{2i})} \qquad (2)$$

where I_1 is the anatomical image of the subject, I_2 the EPI image and n is the number of voxels.

2.3   Computational Platform

The COPE plugin was implemented using C++ 11 code. The data were processed on a MacBook Air with a 1.6 GHz Intel Core i5 processor and 4 GB 1600 MHz DDR3 memory with a macOS 10.13 (High Sierra) operating system. We used COPE v1.1 and `anatabacus` v1.1. Typical processing time for estimation of a VDM by COPE is 3 min (dataset 8).

3   Results

3.1   Distance Measure

The similarities between EPI data and anatomical images, calculated using the fmr2vmrplugin v0.9.1 in BrainVoyager 20.6.2., are shown in Table 2. The 'before' column indicates the similarity between the EPI data and the anatomical image without any EPI distortion correction. The '`anatabacus`' column shows the similarity after fieldmap-based EPI distortion correction via the `anatabacus` plugin. In the 'COPE' column the similarity values are provided after image registration-based EPI distortion correction via the COPE plugin.

Table 2. Similarity values between anatomical image and distorted EPI data (left), between anatomical image and EPI data undistorted via fieldmap-based method (anatabacus) (centre) and between anatomical image and EPI data undistorted via image registration (COPE) (right).

Dataset	Before	anatabacus	COPE
1	0.960059	0.967195	0.961707
2	0.960059	0.967195	0.964098
3	0.960059	0.967195	0.965260
4	0.960059	0.967195	0.963018
5	0.996122	0.997106	0.999763
6	0.884896	0.889236	0.890754
7	0.884390	0.900305	0.911093
8	0.475983	0.491037	0.593685
9	0.665548	0.680071	0.736336
10	0.838839	0.843269	0.915955

In Table 2 we see that in all ten cases, EPI distortion correction improves the match between the shape of the EPI data and the shape of the anatomical data.

Furthermore, in six of the ten cases, the new image registration-based EPI distortion correction method (as implemented in COPE) outperforms the fieldmap-based EPI distortion correction method (as implemented in **anatabacus**), which is shown in the graph in Fig. 3.

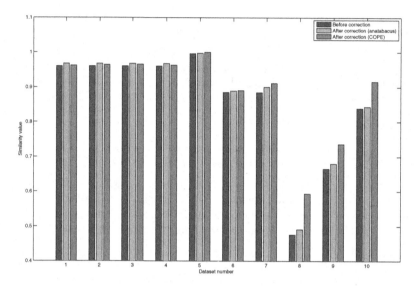

Fig. 3. The graph shows that the image based registration (via COPE) relatively increases similarity between anatomical and functional 7T data the most (datasets 6–10)

3.2 Comparison

We ran a non-parametric test, the Friedman Test, on the distance data. The results showed a significant difference between the groups ($p < 0.001$). Processing was performed via the SciPy library. Posthoc analysis with the Nemenyi test using scikit-posthocs [10] did not provide any further specific significance. All statistical analysis was performed in Python 3.

Figure 4 shows data set 6 after "fine alignment" (normalized gradient field registration) of EPI data to anatomical data (z=135) in BrainVoyager 20.6, where the overlay shows the contours of the EPI image in green. On the left the distorted EPI image is shown; in the centre, the EPI image corrected via image registration-based EPI distortion correction in COPE; on the right, the EPI image corrected via fieldmap-based EPI distortion correction in **anatabacus**. Improvements in the registration with respect to the distorted image on the left are indicated with circles; we see for example an improved fit at the anterior of the corpus callosum. Normalized gradient field registration is an affine image registration method finding global scaling, translation and rotation parameters for the EPI image via Gauss-Newton optimization.

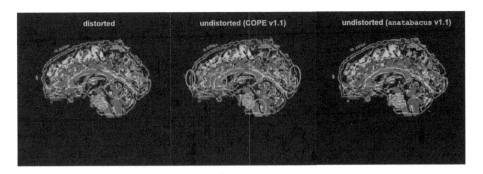

Fig. 4. Slice z = 135 of dataset 6 before EPI distortion correction (left), after EPI distortion correction via COPE v1.1 (centre) and after distortion correction via anatabacus v1.1 (right), where the green lines depict the contours of the EPI image overlaid on the anatomical image in native space (Color figure online)

4   Conclusion

The comparison between fieldmap-based and our novel method of image registration-based distortion correction combined with local cost aggregation indicates that this approach can be a viable alternative to fieldmap-based distortion correction (see also [3]), in particular for 7T data; this eliminates the need for phase data unwrapping and masking. This image registration-based EPI distortion correction variant has been implemented in the COPE plugin for BrainVoyager and can be freely downloaded from the BrainVoyager support website.

Acknowledgements. The authors thank Benedikt Poser and Dimo Ivanov for advice on processing the 32-channel 7T fieldmaps, Faruk Gülban for suggestions to improve the figures and the anonymous reviewers for valuable comments to improve the paper.

References

1. Andersson, J., Skare, S., Ashburner, J.: How to correct susceptibility distortions in spin-echo echo-planar images: application to diffusion tensor imaging. NeuroImage **20**, 870–888 (2003)
2. Bernstein, M., King, K., Zhou, X.: Handbook of MRI Pulse Sequences. Academic Press, Cambridge (2004)
3. Fritz, L., Mulders, J., Breman, H., et al.: Comparison of EPI distortion correction methods at 3T and 7T. In: Presented at the OHBM meeting in Hamburg, Germany (2014)
4. Goebel, R.: BrainVoyager - past, present, future. NeuroImage **62**, 748–756 (2012)
5. Heinrich, M.P., Papież, B.W., Schnabel, J.A., Handels, H.: Non-parametric discrete registration with convex optimisation. In: Ourselin, S., Modat, M. (eds.) WBIR 2014. LNCS, vol. 8545, pp. 51–61. Springer, Cham (2014). https://doi.org/10.1007/978-3-319-08554-8_6
6. Jezzard, P., Balaban, B.: Correction for geometric distortion in echo planar images from B0 field variations. MRM **34**(1), 65–73 (1995)

7. Modersitzki, J.: Numerical Methods for Image Registration. Numerical Mathematics and Scientific Computation. Oxford University Press, Oxford (2004)
8. Nijdam, B., van Buuren, H.: Statistiek voor de sociale wetenschappen, vol. Deel I en II. Alphen aan den Rijn/Zaventem: Samsom Bedrijfsinformatie (1994)
9. Ruthotto, L., Mohammadi, S., Heck, C., Modersitzki, J., Weiskopf, N.: HySCO - hyperelastic susceptibility artifact correction of DTI in SPM. In: Presented at the Bildverarbeitung fuer die Medizin 2013 (2013)
10. Terpilowski, M.: scikit-posthocs: pairwise multiple comparison tests in Python. J. Open Source Softw. 4(36), 1169 (2019). https://doi.org/10.21105/joss.01169

Diffusion Tensor Driven Image Registration: A Deep Learning Approach

Irina Grigorescu[1(✉)], Alena Uus[1], Daan Christiaens[1,2],
Lucilio Cordero-Grande[1], Jana Hutter[1], A. David Edwards[1],
Joseph V. Hajnal[1], Marc Modat[1], and Maria Deprez[1]

[1] School of Biomedical Engineering and Imaging Sciences,
King's College London, London, UK
irina.grigorescu@kcl.ac.uk
[2] Departments of Electrical Engineering, ESAT/PSI, KU Leuven, Leuven, Belgium

Abstract. Tracking microstructural changes in the developing brain relies on accurate inter-subject image registration. However, most methods rely on either structural or diffusion data to learn the spatial correspondences between two or more images, without taking into account the complementary information provided by using both. Here we propose a deep learning registration framework which combines the structural information provided by T_2-weighted (T_2w) images with the rich microstructural information offered by diffusion tensor imaging (DTI) scans. This allows our trained network to register pairs of images in a single pass. We perform a leave-one-out cross-validation study where we compare the performance of our multi-modality registration model with a baseline model trained on structural data only, in terms of Dice scores and differences in fractional anisotropy (FA) maps. Our results show that in terms of average Dice scores our model performs better in subcortical regions when compared to using structural data only. Moreover, average sum-of-squared differences between warped and fixed FA maps show that our proposed model performs better at aligning the diffusion data.

Keywords: Image registration · Diffusion tensor imaging

1 Introduction

Medical image registration is a vital component of a large number of clinical applications. For example, image registration is used to track longitudinal changes occurring in the brain. However, most applications in this field rely on a single modality, without taking into account the rich information provided by other modalities. Although T_2w magnetic resonance imaging (MRI) scans provide good contrast between different brain tissues, they do not have knowledge of the extent or location of white matter tracts. Moreover, during early life, the brain undergoes dramatic changes, such as cortical folding and myelination, processes which affect not only the brain's shape, but also the MRI tissue contrast.

© Springer Nature Switzerland AG 2020
Ž. Špiclin et al. (Eds.): WBIR 2020, LNCS 12120, pp. 131–140, 2020.
https://doi.org/10.1007/978-3-030-50120-4_13

In order to establish correspondences between images acquired at different gestational ages, we propose a deep learning image registration framework which combines both T_2w and DTI scans. More specifically, we build a neural network starting from the popular diffeomorphic VoxelMorph framework [2], on which we add layers capable of dealing with diffusion tensor (DT) images. The key novelties in our proposed deep learning registration framework are:

- The network is capable of dealing with higher-order data, such as DT images, by accounting for the change in orientation of diffusion tensors induced by the predicted deformation field.
- During inference, our trained network can register pairs of T_2w images without the need to provide the extra microstructural information. This is helpful when higher-order data is missing in the test dataset.

Throughout this work we use 3-D MRI brain scans acquired as part of the developing Human Connectome Project[1] (dHCP). We showcase the capabilities of our proposed framework on images of infants born and scanned at different gestational ages and we compare the results against the baseline network trained on only T_2w images. Our results show that by using both modalities to drive the learning process we achieve superior alignment in subcortical regions and a better alignment of the white matter tracts.

2   Method

Let F, M represent the fixed (target) and the moving (source) magnetic resonance (MR) volumes, respectively, defined over the 3-D spatial domain Ω, and let ϕ be the deformation field. In this paper we focus on T_2w images (F^{T2w} and M^{T2w} which are single channel data) and DT images (F^{DTI} and M^{DTI} which are 6 channels data) acquired from the same subjects. Our aim is to align pairs of T_2w volumes using similarity metrics defined on both the T_2w and DTI data, while only using the structural data as input to the network.

In order to achieve this, we model a function $g_\theta(F^{T2w}, M^{T2w}) = v$ a velocity field (with learnable parameters θ) using a convolutional neural network (CNN) architecture based on VoxelMorph [2]. In addition to the baseline architecture, we construct layers capable of dealing with the higher-order data represented by our DT images. Throughout this work we use T_2w and DTI scans that have been affinely aligned to a common 40 weeks gestational age atlas space [14], prior to being used by the network.

Figure 1 shows the general architecture of the proposed network. During training, our model uses pairs of T_2w images to learn a velocity field v, while the *squaring and scaling layers* [2] transform it into a topology-preserving deformation field ϕ. The moving images M are warped by the deformation field using a *SpatialTransform* layer [5] which outputs the moved (linearly resampled) T_2w and DT images. The DT images are further processed to obtain the final moved and reoriented image.

---

[1] http://www.developingconnectome.org/.

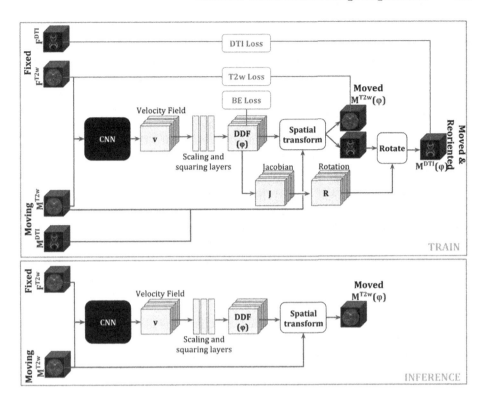

Fig. 1. The proposed network architecture at both training and inference time.

The model is trained using stochastic gradient descent to find the optimal parameters $\hat{\theta}$ that minimize a sum of three loss functions, representing the tensor similarity measure, the scalar-data similarity measure and a regulariser applied on the predicted deformation field. The DTI data is not used as input to our CNN, but only used to drive the learning process through calculating the similarity measure. During inference, our model uses only T_2w images to predict the deformation field, without the need for a second modality. In the following subsections, we describe our model in further detail.

Network Architecture. The baseline architecture of our network is a 3-D UNet [12] based on VoxelMorph [2]. The encoding branch is made up of four 3D convolutions of $16, 32, 32$, and 32 filters, respectively, with a kernel size of $3 \times 3 \times 3$, followed by *Leaky ReLU* ($\alpha = 0.2$) activations [18]. The decoding branch contains four transverse 3D convolutions of 32 filters each, with the same kernel size and activation function. Skip connections are used to concatenate the encoding branch's information to the decoder branch. Two more convolutional layers, one with 16 filters and a second one with 3 filters, are added at the end, both with the same kernel size and activation function as before.

A pair of T_2w images are concatenated on the channel axis and become a $96 \times 96 \times 64 \times 2$ input for the CNN network. The output is a three channel velocity field of the same size as the input images. The velocity field is smoothed with a $3 \times 3 \times 3$ Gaussian kernel (with $\sigma = 1.2\,\text{mm}$), and passed onto seven *squaring and scaling layers* [2], which transform it into a topology-preserving deformation field. The *SpatialTransform* layer [5] receives as input the predicted field ϕ and the moving scalar-valued T_2w image, and outputs the warped and resampled image. A similar process is necessary to warp the moving DT image, with a few extra steps which are explained in the next subsection.

Tensor Reorientation. Registration of DT images is not as straightforward to perform as scalar-valued data. When transforming the latter, the intensities in the moving image are interpolated at the new locations determined by the deformation field ϕ and copied to the corresponding location in the target image space. However, after interpolating DT images, the diffusion tensors need to be reoriented to remain anatomically correct [1]. In this work we use the *finite strain* (FS) strategy [1].

When the transformation is non-linear, such as in our case, the reorientation matrix can be computed at each point in the deformation field ϕ through a polar decomposition of the local Jacobian matrix. This factorisation transforms the non-singular matrix J into a unitary matrix R (the pure rotation) and a positive-semidefinite Hermitian matrix P, such that $J = RP$ [15]. The rotation matrices R are then used to reorient the tensors without changing the local microstructure.

Loss Function. We train our model using a loss function composed of three parts. First, the structural loss $\mathcal{L}_{struct}$ (applied on the T_2w data only) is a popular similarity measure used in medical image registration, called normalised cross correlation (NCC). We define it as:

$$NCC(F, M(\phi)) = -\frac{\sum_{\mathbf{x} \in \Omega}(F(\mathbf{x}) - \overline{F}) \cdot (M(\phi(\mathbf{x})) - \overline{M})}{\sqrt{\sum_{\mathbf{x} \in \Omega}(F(\mathbf{x}) - \overline{F})^2 \cdot \sum_{\mathbf{x} \in \Omega}(M(\phi(\mathbf{x})) - \overline{M})^2}}$$

where $\overline{F}$ is the mean voxel value in the fixed image F and $\overline{M}$ is the mean voxel value in the transformed moving image $M(\phi)$.

Second, to encourage a good alignment between the DT images, we set $\mathcal{L}_{tensor}$ to be one of the most commonly used diffusion tensor similarity measures, known as the Euclidean distance squared. We define it as:

$$EDS(F, M(\phi)) = \sum_{\mathbf{x} \in \Omega} ||F(\mathbf{x}) - M(\phi(\mathbf{x}))||_C^2$$

where the euclidean distance between two pairs of tensors $\mathbf{D_1}$ and $\mathbf{D_2}$ is defined as $||\mathbf{D_1} - \mathbf{D_2}||_C = \sqrt{Tr((\mathbf{D_1} - \mathbf{D_2})^2)}$ [19].

Finally, to ensure a smooth deformation field ϕ we use a regularisation penalty $\mathcal{L}_{reg}$ in the form of bending energy [13]:

$$BE(\phi) = \sum_{\mathbf{x} \in \Omega} \left[\left(\frac{\partial^2 \phi(\mathbf{x})}{\partial x^2} \right)^2 + \left(\frac{\partial^2 \phi(\mathbf{x})}{\partial y^2} \right)^2 + \left(\frac{\partial^2 \phi(\mathbf{x})}{\partial z^2} \right)^2 + \right.$$
$$\left. 2\left(\frac{\partial^2 \phi(\mathbf{x})}{\partial xy} \right)^2 + 2\left(\frac{\partial^2 \phi(\mathbf{x})}{\partial xz} \right)^2 + 2\left(\frac{\partial^2 \phi(\mathbf{x})}{\partial yz} \right)^2 \right]$$

Thus, the final loss function is:

$$\mathcal{L}(F, M(\phi)) = \alpha \, EDS(F^{DTI}, M^{DTI}(\phi)) + \beta \, NCC(F^{T2w}, M^{T2w}(\phi)) + \lambda \, BE(\phi)$$

We compare our network with a baseline trained on T_2w data only. For the latter case the loss function becomes: $\mathcal{L}(F, M(\phi)) = \beta \, NCC(F^{T2w}, M^{T2w}(\phi)) + \lambda \, BE(\phi)$. In all of our experiments we set the weights to $\alpha = 1.0$, $\beta = 1.0$ and $\lambda = 0.001$ when using both DTI and T_2w images, and to $\beta = 1.0$ and $\lambda = 0.001$ when using T_2w data only. These hyper-parameters were found to be optimal on our validation set.

3   Experiments

Dataset. The image dataset used in this work is part of the developing Human Connectome Project. Both the T_2w images and the diffusion weighted (DW) images were acquired using a 3T Philips Achieva scanner and a 32-channels neonatal head coil [6]. The structural data was acquired using a turbo spin echo (TSE) sequence in two stacks of 2D slices (sagittal and axial planes), with parameters: $T_R = 12$ s, $T_E = 156$ ms, and SENSE factors of 2.11 for the axial plane and 2.58 for the sagittal plane. The data was subsequently corrected for motion [4,8] and resampled to an isotropic voxel size of 0.5 mm.

The DW images were acquired using a monopolar spin echo echo-planar imaging (SE-EPI) Stejksal-Tanner sequence [7]. A multiband factor of 4 and a total of 64 interleaved overlapping slices (1.5 mm in-plane resolution, 3 mm thickness, 1.5 mm overlap) were used to acquire a single volume, with parameters $T_R = 3800$ ms, $T_E = 90$ ms. This data underwent outlier removal, motion correction and it was subsequently super-resolved to a 1.5 mm isotropic voxel resolution [3]. All resulting images were checked for abnormalities by a paediatric neuroradiologist.

For this study, we use a total of 368 T_2w and DT volumes of neonates born between 23–42 weeks gestational age (GA) and scanned at term-equivalent age (37–45 weeks GA). The age distribution in our dataset is found in Fig. 2, where GA at birth is shown in blue, and post-menstrual age (PMA) at scan is shown in orange. In order to use both the T_2w and DT volumes in our registration network, we first resampled the T_2w data into the DW space of 1.5 mm voxel resolution. Then, we affinely registered all of our data to a common 40 weeks

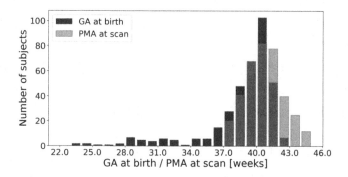

Fig. 2. Distribution of gestational ages at birth (GA) and post-menstrual ages at scan (PMA) in our dataset. (Color figure online)

gestational age atlas space [14] available in the MIRTK[2] software toolbox [13] and obtained the DT images using the DWI2TENSOR [17] command available in the MRTRIX[3] toolbox. Finally, we performed skull-stripping using the available dHCP brain masks [3] and we cropped the resulting images to a $96 \times 96 \times 64$ volume size.

Training. We trained our models using the rectified Adam (RAdam) optimiser [9] with a cyclical learning rate [16] varying from 10^{-9} to 10^{-4}, for $90,000$ iterations. Out of the 368 subjects in our entire dataset, 318 were used for training, 25 for validation and 25 for test. The subjects in each category were chosen such that their GA at birth and PMA at scan were distributed across the entire range. The validation set was used to help us choose the best hyperparameters for our network and the best performing models. The results reported in the next section are on the test set.

Final Model Results. In both our T_2w-only and T_2w+DTI cases we performed a leave-one-out cross-validation, where we aligned 24 of the test subjects to a single subject, and repeated until all the subjects were used as target. Each of the 25 subjects had tissue label segmentations (obtained using the Draw-EM pipeline for automatic brain MRI segmentation of the developing neonatal brain [10]) which were propagated using NIFTYREG[4] [11] and the predicted deformation fields. The average resulting Dice scores are summarised in Fig. 3, where the initial pre-alignment is shown in pink, the T_2w-only results are shown in light blue and the T_2w+DTI are shown in purple. Our proposed model performs better than the baseline model for all subcortical structures (cerebellum, deep gray matter, brainstem and hippocampi and amygdala), while performing similarly well in white matter structures. In contrast, cortical gray matter regions were better aligned when using the T_2w-only model, as structural data has higher contrast than DTI in these areas.

---

[2] https://mirtk.github.io/.

[3] https://mrtrix.readthedocs.io/.

[4] https://github.com/KCL-BMEIS/niftyreg/.

We also computed the FA maps for all the initial affinely aligned and all the warped subjects in the cross-validation study and calculated the sum-of-squared differences (SSD) between the moved FA maps and the fixed FA maps. The resulting average values are summarised in Table 1, which shows that our proposed model achieved better alignment in terms of FA maps.

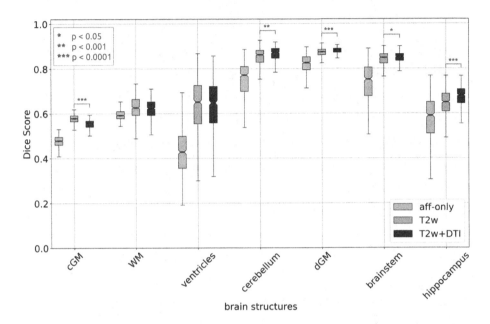

Fig. 3. Average Dice scores for our cross-validation study for 7 tissue types: cortical gray matter (cGM), white matter (WM), ventricles, cerebellum, deep gray matter (dGM), brainstem and the hippocampus. For both of our trained models the input images, $F^{T2w|DTI}$ and $M^{T2w|DTI}$, have been affinely aligned to a template, prior to being used by the models. Our proposed model outperforms the T_2w-only training in terms of obtaining higher Dice scores for the cerebellum, dGM, brainstem and hippocampus. (Color figure online)

Finally, Fig. 4 shows two example registrations. The target images are from two term-born infants with GA = 40.86 weeks and PMA = 41.43 weeks, and GA = 40.57w and PMA = 41w, respectively, while the moving images are from infants with GA = 40.57 weeks and PMA = 41 weeks, and GA = 37.14w and PMA = 37.28w, respectively. The figure shows both T_2w and FA maps of axial slices of the fixed (first column), the moving (second column) and the warped images by our proposed method (third column) and the baseline method (fourth column), respectively. The moved FA maps show that by using DTI data to drive the learning process of a deep learning registration framework, we were able to achieve good alignment not only on the structural data, but also on the diffusion data as well.

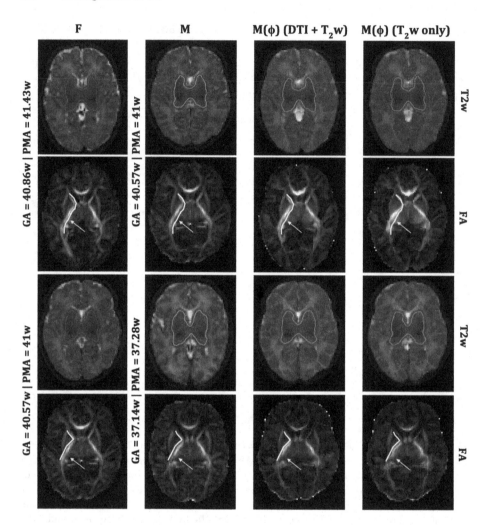

Fig. 4. First two rows show an example registration between a neonate with GA = 40.57w and PMA = 41w as moving, and one with GA = 40.86w and PMA = 41.43w as fixed, last two rows show an example where the moving image is from a neonate with GA = 37.14w and PMA = 37.28w, and fixed is a neonate with GA = 40.57w and PMA = 41w. First column shows axial slices of the fixed T_2w images and FA maps, the second column shows axial slices of the moving T_2w images and FA maps, and the third and fourth columns show the moved images using our proposed network and the baseline network, respectively. In the T_2w maps the deep gray matter (dGM) labels are shown for the fixed images in dark blue and for the moving and moved in cyan. In both cases a higher dGM Dice score was obtained for the T_2w+DTI model (0.88 and 0.88, respectively), than when using T_2w-only (0.84 and 0.87, respectively). The arrows point at areas where the underlying anatomy was better preserved when using T_2w+DTI, than when using T_2w-only. (Color figure online)

Table 1. Average sum-of-squared differences between warped and fixed FA maps in our leave-one-out cross-validation study. The first line shows mean and standard deviation SSD values for the initial affine alignment.

Method	Mean (SSD)	Std.Dev. (SSD)	p-value		
Affine	1087	174	Affine vs T2w		$p < 1e^{-5}$
T2w	1044	168	Affine vs T2w+DTI		$p < 1e^{-5}$
T2w+DTI	981	181	T2w vs T2w+DTI		$p < 1e^{-5}$

4   Discussion and Future Work

In this work we showed for the first time a deep learning registration framework capable of aligning both structural (T2w) and microstructural (DTI) data, while using only T_2w data at inference time. A key result from our study is that our proposed T_2w+DTI model performed better in terms of aligning subcortical structures, even though the labels for these regions were obtained from structural data only. For future work we plan to focus on improving the registration in the cortical regions, and to compare our deep learning model with classic registration algorithms.

Acknowledgments. This work was supported by the Academy of Medical Sciences Springboard Award (SBF004\1040), European Research Council under the European Union's Seventh Framework Programme (FP7/ 20072013)/ERC grant agreement no. 319456 dHCP project, the Wellcome/EPSRC Centre for Medical Engineering at King's College London (WT 203148/Z/16/Z), the NIHR Clinical Research Facility (CRF) at Guy's and St Thomas' and by the National Institute for Health Research Biomedical Research Centre based at Guy's and St Thomas' NHS Foundation Trust and King's College London. The views expressed are those of the authors and not necessarily those of the NHS, the NIHR or the Department of Health.

References

1. Alexander, D.C., Pierpaoli, C., Basser, P.J., Gee, J.C.: Spatial transformations of diffusion tensor magnetic resonance images. IEEE Trans. Med. Imaging **20**(11), 1131–1139 (2001)
2. Balakrishnan, G., Zhao, A., Sabuncu, M.R., Guttag, J., Dalca, A.V.: Voxelmorph: a learning framework for deformable medical image registration. IEEE Trans. Med. Imaging **38**(8), 1788–1800 (2019)
3. Christiaens, D., et al.: Scattered slice shard reconstruction for motion correction in multi-shell diffusion MRI of the neonatal brain. arXiv preprint arXiv:1905.02996 (2019)
4. Cordero-Grande, L., Hughes, E.J., Hutter, J., Price, A.N., Hajnal, J.V.: Three-dimensional motion corrected sensitivity encoding reconstruction for multi-shot multi-slice MRI: application to neonatal brain imaging. Magnet. Reson. Med. **79**(3), 1365–1376 (2018)

5. Dalca, A.V., Balakrishnan, G., Guttag, J., Sabuncu, M.R.: Unsupervised learning for fast probabilistic diffeomorphic registration. In: Frangi, A.F., Schnabel, J.A., Davatzikos, C., Alberola-López, C., Fichtinger, G. (eds.) MICCAI 2018. LNCS, vol. 11070, pp. 729–738. Springer, Cham (2018). https://doi.org/10.1007/978-3-030-00928-1_82

6. Hughes, E.J., et al.: A dedicated neonatal brain imaging system. Magnet. Reson. Med. **78**(2), 794–804 (2017)

7. Hutter, J., et al.: Time-efficient and flexible design of optimized multishell hardi diffusion. Magnet. Reson. Med. **79**(3), 1276–1292 (2018)

8. Kuklisova-Murgasova, M., Quaghebeur, G., Rutherford, M.A., Hajnal, J.V., Schnabel, J.A.: Reconstruction of fetal brain MRI with intensity matching and complete outlier removal. Med. Image Anal. **16**(8), 1550–1564 (2012)

9. Liu, L., et al.: On the variance of the adaptive learning rate and beyond (2019)

10. Makropoulos, A., et al.: Automatic whole brain MRI segmentation of the developing neonatal brain. IEEE Trans. Med. Imaging **33**(9), 1818–1831 (2014)

11. Modat, M., et al.: Fast free-form deformation using graphics processing units. Comput. Methods Programs Biomed. **98**(3), 278–284 (2010)

12. Ronneberger, O., Fischer, P., Brox, T.: U-Net: convolutional networks for biomedical image segmentation. In: Navab, N., Hornegger, J., Wells, W.M., Frangi, A.F. (eds.) MICCAI 2015. LNCS, vol. 9351, pp. 234–241. Springer, Cham (2015). https://doi.org/10.1007/978-3-319-24574-4_28

13. Rueckert, D., Sonoda, L.I., Hayes, C., Hill, D.L.G., Leach, M.O., Hawkes, D.J.: Nonrigid registration using free-form deformations: application to breast MR images. IEEE Trans. Med. Imaging **18**(8), 712–721 (1999)

14. Schuh, A., et al.: Unbiased construction of a temporally consistent morphological atlas of neonatal brain development. bioRxiv (2018)

15. Shoemake, K., Duff, T.: Matrix animation and polar decomposition. In: Proceedings of the Conference on Graphics Interface, vol. 92, pp. 258–264. Citeseer (1992)

16. Smith, L.N.: Cyclical learning rates for training neural networks (2015)

17. Veraart, J., Sijbers, J., Sunaert, S., Leemans, A., Jeurissen, B.: Weighted linear least squares estimation of diffusion MRI parameters: strengths, limitations, and pitfalls. NeuroImage **81**, 335–346 (2013)

18. Xu, B., Wang, N., Chen, T., Li, M.: Empirical evaluation of rectified activations in convolutional network (2015)

19. Zhang, H., Yushkevich, P.A., Alexander, D.C., Gee, J.C.: Deformable registration of diffusion tensor mr images with explicit orientation optimization. Med. Image Anal. **10**(5), 764–785 (2006)

Multimodal MRI Template Creation in the Ring-Tailed Lemur and Rhesus Macaque

Frederik J. Lange[1(✉)], Stephen M. Smith[1], Mads F. Bertelsen[2],
Alexandre A. Khrapitchev[3], Paul R. Manger[4], Rogier B. Mars[1,5],
and Jesper L. R. Andersson[1]

[1] Oxford Centre for Functional MRI of the Brain (FMRIB),
Wellcome Centre for Integrative Neuroimaging, Nuffield Department
of Clinical Neurosciences, University of Oxford, Oxford, UK
frederik.lange@dtc.ox.ac.uk
[2] Centre for Zoo and Wild Animal Health, Copenhagen Zoo, Frederiksberg, Denmark
[3] CRUK/MRC Oxford Institute for Radiation Oncology, Department of Oncology,
University of Oxford, Oxford, UK
[4] School of Anatomical Sciences, Faculty of Health Sciences,
University of the Witwatersrand, Johannesburg, South Africa
[5] Donders Institute for Brain, Cognition and Behaviour,
Radboud University Nijmegen, Nijmegen, The Netherlands

Abstract. We present a multimodal registration algorithm for simultaneous alignment of datasets with both scalar and tensor MRI images. We employ a volumetric, cubic B-spline parametrised transformation model. Regularisation is based on the logarithm of the singular values of the local Jacobian and ensures diffeomorphic warps. Tensor registration takes reorientation into account during optimisation, through a finite-strain approximation of rotation due to the warp. The combination of scalar, tensor and regularisation cost functions allows us to optimise the deformations in terms of tissue matching, orientation matching and distortion minimisation simultaneously. We apply our method to creating multimodal T2 and DTI MRI brain templates of two small primates (the ring-tailed lemur and rhesus macaque) from high-quality, *ex vivo*, 0.5/0.6 mm isotropic data. The resulting templates are of very high quality across both modalities and species. Tissue contrast in the T2 channel is high indicating excellent tissue-boundary alignment. The DTI channel displays strong anisotropy in white matter, as well as consistent left/right orientation information even in relatively isotropic grey matter regions. Finally, we demonstrate where the multimodal templating approach overcomes anatomical inconsistencies introduced by unimodal only methods.

Keywords: Registration · Multimodal · Lemur · Macaque ·
Template · MRI

© Springer Nature Switzerland AG 2020
Ž. Špiclin et al. (Eds.): WBIR 2020, LNCS 12120, pp. 141–150, 2020.
https://doi.org/10.1007/978-3-030-50120-4_14

1   Introduction

The most common approach to spatial normalisation of multimodal MRI datasets is to register a single, scalar modality to a template and then transform all modalities through the resulting warp. However, this approach is only valid when the within-tissue information is comparable across modalities (*e.g.*, T1 and T2-weighted scans). When a modality contains additional within-tissue information compared to the registered modality (*e.g.*, orientation in DTI), then there is no reason to believe that the resulting warps will modulate this information in a consistent manner across subjects.

One method of overcoming this issue is to register each modality independently. However, from a generative modelling perspective there is only a *single* true warp which maps each subject to the template. This true warp cannot be estimated by averaging the unimodal warps as the result would not guarantee the preservation of desirable properties such as diffeomorphism. A preferable approach is to simultaneously optimise over all modalities, thereby finding the solution which jointly maximises the similarity across all modalities.

To our knowledge, there is currently only one method (DR-TAMAS) capable of performing such joint optimisations [1]. This is an extension of the SyN method [2] to include a similarity term sensitive to local rotations due to warping. One limitation of DR-TAMAS's *plastic* transformation model is that desirable measures of deformation, such as the local Jacobian determinant, are prohibitively difficult to regularise explicitly [1]. This necessitates using a simpler but less biologically meaningful regularisation of the velocity field (*e.g.*, Gaussian smoothing).

Our method overcomes this limitation by employing a cubic B-spline, *elastic* transformation which allows for direct regularisation of the Jacobian field, whilst simultaneously explicitly optimising for local rotations.

A prerequisite for making multimodal registration useful is the existence of multimodal templates. This work aims to present how our method can be used to generate such templates, and demonstrate some benefits they provide over their unimodal counterparts.

2   Registration Method

2.1   Framework

Transformation Model. Our registration framework utilises a 3D cubic B-spline parametrised transformation $\mathbf{t}(\mathbf{x})$. The finite spatial support of B-splines results in predictable sparseness of the Hessian of the cost function, which we leverage during optimisation. Additionally, this transformation has analytical derivatives, which allows for the formulation of explicit relationships between the transformation parameters and the local Jacobian field. We overcome historical concerns regarding diffeomorphism of elastic transformations through explicit regularisation of the Jacobian field as described in Sect. 2.4.

Optimisation Strategy. We employ the Levenberg-Marquardt variant of Gauss-Newton optimisation due to its robustness and rapid convergence properties [3]. Additionally, it does not require manually choosing a learning rate or performing a line search as is necessary when employing gradient only methods. This necessitates manipulating the cost function into the form $C(\mathbf{w}) = f^2(\mathbf{w})$ and iteratively updating the warp parameters $\mathbf{w}$ according to $\Delta\mathbf{w} = -\mathbf{H}^{-1}\mathbf{b}$, where $\mathbf{b}$ is the gradient and $\mathbf{H}$ is the Hessian of C. The Gauss-Newton Hessian is then $\mathbf{H}_{GN} = 2\frac{\delta f}{\delta \mathbf{w}}^{\mathsf{T}}\frac{\delta f}{\delta \mathbf{w}}$, and the Levenberg-Marquardt variant is $\mathbf{H}_{LM} = \mathbf{H}_{GN} + \lambda_{LM}\mathbf{I}$. Calculating $\mathbf{H}_{GN}$ is, in general, computationally expensive. However, this is aided by our choice of B-spline parametrisation as described in Sect. 2.1. At higher resolutions $\mathbf{H}_{GN}$ may become too large to store in memory (despite its sparseness). At this point we transition to using a *majorising* approximation $\mathbf{H}_{MM} = \mathtt{diag}(\mathtt{abs}(\mathbf{H}_{LM})\mathbf{1})$ [5], where $\mathbf{1}$ is a column vector of ones. $\mathbf{H}_{MM}$ is then a diagonal matrix where the diagonal entries are the sum of the absolute values across each row of $\mathbf{H}_{LM}$. This has the property that $\mathbf{H}_{MM} \succeq \mathbf{H}_{LM}$, and is therefore compatible with the Gauss-Newton family of algorithms. This greatly reduces memory requirements whilst allowing for a consistent optimisation strategy across all warp resolutions.

Cost Function Weighting. The relative weighting of each modality and the regularisation penalty can be set globally (*i.e.*, the importance of each modality to the overall cost function, controlled by a modality specific λ) as well as locally (*i.e.*, the importance of each area within a modality to that modality's cost) controlled by a spatially varying multiplicative mask.

2.2 Scalar Cost Function

The cost function for scalar modalities is the mean-squares dissimilarity, shown in Eq. (1) for a reference image f and moving image g defined over $N_\mathbf{x}$ voxels, where $\mathbf{x} \in \mathbb{R}^3$. This requires bias corrected images with the same nominal contrast. Residual differences in tissue intensities are modelled using quartic-polynomial intensity matching. This is re-evaluated at each iteration of the optimisation. The weight applied to the scalar cost can be modulated by the voxel-wise variance after each iteration to effectively up- or down-weight the regularisation prior.

$$C_S = \lambda_S \frac{1}{N_\mathbf{x}} \sum_{\mathbf{x} \in \mathbb{R}^3} \Big(f(\mathbf{x}) - g\big(\mathbf{t}(\mathbf{x})\big) \Big)^2 \tag{1}$$

2.3 Tensor Cost Function

The tensor cost function can be chosen as either the Euclidean, equation (2), or log-Euclidean, equation (3), distance between two tensor volumes $\mathbf{F}$ and $\mathbf{G}$. These metrics are sensitive to both scalar and vector characteristics of the tensor, relatively insensitive to variations in tensor fitting, and efficient to implement [4,6]. The transformation affects these cost functions in two ways: through displacement of the tensor elements as if they were individual scalar modalities

$(\mathbf{t}_{dis})$, and through the local rotation of tensors $(\mathbf{t}_{rot})$. The method proposed by Yeo [7] allows us to calculate analytical forms of the gradient and Hessian as a function of the transformation parameters, facilitating efficient implementation within our optimisation framework. The results in this work were generated using C_E.

$$C_E = \lambda_E \frac{1}{N_\mathbf{x}} \sum_{\mathbf{x} \in \mathbb{R}^3} \mathrm{tr}\left(\left(\mathbf{F}\big(\mathbf{t}_{rot}(\mathbf{x})\big) - \mathbf{G}\big(\mathbf{t}_{dis}(\mathbf{x})\big) \right)^2 \right) \tag{2}$$

$$C_{LE} = \lambda_{LE} \frac{1}{N_\mathbf{x}} \sum_{\mathbf{x} \in \mathbb{R}^3} \mathrm{tr}\left(\left(\log\big(\mathbf{F}\big(\mathbf{t}_{rot}(\mathbf{x})\big)\big) - \log\big(\mathbf{G}\big(\mathbf{t}_{dis}(\mathbf{x})\big)\big) \right)^2 \right) \tag{3}$$

2.4 Regularisation

The regularisation cost in Eq. (4) is based on work by Ashburner [8], and penalises the log singular values s_i of the local Jacobian $\mathbf{J}$. This imposes a log-normal prior on lineal, areal and volumetric changes, centred at a value of 1. Expansions and contractions are therefore penalised symmetrically. Additionally, the penalty tends to ∞ as $|\mathbf{J}|$ approaches both 0 and ∞, ensuring the warps remain diffeomorphic. By penalising s_i rather than simply $|\mathbf{J}|$ we ensure that the shape as well as the volume of the transformed images is kept within reasonable limits. Finally, the highly non-linear nature of the penalty allows for larger deformations than traditional linear elastic models, bringing our method in line with the capabilities of LDDMM-based transformation methods.

$$C_R = \lambda_R \frac{1}{N_\mathbf{x}} \sum_{\mathbf{x} \in \mathbb{R}} \left(1 + \big| \mathbf{J}\big(\mathbf{t}(\mathbf{x})\big) \big| \right) \sum_{i=1}^{3} \log^2 s_i\big(\mathbf{t}(\mathbf{x})\big) \tag{4}$$

3 Methods

3.1 Data Acquisition

Full extracted brains from three ring-tailed lemurs (Lemur catta) and three rhesus macaques (Macaca mulatta) were obtained. Brains were perfusion fixed using paraformaldehyde after euthanasia for causes unrelated to the current research. Data were acquired on a 7T magnet with an Agilent DirectDrive console[1]. A 2D diffusion-weighted spin-echo protocol with single line readout was used (DW-SEMS; TE/TR: 25 ms/10 s; matrix size: 128×128; number of slices: 128; resolution: 0.5 mm (lemur) or 0.6 mm (macaque) isotropic. Sixteen non-diffusion-weighted (b $= 0$ s/mm^2) and 128 diffusion-weighted (b $= 4000$ s/mm^2) volumes were acquired with diffusion directions distributed over the whole sphere. The brains were stored in PBS before scanning and placed in Fluorinert during the scan.

---

[1] Agilent Technologies, Santa Clara, CA, USA.

3.2   Data Preprocessing

Diffusion tensors were fit to the data using the FSL FDT toolbox [9]. Additionally, FDT was used to generate a "no-diffusion" b = 0 image with T2 contrast. The T2 images were then bias-field corrected using FSL FAST [10]. Note that T2 and DTI images *within* each subject are already co-registered.

3.3   Template Creation

A combined T2 and DTI template was created for each species individually, using three subjects per species. Template creation followed a multi-resolution iterative approach. An initial template space was chosen by affine alignment of the T2 images to one randomly chosen subject using FSL FLIRT [11]. T2 images were intensity normalised before being resampled into this space, followed by voxelwise averaging across subjects. DTI images were resampled with reorientation using FSL vecreg, followed by log-tensor averaging. Each subject was then non-linearly aligned to the initial template at a warp resolution of 16 mm isotropic, and averaged in the same way to create a new template. This process was repeated, doubling the warp resolution each time, to a final resolution of 0.5 mm isotropic. At each iteration all images were smoothed using an isotropic Gaussian kernel, with a full width at half maximum equal to a quarter of the current warp resolution. The amount of regularisation was empirically decreased as warp resolution increased.

Spatial unbiasing of the template was carried out after each iteration, such that the average displacement of every voxel in the template was approximately 0. The methodology followed is given in Eqs. (5) and (6), where W_m is the warp from the template $\tilde{f}$ to m^{th} subject.

$$\bar{W}(\mathbf{x}) = \frac{1}{M} \sum_{m=1}^{M} W_m(\mathbf{x}) \tag{5}$$

$$\tilde{f}_{unbiased}(\mathbf{x}) = \tilde{f}_{biased}\left(\bar{W}^{-1}(\mathbf{x})\right) \tag{6}$$

Although $\bar{W}^{-1}(\mathbf{x})$ is not guaranteed to be diffeomorphic, we enforced diffeomorphism by projecting this field onto its closest diffeomorphic representation using the method proposed by Karacali [12].

Relative modality weighting was determined in two steps. First, by setting $\lambda_S = 1$, $\lambda_E = 0$ and varying λ_R until the T2 template appeared visually acceptable. Second, by setting $\lambda_S = 0$, fixing λ_R to the final value from step 1, and varying λ_E until the range of $|\mathbf{J}|$ for the warps was similar to that in step 1. In this way, we aimed to weight the influence of the T2 and DTI modalities on the warp approximately equally.

The template creation process was carried out three times using different combinations of the modalities to drive the registration: T2 image only, DTI image only, and multimodal using both T2 and DTI. We will refer to these methods and resulting templates as T_{T2}, T_{DT} and T_{MM} respectively. The weighting of individual modalities and the amount of regularisation was constant across all methods.

3.4   Template Quality Assessment

The quality of the T2 and DTI templates were visually evaluated, and examined for obvious inconsistencies. The T2 template quality was then quantified using the average *mutual information* (MI) between each warped subject and the template as calculated by FSL `FLIRT`. MI ranges between 0 (worst) and ∞. The DTI template quality was evaluated using the average *overlap of eigenvalue-eigenvector pairs* (OVL) metric between each warped subject and the template [1,13]. OVL is defined in Eq. (7), where λ_i and $\mathbf{e}_i$ are the ith eigenvalue and eigenvector of the tensor respectively. This provides a voxelwise similarity measure of the complete eigenvalue-eigenvector tensor descriptor. It ranges between 0 and 1, with 0 representing complete dissimilarity and 1 representing identical tensors. OVL was evaluated in 3 regions, namely the entire brain, the entire brain weighted by FA, and within a mask where FA > 0.2.

$$OVL = \frac{1}{N_{\mathbf{x}}} \sum_{\mathbf{x} \in \mathbb{R}^3} \frac{\sum_{i=1}^{3} \lambda_i^F(\mathbf{x}) \lambda_i^G(\mathbf{x}) \left(\mathbf{e}_i^F(\mathbf{x})^{\mathsf{T}} \mathbf{e}_i^G(\mathbf{x}) \right)^2}{\sum_{i=1}^{3} \lambda_i^F(\mathbf{x}) \lambda_i^G(\mathbf{x})} \tag{7}$$

4   Results and Discussion

4.1   Visual Evaluation

Figure 1 shows the DTI, FA and T2 volumes of the final T_{MM} template for both the lemur and macaque. We do not show the entire T_{T2} and T_{DT} templates as at this scale they are visually difficult to distinguish from one another. Instead, we first describe the common appearance of the templates, and then focus on select regions which demonstrate difference between the methods.

Visually the T2 volumes are sharp, showing good contrast between tissue types, even within fairly complex structures such as the cerebellum. This is particularly true for the lemur template where the relatively simpler gyrification leads to smaller differences between subjects making spatial normalisation somewhat easier. The posterior of the macaque brain showed the highest variability between subjects and thus is unsurprisingly the least sharp template region. In general the T2 volume of the T_{MM} and and T_{T2} templates did appear slightly sharper than T_{DT}. This is in line with what might be expected: the contrast between signal from grey matter and from fluid in the sulci and ventricles in the DTI volume may be insufficient to overcome regularisation. A clear example of this in the lemur is shown in the bottom left of Fig. 1. Here, T_{DT} has been unable to correctly align one of the sulci, whereas both T_{MM} and T_{T2} have had no such difficulty.

The DTI volumes are of excellent quality. High FA within white matter indicates that not only are the anisotropic regions of the individual subjects brought to the correct positions, but that they arrive there with a consistent orientation. Perhaps somewhat surprisingly, the T_{T2} DTI template is not clearly worse than the other methods within these high FA regions. We suggest two possible reasons

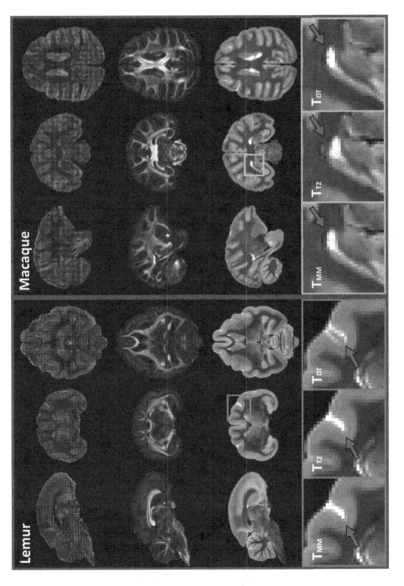

Fig. 1. DTI (1st row), FA (2nd row) and T2 (3rd row) images from the T_{MM} template for lemur (left) and macaque (right). In the lemur we highlight a region where T_{DT} was unable to correctly align the sulci due to insufficient contrast between grey matter and the exterior fluid. In the macaque we highlight a region where T_{T2} was unable to correctly align the ventricles due to differences in T2 contrast of the ventricular fluid between subjects. In both cases the T_{MM} template has aligned the region correctly.

for this. Firstly, the regularisation method is primarily focussed on maintaining plausible deformations. This means that the interior of the white matter is transformed in a sensible manner as it follows the tissue boundaries during registration of the T2 images. Secondly, the areas of anisotropy are always quite near tissue boundaries due to the small size of the lemur and macaque brains. Therefore, the possible deformations which correctly match tissue types are constrained in terms of allowable rotational effects. However, within some comparatively isotropic regions we do observed larger differences. In the macaque, the fluid in the ventricle of one subject had a significantly different (darker) T2 contrast than the others. The bottom right of Fig. 1 shows how this has led to ghosting around the ventricle in T_{T2}. In contrast, information in the DTI modality has allowed both T_{MM} and T_{DT} to correctly align the structure.

From this we can see a clear benefit in terms of anatomical correctness that the multimodal registration approach provides over its unimodal counterparts.

4.2 Quantitative Evaluation

Quantification of how well the subject data aligns to the templates is shown for the lemur in Table 1 and for the macaque in Table 2. Both species show similar trends between the methods indicating that these results generalise well.

Unsurprisingly, T_{T2} has the highest average MI, followed by T_{MM} and finally T_{DT}. This is in line with the visual observations of the T2 image sharpness in the respective templates. However, as shown by the ventricular ghosting above, the higher MI value does not necessarily mean better global anatomical correctness.

Whole brain OVL is consistently highest for T_{MM} indicating that both high and low FA regions are being well aligned by this method. The lower performance of unimodal methods can be attributed on the one hand to T_{T2} having no knowledge of rotations introduced by the warps, and on the other hand to poorer overlap of tissue types in T_{DT}.

When the OVL calculation is restricted to high-FA regions, either though FA-weighting or explicit FA masking, the results for all methods is higher than for the brain as a whole. As might be expected, T_{DT} performance is very similar to T_{MM} in these regions, and yet the multimodal approach still has an advantage. Interestingly, the performance deficit between T_{T2} and the other methods is greater for the macaque brain compared to the lemur. This may be due to an increase in the amount of uncontrolled rotation induced by the T_{T2} warps during alignment of the comparatively more complex cortical folding patterns in the macaque.

4.3 Overall Evaluation

Using multimodal data to drive the registration successfully overcame shortcomings in both the scalar and tensor only methods, whilst preserving the best aspects of each. DTI similarity measures improved across all areas of the template brains, and we therefore believe that a multimodal approach to registration can only be an advantage in the analysis of diffusion MRI data. Whilst scalar

Table 1. Average MI and OVL measures in the lemur

	MM template	T2 template	DTI template
T2 Mutual Information	1.357	1.407	1.268
OVL Whole Brain	0.859	0.854	0.850
OVL FA Weighted	0.968	0.966	0.967
OVL FA Masked	0.946	0.940	0.944

Table 2. Average MI and OVL measures in the macaque

	MM template	T2 template	DTI template
T2 Mutual Information	1.151	1.210	1.072
OVL Whole Brain	0.784	0.769	0.774
OVL FA Weighted	0.964	0.949	0.960
OVL FA Masked	0.891	0.870	0.880

registration appears to have a slight advantage over multimodal in terms of MI scores, the lower OVL scores and some clear anatomical inconsistencies in the T2 driven template suggest that this might be attributable to over-fitting. As the goal of registration in neuroimaging is anatomical consistency rather than outright image similarity, this regularisation effect of the tensor data in the multimodal method is in fact a desirable quality.

5   Conclusion and Future Work

We have shown that multimodal registration is a powerful tool for template creation, capable of leveraging complimentary imaging contrasts to find a common space which is truly representative of the group data. Our combination of scalar, tensor and regularisation cost functions allows us to optimise multiple aspects of the deformations simultaneously such that the most anatomically plausible mapping to this common space can be found. The multimodal-driven lemur and macaque templates we created show improved consistency with individual subject scans compared to both unimodal scalar and tensor driven templates.

The data used to create these templates is quite unique, with the lemur template in particular being the first of its kind for this species. We hope that by having a multimodal template available, any future analysis done on this species will be able to take advantage of increased anatomical consistency when analysing and reporting results of both individual and group studies.

Future work will focus on applying these same techniques to large human cohorts such as the Human Connectome Project and UK Biobank where we hope the benefits of multimodal templating will be even more apparent.

Acknowledgements. The Wellcome Centre for Integrative Neuroimaging is supported by core funding from the Wellcome Trust [203139/Z/16/Z]. This work was supported by funding from the EPSRC and MRC [EP/L016052/1]. FJL is supported by The Oppenheimer Memorial Trust and St Catherine's College, Oxford. RBM is supported by funding from the BBSRC [BB/N019814/1]. JLRA is supported by a Wellcome Trust Strategic Award [098369/Z/12/Z]; and the NIH Human Connectome Project [1U01MH109589-01 and 1U01AG052564-01].

Ethical Approval. All brains were obtained from animals that were euthanised for causes unrelated to research and treated in accordance with appropriate guidelines.

References

1. Irfanoglu, M.O., et al.: DR-TAMAS: diffeomorphic registration for tensor accurate alignment of anatomical structures. Neuroimage **132**, 439–454 (2016)
2. Avants, B.B., Epstein, C.L., Grossman, M., Gee, J.C.: Symmetric diffeomorphic image registration with cross-correlation: evaluating automated labeling of elderly and neurodegenerative brain. Med. Image Anal. **12**(1), 26–41 (2008)
3. Chen, P.: Hessian matrix vs. Gauss-Newton Hessian matrix. SIAM **49**(4), 1417–1435 (2011)
4. Beg, M.F., Miller, M.I., Trouvé, A., Younes, L.: Computing large deformation metric mappings via geodesic flows of diffeomorphisms. Int. J. Comput. Vis. **61**(2), 139–157 (2005)
5. Chun, I.Y., Fessler, J.A.: Convolutional dictionary learning: acceleration and convergence. IEEE Trans. Image Process. **27**(4), 1697–1712 (2018)
6. Peeters, T.H.J.M., Rodrigues, P.R., Vilanova, A., ter Haar Romeny, B.M.: Analysis of distance/similarity measures for diffusion tensor imaging. In: Laidlaw, D., Weickert, J. (eds.) Visualization and Processing of Tensor Fields. MATHVISUAL, pp. 113–136. Springer, Heidelberg (2009)
7. Yeo, B., et al.: DT-REFinD: diffusion tensor registration with exact finite-strain differential. IEEE Trans. Med. Imaging **28**(12), 1914–1928 (2009)
8. Ashburner, J., Andersson, J.L., Friston, K.J.: Image registration using a symmetric prior-in three dimensions. Hum. Brain Mapp. **9**(4), 212–25 (2000)
9. Jenkinson, M., Beckmann, C.F., Behrens, T.E., Woolrich, M.W., Smith, S.M.: FSL. Neuroimage **62**(2), 782–790 (2012)
10. Zhang, Y., Brady, M., Smith, S.: Segmentation of brain MR images through a hidden Markov random field model and the expectation-maximization algorithm. IEEE Trans. Med. Imaging **20**(1), 45–57 (2001)
11. Jenkinson, M., Smith, S.: A global optimisation method for robust affine registration of brain images. Med. Image Anal. **5**(2), 143–156 (2001)
12. Karacali, B., Davatzikos, C.: Estimating topology preserving and smooth displacement fields. IEEE Trans. Med. Imaging **23**(7), 868–880 (2004)
13. Basser, P.J., Pajevic, S.: Statistical artifacts in diffusion tensor MRI (DT-MRI) caused by background noise. Magn. Reson. Med. **44**(1), 41–50 (2000)

Sliding Motion

An Unsupervised Learning Approach to Discontinuity-Preserving Image Registration

Eric Ng and Mehran Ebrahimi[✉]

Imaging Lab, Faculty of Science, Ontario Tech University,
2000 Simcoe Street North, Oshawa, ON L1H 7K4, Canada
{eric.ng,mehran.ebrahimi}@ontariotechu.ca
http://www.ImagingLab.ca

Abstract. Most traditional image registration algorithms aimed at aligning a pair of images impose well-established regularizers to guarantee smoothness of unknown deformation fields. Since these methods assume global smoothness within the image domain, they pose issues for scenarios where local discontinuities are expected, such as the sliding motion between the lungs and the chest wall during the respiratory cycle. Furthermore, an objective function must be optimized for each given pair of images, thus registering multiple sets of images become very time-consuming and scale poorly to higher resolution image volumes.

Using recent advances in deep learning, we propose an unsupervised learning-based image registration model. The model is trained over a loss function with a custom regularizer that preserves local discontinuities, while simultaneously respecting the smoothness assumption in homogeneous regions of image volumes. Qualitative and quantitative validations on 3D pairs of lung CT datasets will be presented.

1 Introduction

Image registration is an invaluable tool for medical image analysis and has received vast attention in imaging research for the past several decades. Image registration is used as a tool to find meaningful temporal transformations to align images taken at different time frames. Traditionally, registration algorithms assume smooth transformations. This assumption quickly falls apart for many cases, since different organs move, to a certain degree, independently from one another. Image misalignment becomes inevitable if smoothness is assumed at regions where discontinuities are expected, such as organ boundaries [4]. In this paper, we introduce an unsupervised learning model that learns the relationship between image pairs and a corresponding displacement field. We propose a regularizer that accounts for local image discontinuities while simultaneously respecting local homogeneity. This approach drastically decreases registration time, as the registration task is no longer an optimization task, but becomes a simple function evaluation.

© Springer Nature Switzerland AG 2020
Ž. Špiclin et al. (Eds.): WBIR 2020, LNCS 12120, pp. 153–162, 2020.
https://doi.org/10.1007/978-3-030-50120-4_15

2   Related Work

In traditional image registration, the most common approach is to solve an optimization problem, where the objective function is comprised of two terms, an image dissimilarity term and a regularization term to restrict the solution space. Common methods include elastic and diffusion models [16], free-form deformations using b-splines [3], and more recently, kernel methods [11–13]. Because all of these methods optimize an energy function for every image pair, large-scale or successive registration tasks becomes very time consuming. Specialized algorithms such as Thirion's Demons [5,17,22] allow significant reduction in computational time by estimating force vectors that acts to drive the deformation followed by Gaussian smoothing during the optimization process. Unfortunately, this algorithm restricts models to be diffusion-based models only.

With the rise of deep learning over the past decade, learning-based approaches have become extremely popular. Several models are trained in a supervised manner which required ground truth transformations to be available [6,15,18]. Although these methods showed promising results, the task of obtaining ground truth transformation fields is cumbersome and highly prone to error. Thus, recent methods have shifted to an unsupervised approach instead, where models are trained based on how transformation fields act on images, rather than strictly on the transformations [1,9,25]. For a survey of learning-based image registration methods, refer to the article by Haskins *et al.* [10].

3   Method

Our model follows a framework popularized by Voxelmorph [2]. Let I_F and I_M denote fixed and moving images. We find a function $g_\theta(I_F, I_M)$ that produces the displacement field $\mathbf{u}$, i.e. $\mathbf{u} = g_\theta(I_F, I_M)$. The deformation ϕ can then expressed as the mapping $\phi = Id + \mathbf{u}$ where Id is the identity mapping. The deformation field is applied to I_M to produce the warped image $I_M \circ \phi$ where $I_F(x)$ is similar to $[I_M \circ \phi](x)$ for all voxel locations $x \in \Omega$. Since ϕ may map the original coordinate system to non-integer valued voxel locations, interpolation is required to warp I_M under ϕ. For our experiments, we use trilinear interpolation due to its simplicity. An overview of the model is shown in Fig. 1.

3.1   Network Architecture

The function g_θ is modeled using a convolutional neural network where θ denotes the network parameters. The neural network follows a modified version of U-Net [19], which contains an encoder and a decoder structure that mirror each other and are connected by skip connections at each layer (Fig. 2). The encoder/decoder architecture is motivated by image pyramid techniques in many computer vision algorithms, where each encoding and decoding layer operate from coarse to fine representations of the input.

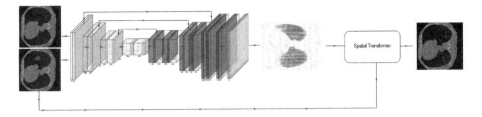

Fig. 1. Overview of the model. Fixed and moving images I_F, I_M are passed into a convolutional neural network which produces the displacement field $\mathbf{u}(x)$. The spatial transformer morphs I_M based on the displacement field. The loss is measured over the dissimilarity between the fixed and morphed moving images, as well as additional penalty functions defined over $\mathbf{u}$.

The encoder consists of three convolution layers by applying $3 \times 3 \times 3$ convolutions with stride 2 for downsampling, followed by LeakyReLU with slope of 0.2 at each layer. Each convolution layer has 32 output channels except the first layer which contains 16 output channels.

The decoder follows a similar structure as the encoder but in reverse order. In the first decoding layer, we simply use the output of the final encoding layer as the input. In subsequent decoding layers, we first upsample the output of the previous decoding layer. Skip connections are constructed by concatenating layer outputs with that of the mirroring encoding layer. This effectively uses representations of the encoding layers to enforce more precise outputs in the decoding layers. Similar to the encoder, each decoding layer applies $3 \times 3 \times 3$ convolutions followed by LeakyReLU of slope 0.2, but with stride 1 to preserve resolution at each layer. The output of the final decoding layer is passed into an additional convolution layer with 3 output channels, where each output channel contains the coordinate components of the displacement field $\mathbf{u}$.

3.2 Loss Function

We train our model using a loss function in the form

$$\mathcal{L}(I_F, I_M, \mathbf{u}) = \lambda_{sim}\mathcal{L}_{sim}(I_F, I_M, \mathbf{u}) + \lambda_{disc}\mathcal{L}_{disc}(\mathbf{u}) + \lambda_{mag}\mathcal{L}_{mag}(\mathbf{u}), \qquad (1)$$

where $\mathcal{L}_{sim}$ measures image dissimilarity, $\mathcal{L}_{disc}$ is a discontinuity preserving regularizer, and $\mathcal{L}_{mag}$ is a second loss term that manages the (ir)regularities in the magnitude of the displacement fields. $\lambda_{sim}, \lambda_{disc}$, and λ_{mag} are corresponding regularization constants.

Similarity Loss. To measure image similarity/dissimilarity, we use a local normalized cross correlation which is defined as

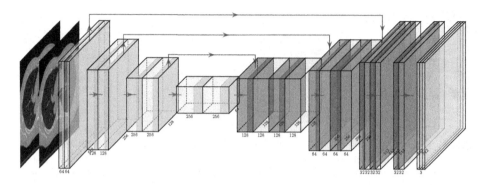

Fig. 2. Network architecture of g_θ based on a modified version of U-Net. The network receives I_M and I_F to produce the displacement field $\mathbf{u}$. The input and output of the network are of dimensions $D \times H \times W \times 2$ and $D \times H \times W \times 3$ respectively. The architecture consists of a contractive path (encoder) and a mirroring expansive path (decoder) connected by skip connections at each layer.

$$\text{LNCC}(I_M, I_F) = \sum_{x \in \Omega} \frac{\left[\sum_{y \in \mathcal{N}(x)} (I_M(y) - \mu_M(x)) (I_F(y) - \mu_F(x))\right]^2}{\left[\sum_{y \in \mathcal{N}(x)} (I_M(y) - \mu_M(x))^2\right] \left[\sum_{y \in \mathcal{N}(x)} (I_F(y) - \mu_F(x))^2\right]} \tag{2}$$

where x is any voxel in the image domain Ω, and $y \in \mathcal{N}(x)$ are the neighborhood points around voxel x, and $\mu_M(x)$ and $\mu_F(x)$ are the average local intensities around x in the moving and fixed images, respectively. LNCC is maximized when $I_F = I_M$ which measures similarity, thus we define the dissimilarity measure as $\mathcal{L}_{\text{sim}} = 1 - \text{LNCC}$.

Discontinuous Loss. In designing the discontinuous loss, we first assume that there are no topological changes, i.e. no new tissue is introduced nor destroyed. We then consider the requirements based on these physical scenarios: 1. Homogeneous movement, 2. Movement along rigid structures, and 3. Sliding organs.

These scenarios help us define the requirements for our regularizer. Firstly, the regularizer must preserve smooth local deformations that occur locally within organ interiors. Secondly, the regularizer must not penalize large local changes in deformation magnitude as long as the movement is in a similar direction. This is to mimic the movement of soft tissues or organs against rigid structures such as the rib cage or the spinal column. Finally, the regularizer must be able to account for movements in the opposite directions along organ boundary. This final requirement is perhaps the most significant as there are many scenarios where sliding organs exist. Common examples include the sliding of the lungs against the chest wall during the respiratory cycle, and the movement of organs against one another in the abdominal region. Figure 3 visually summarizes possible desired behaviors of a discontinuous displacement field.

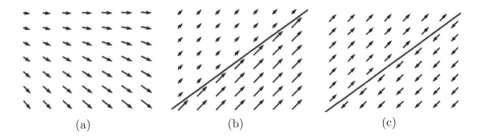

(a)   (b)   (c)

Fig. 3. Desired behaviors of the discontinuous displacement field. Figure 4(a) demonstrates local homogeneity which is expected within organs. Figure 4(b) allows displacement vectors of different magnitudes as long as they are in a similar direction, which represents soft tissue moving against rigid structures. (c) depicts sliding boundary conditions as displacement vectors on opposite sides of the boundary travel in opposite directions.

Let $\mathbf{u}$ be represented by a collection of displacement vectors $\{u_i\}_{i=1,\dots,N}$, where N is the number of voxels in the image. Now consider two arbitrary vectors u_i and u_j, respectively corresponding to locations x_i and x_j in the image domain. The area of the parallelogram spanned by u_i and u_j is maximized when u_i and u_j is orthogonal to one another, and minimized when they are parallel. Thus the three conditions are encouraged for any regularizer in the form

$$\mathcal{L}_{disc} = \sum_{i,j=1}^{N} g(\mathcal{P}(u_i, u_j)) \tag{3}$$

where $\mathcal{P}$ the unsigned area of the parallelogram spanned by u_i and u_j, and $g : \mathbb{R} \to \mathbb{R}$ is a strictly increasing function satisfying $g(0) = 0$. $\mathcal{P}$ is computed as

$$\mathcal{P}(u_i, u_j) = \|u_i \times u_j\|_2 \tag{4}$$

where $\times$ denotes the cross product. We propose the regularizer

$$\mathcal{L}_{disc} = \sum_{i,j=1}^{N} \frac{1}{2} \log\left(1 + \mathcal{P}(u_i, u_j)^2\right) k(x_i, x_j) \tag{5}$$

where $k(x_i, x_j)$ is a decreasing weight function that depends on the proximity between the locations x_i and x_j. For our experiments, we choose the C^4 Wendland kernel [26] for $k(x_i, x_j)$.

Magnitude Loss. During preliminary stages of our experiments, we noticed that deformations in large dark image regions (background of CT image, for instance) behave erratically. We found that imposing an additional magnitude-based regularizer is needed to suppress this unpredictable behavior. Thus we add the following term to our loss function

$$\mathcal{L}_{mag}(u) = \max_i(\|u_i\|_2). \tag{6}$$

This effectively discourages large magnitudes of u. Evidently, this additional term may become problematic for coarse registration where large-scale movement may be expected. However, since this is aimed towards addressing local discontinuities, it is safe to assume that deformations remain relatively small.

4   Experiments

4.1   Setup

Our model is implemented using PyTorch 1.3.0 and trained using an NVIDIA GeForce GTX 1080Ti with 11 GB of graphics memory. CPU tests are performed on an Intel Xeon E5-1620 at 3.7 GHz. We trained our model using Adam optimizer [14] with $\lambda_{sim} = 100, \lambda_{disc} = \lambda_{mag} = 1$, and learning rate 10^{-4}.

The model is evaluated over 4DCT datasets provided by DIR-Lab [7,8] and the POPI-model [23]. The DIR-Lab Reference 4DCT datasets contain ten sets of image volumes of sizes 256×256 and 512×512 with various number of axial slices (average of 100 and 128 for the two respective resolutions). To account for these variations, we only keep the middle 96 axial slices of the 256×256 volume, and the middle 112 axial slices of the 512×512 volumes. Each set of image volumes are taken over 10 time steps over the period of a single respiratory cycle. Since the input is a pair of image volumes, I_F is chosen as the image volume with a randomly chosen case number and time step, and I_M is selected based on the same case number with a different time step. By choosing eight cases as training data, this allows $8 \times 10 \times 9 = 720$ training samples and $2 \times 10 \times 9 = 180$ test samples, despite only having ten available cases. The POPI-Model contains six image volumes of sizes 512×512 with 140 to 190 axial slices. For consistency, we only keep the middle 136 axial slices and use five of the six cases as training data. We follow the same approach as DIR-Lab in choosing I_F and I_M.

4.2   Results

We first compare our discontinuity-preserving model with one that assumes global smoothness. As a baseline, we trained a second model using the DIR-lab dataset with an identical configuration, with the exception where the discontinuous loss $\mathcal{L}_{disc}$ is replaced with a total variation loss $\mathcal{L}_{TV}$ defined as

$$\mathcal{L}_{TV} = \sum_i \|\nabla u_i\|_2 \tag{7}$$

where the summation is over all voxels indexed by i. Figure 4 shows a comparison between our model trained using $\mathcal{L}_{TV}$ and $\mathcal{L}_{disc}$. One can quickly identify sudden changes in the displacement field near the lung's boundaries especially near the lung/vertebrae interface. Additional registration results are shown in Fig. 5. We compare our results (Table 1) quantitatively to the following methods: Free-Form Deformations (FFD) [20], isotropic parametric Total Variation (pTV) [24], and Sparse Kernel Machines (SKM) [12]. For comparison, we fixed frame

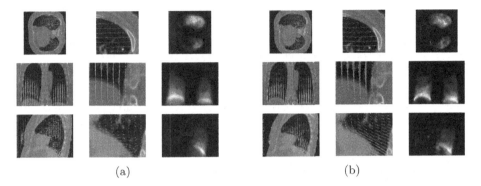

(a)   (b)

Fig. 4. Results obtained using $\mathcal{L}_{TV}$ (a) and $\mathcal{L}_{disc}$ (b). Columns 1 and 4 show an overlay of $\mathbf{u}$ over I_M. Columns 2 and 5 show a magnified local region where transformation discontinuities are expected. Columns 3 and 6 are heatmaps of the displacement field's local magnitudes.

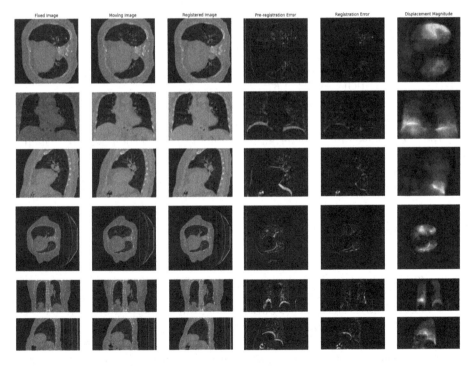

Fig. 5. Qualitative results of proposed model. From left to right: fixed image I_F, moving image I_M, registered image $I_M \circ \phi$, absolute error before registration $|I_F - I_M|$, absolute error after registration $|I_F - I_M \circ \phi|$, heatmap of displacement field $\mathbf{u}$.

Table 1. Target Registration Error (TRE) in millimeters (mm) against FFD [20], pTV [24], and SKM [12] on the DIR-Lab and POPI 4DCT Model. Baseline model is the same configuration but trained with $\mathcal{L}_{TV}$ in place of $\mathcal{L}_{disc}$.

Frame	DIR-Lab 256					DIR-Lab 512					POPI				
	FFD	pTV	SKM	Base	Ours	FFD	pTV	SKM	Base	Ours	FFD	pTV	SKM	Base	Ours
0	1.01	0.92	1.06	1.10	1.04	0.79	0.62	0.59	0.77	0.65	0.79	0.72	0.66	0.77	0.76
2	0.99	0.89	0.85	0.94	0.91	0.81	0.63	0.57	0.73	0.64	0.81	0.71	0.65	0.73	0.74
3	1.29	1.34	1.32	1.26	1.24	1.14	0.99	1.01	0.97	1.00	1.14	1.12	1.17	1.08	1.11
4	1.26	1.27	1.25	1.23	1.26	1.11	0.92	0.93	0.96	0.95	1.11	1.01	1.07	1.04	1.07
5	1.27	1.29	1.35	1.29	1.31	1.11	1.00	1.01	0.99	1.02	1.11	1.11	1.13	1.10	1.16
6	1.31	1.17	1.18	1.27	1.25	1.20	0.90	0.89	1.02	0.92	1.20	1.03	1.00	1.11	1.06
7	1.36	1.19	1.22	1.25	1.30	1.20	0.95	0.93	1.00	1.01	1.20	1.06	1.05	1.09	1.13
8	1.10	1.05	0.94	1.04	1.07	0.88	0.73	0.67	0.78	0.79	0.88	0.84	0.75	0.88	0.90
9	1.09	0.97	0.99	1.07	1.09	0.92	0.70	0.75	0.78	0.80	0.92	0.81	0.83	0.86	0.89

Table 2. Comparison of registration time between learning-based model and inverse model. For the learning-based model, we used our proposed model for evaluation. For the inverse model, we perform pairwise registration with diffusion regularizer over 1,000 iterations. The inverse model is evaluated using the AIRLab framework [21]. The CPU time for the classical model over DIR-Lab 512 and POPI Model is not computed, as they were much higher than the corresponding GPU time. Time is measured in seconds.

	Learning-based		Inverse Model	
	GPU	CPU	GPU	CPU
DIR-lab 256	0.33	15.70	82.57	5724.36
DIR-lab 512	1.38	63.14	532.41	–
POPI Model	1.67	76.45	702.86	–

1 as the fixed image, and register all remaining frames to the reference. Finally, we compare the time required to register a pair of images using our approach versus a classical registration algorithm using minimization (Table 2). Classical registration is applied using the AIRLab framework [21] via diffusion regularizer.

5   Conclusion and Future Work

We presented an unsupervised learning-based model for discontinuity preserving image registration. Although the training set was relatively small, our model performed on par with existing methods while begin able to handle locations where discontinuities may occur. Furthermore, our model significantly reduced computation by several orders of magnitude, allowing successive registration to be performed within a relatively short time frame. A drawback of the model is its sensitivity to noise. In particular, since $\mathcal{L}_{disc}$ is computed by comparing local displacement vectors with neighboring displacement vectors individually, there are no mechanisms to discourage local chaotic behaviors in the displacement field. A possible remedy is to extend the current model to incorporate additional information, such as segmentation masks and edge information. This allows image discontinuities to be defined rather than relying on only image intensities to predict boundary regions.

Acknowledgments. This research was supported by an NSERC Discovery Grant for M. Ebrahimi. We acknowledge the support of NVIDIA Corporation for the donation of GPUs used in this research.

References

1. Balakrishnan, G., Zhao, A., Sabuncu, M.R., Guttag, J., Dalca, A.V.: An unsupervised learning model for deformable medical image registration. In: Proceedings of the IEEE Conference on CVPR, pp. 9252–9260 (2018)
2. Balakrishnan, G., Zhao, A., Sabuncu, M.R., Guttag, J., Dalca, A.V.: VoxelMorph: a learning framework for deformable medical image registration. IEEE Trans. Med. Imaging **38**, 1788–1800 (2019)
3. Balci, S.K., Golland, P., Shenton, M.E., Wells, W.M.: Free-form B-spline deformation model for groupwise registration. In: MICCAI (2007)
4. Berendsen, F.F., Kotte, A.N., Viergever, M.A., Pluim, J.P.: Registration of organs with sliding interfaces and changing topologies. In: Medical Imaging 2014, vol. 9034, p. 90340E. International Society for Optics and Photonics (2014)
5. Cahill, N.D., Noble, J.A., Hawkes, D.J.: A demons algorithm for image registration with locally adaptive regularization. In: Yang, G.-Z., Hawkes, D., Rueckert, D., Noble, A., Taylor, C. (eds.) MICCAI 2009. LNCS, vol. 5761, pp. 574–581. Springer, Heidelberg (2009). https://doi.org/10.1007/978-3-642-04268-3_71
6. Cao, X., et al.: Deformable image registration based on similarity-steered CNN regression. In: Descoteaux, M., Maier-Hein, L., Franz, A., Jannin, P., Collins, D.L., Duchesne, S. (eds.) MICCAI 2017. LNCS, vol. 10433, pp. 300–308. Springer, Cham (2017). https://doi.org/10.1007/978-3-319-66182-7_35
7. Castillo, E., Castillo, R., Martinez, J., Shenoy, M., Guerrero, T.: Four-dimensional deformable image registration using trajectory modeling. Phys. Med. & Biol. **55**(1), 305 (2009)
8. Castillo, R., et al.: A framework for evaluation of deformable image registration spatial accuracy using large landmark point sets. Phys. Med. Biol. **54**(7), 1849 (2009)
9. Dalca, A.V., Balakrishnan, G., Guttag, J., Sabuncu, M.R.: Unsupervised learning for fast probabilistic diffeomorphic registration. In: Frangi, A.F., Schnabel, J.A., Davatzikos, C., Alberola-López, C., Fichtinger, G. (eds.) MICCAI 2018. LNCS, vol. 11070, pp. 729–738. Springer, Cham (2018). https://doi.org/10.1007/978-3-030-00928-1_82
10. Haskins, G., Kruger, U., Yan, P.: Deep learning in medical image registration: a survey. arXiv preprint arXiv:1903.02026 (2019)
11. Jud, C., Möri, N., Bitterli, B., Cattin, P.C.: Bilateral regularization in reproducing kernel hilbert spaces for discontinuity preserving image registration. In: Wang, L., Adeli, E., Wang, Q., Shi, Y., Suk, H.-I. (eds.) MLMI 2016. LNCS, vol. 10019, pp. 10–17. Springer, Cham (2016). https://doi.org/10.1007/978-3-319-47157-0_2
12. Jud, C., Mori, N., Cattin, P.C.: Sparse kernel machines for discontinuous registration and nonstationary regularization. In: Proceedings of the IEEE Conference on CVPR Workshops, pp. 9–16 (2016)

13. Jud, C., Sandkühler, R., Möri, N., Cattin, P.C.: Directional averages for motion segmentation in discontinuity preserving image registration. In: Descoteaux, M., Maier-Hein, L., Franz, A., Jannin, P., Collins, D.L., Duchesne, S. (eds.) MICCAI 2017. LNCS, vol. 10433, pp. 249–256. Springer, Cham (2017). https://doi.org/10.1007/978-3-319-66182-7_29

14. Kingma, D.P., Ba, J.: Adam: a method for stochastic optimization. In: International Conference on Learning Representations (ICLR) (2015)

15. Krebs, J., et al.: Robust non-rigid registration through agent-based action learning. In: Descoteaux, M., Maier-Hein, L., Franz, A., Jannin, P., Collins, D.L., Duchesne, S. (eds.) MICCAI 2017. LNCS, vol. 10433, pp. 344–352. Springer, Cham (2017). https://doi.org/10.1007/978-3-319-66182-7_40

16. Modersitzki, J.: FAIR: flexible algorithms for image registration, vol. 6. SIAM (2009)

17. Pennec, X., Cachier, P., Ayache, N.: Understanding the "Demon's Algorithm": 3D non-rigid registration by gradient descent. In: Taylor, C., Colchester, A. (eds.) MICCAI 1999. LNCS, vol. 1679, pp. 597–605. Springer, Heidelberg (1999). https://doi.org/10.1007/10704282_64

18. Rohé, M.-M., Datar, M., Heimann, T., Sermesant, M., Pennec, X.: SVF-Net: learning deformable image registration using shape matching. In: Descoteaux, M., Maier-Hein, L., Franz, A., Jannin, P., Collins, D.L., Duchesne, S. (eds.) MICCAI 2017. LNCS, vol. 10433, pp. 266–274. Springer, Cham (2017). https://doi.org/10.1007/978-3-319-66182-7_31

19. Ronneberger, O., Fischer, P., Brox, T.: U-Net: convolutional networks for biomedical image segmentation. In: Navab, N., Hornegger, J., Wells, W.M., Frangi, A.F. (eds.) MICCAI 2015. LNCS, vol. 9351, pp. 234–241. Springer, Cham (2015). https://doi.org/10.1007/978-3-319-24574-4_28

20. Rueckert, D., Sonoda, L.I., Hayes, C., Hill, D.L., Leach, M.O., Hawkes, D.J.: Non-rigid registration using free-form deformations: application to breast MR images. IEEE Trans. Med. Imaging 18(8), 712–721 (1999)

21. Sandkühler, R., Jud, C., Andermatt, S., Cattin, P.C.: AirLab: autograd image registration laboratory. arXiv preprint arXiv:1806.09907 (2018)

22. Thirion, J.P.: Image matching as a diffusion process: an analogy with Maxwell's demons. Med. Image Anal. 2(3), 243–260 (1998)

23. Vandemeulebroucke, J., Rit, S., Kybic, J., Clarysse, P., Sarrut, D.: Spatiotemporal motion estimation for respiratory-correlated imaging of the lungs. Med. Phys. 38(1), 166–178 (2011)

24. Vishnevskiy, V., Gass, T., Szekely, G., Tanner, C., Goksel, O.: Isotropic total variation regularization of displacements in parametric image registration. IEEE Trans. Med. Imaging 36(2), 385–395 (2016)

25. de Vos, B.D., Berendsen, F.F., Viergever, M.A., Staring, M., Išgum, I.: End-to-end unsupervised deformable image registration with a convolutional neural network. In: Cardoso, M.J., et al. (eds.) DLMIA/ML-CDS -2017. LNCS, vol. 10553, pp. 204–212. Springer, Cham (2017). https://doi.org/10.1007/978-3-319-67558-9_24

26. Wendland, H.: Piecewise polynomial, positive definite and compactly supported radial functions of minimal degree. Adv. Comput. Math. 4(1), 389–396 (1995)

An Image Registration Framework for Discontinuous Mappings Along Cracks

Hari Om Aggrawal[1(✉)], Martin S. Andersen[3], and Jan Modersitzki[1,2]

[1] Institute of Mathematics and Image Computing,
University of Lübeck, Lübeck, Germany
hariom85@gmail.com
[2] Fraunhofer Institute for Digital Medicine MEVIS, Lübeck, Germany
[3] Technical University of Denmark, Lyngby, Denmark

Abstract. A novel crack capable image registration framework is proposed. The approach is designed for registration problems suffering from cracks, gaps, or holes. The approach enables discontinuous transformation fields and also features an automatically computed crack indicator function and therefore does not require a pre-segmentation. The new approach is a generalization of the commonly used variational image registration approach. New contributions are an additional dissipation term in the overall energy, a proper balancing of different ingredients, and a joint optimization for both, the crack indicator function and the transformation. Results for histological serial sectioning of marmoset brain images demonstrate the potential of the approach and its superiority as compared to a standard registration.

Keywords: Discontinuous deformations · Non-smooth deformations · Image registration · Cracks · Holes · Digital pathology · Histology

1 Introduction

Image registration for smooth displacements is a very well explored topic in the literature; see, e.g. [9,13], and references therein. There also exists work on discontinuous deformations for applications such as lung motion compensation (sliding motion) or partially constrained registration (local rigidity); see, e.g. [12, 14] and [5,7]. However, to our best knowledge, the stage for images showing cracks has not yet been set although cracks frequently appear in applications with very thin and fragile objects such as histological serial sectioning [15].

Histological sections are still a very important foundation of the analysis of organs and diseases and are often considered as ultimate ground truth. Tissue is being sectioned into very thin ($1-20\,\mu$m), essentially 2D slices which are then analyzed using high-resolution microscopes; see, e.g., [15] for the histological background and Fig. 3 for an example. Our objective is to regain the 3D information of the findings. This is achieved by registering the slices to compensate non-linear tissue deformation introduced by the sectioning process; see also [15].

© Springer Nature Switzerland AG 2020
Ž. Špiclin et al. (Eds.): WBIR 2020, LNCS 12120, pp. 163–173, 2020.
https://doi.org/10.1007/978-3-030-50120-4_16

With this fragile material, crack formation related to distortions, movements, and in particular drying processes is common [15].

An example is an animal model for brain behavior. The interest in brain models for studying diseases such as degeneration is enormous. Typically, primate species, such as marmoset monkey, are used to build these models [11]. These models obtain mesoscale neuro-anatomical information through the study of histological images. To this end, sliced brain tissue is stained with different chemical dyes to highlight key biomarkers and digitized to an appropriate image format. Afterward, the image stack has to be registered to correct for the deformations introduced by the sectioning process and to gain 3D information. The alignment of these sections is difficult, as the tissue undergoes several deformations steps during sectioning and preparation. The tissues may suffer from non-linear deformations including cracking, tearing, or splitting; see Fig. 3 for an example. The registration of histological serial section is hence an important task and well explored in the literature; see, e.g., [13,15], and references therein.

The picture changes when cracks appear. One of the obstacles is that a solid mathematical model is non-trivial and still missing. We consider a crack as an interface along which material breaks apart. The formation of a crack is a non-smooth process and the deformation map attains a jump discontinuity at the crack interface [4]. This process develops a gap or a hole in the material. Note that a crack might be viewed as an opening of the material and registration may aim to mimic this formation process (opening) or its inverse (closing).

Borrowing ideas from damage mechanics [8], we present a mathematical model for the registration with discontinuous deformations along cracks. A first attempt is proposed in [6], where the global regularization parameter is made spatially-dependent. This enables to relax the regularity along crack interfaces, but it also requires a pre-segmentation of the crack. Spatially-dependent regularization has also been used in several studies [12,14], mainly to handle discontinuity due to sliding motion. However, these studies assume that a one-to-one correspondence exists almost everywhere for the given images. But, this assumption is not valid for the images with cracks.

Our work differs from the approach in [6]. First of all, we assume a crack to be a set of measure zero. We find this a more natural assumption, but it also provides challenges when dealing with integral measures. Next, our framework estimates both the deformation map and the location of the cracks and holes. Therefore, additional segmentation is not required. Note that the identification of the crack and in particular, its origin is non-trivial; see also our estimated crack interfaces in the result section. The new model utilizes the physical principles underlying crack propagation in material as studied in damage mechanics; see, e.g., [8]. These principles provide insight into the deformation processes. A damage mechanic model enables discontinuities in the deformation map by varying the stiffness of a material. This approach is thus similar to the spatially-varying regularization idea used in image registration. But the damage model also assumes that the material dissipates energy during the formation of a crack. This energy model the properties of a crack in terms of a crack indicator function. Finally and similarly to [3], we also introduce an adaptive spatially-varying dissimilarity weight to handle non-correspondences due to cracks and/or holes.

The proposed framework belongs to the class of joint segmentation and registration problems, where both an indicator function and the deformation map are unknown. Such frameworks are also explored for image denoising and fracture mechanics problems. In particular, the approach of Mumford and Shah [10] is common. We use ideas similar to the Ambrosio and Tortorelli [1] approximation of the Mumford Shah functional to avoid numerical difficulties arising from the low dimensional cracks. More specifically, we follow a damage mechanics framework [8], which is closely related to the Ambrosio and Tortorelli approximation.

In this paper, the focus is on the mathematical model and its properties and less on a particular application and parameterization. Therefore, we show results for 1D test case, where analytical solutions are known and can be used for objective comparison and parameter estimation. We also show preliminary results for marmoset brain images for which parameters are hand-tuned. The results confirm our expectations: the new approach is much better suited for the registration of images with cracks than a generic approach.

The paper is organized as follows. In Sect. 2, we outline the generic registration approach and describe our modifications to handle images with cracks. We introduce the new model and its parameterization. Sect. 3 comments on the numerical scheme to solve the new model. We demonstrate the superiority of our model on the 1D and 2D datasets in Sect. 4 and conclude our findings in Sect. 5.

2   Problem Statement

We begin by briefly outlining a generic image registration approach, which is based on a variational formulation of the correspondence problem; see [9] for details. As our focus is on images with cracks, we state the framework in its simplest form and even restrict to the 1D case. We stress that our concepts are generic and cover the general setting.

We next describe our modifications that enable us to handle images with cracks. The central idea is to decompose the image domain into a crack part Γ and its complement Γ^c. Following ideas from damage mechanic, we add a dissipation energy with is essentially based on the $(d-1)$-dimensional volume of the crack. Using ideas similar to the Ambrosio and Tortorelli approximation, we end up with our new model (3). Finally, we discuss our parameterization. We propose a particular parameter setting, such that only two parameters (regularization and crack weight) need to be specified.

We remark that the inverse mapping z may provide additional insight; see Fig. 1. Due to page limitations, we do not explore this mapping further.

2.1   Generic Registration Problem

We only briefly outline the variational image registration approach; see e.g. [9] for details. In our setting $\Omega \subset \mathbb{R}$ is a bounded domain, say $\Omega =]-1, 1[$, and

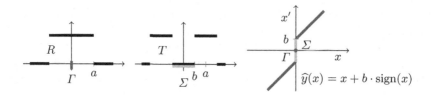

Fig. 1. A 1D function $R = \chi_{[-a,a]}$ (left) is mapped to T (center) by $\widehat{y}$ (right). Due to the discontinuity at the crack $\Gamma = \{0\}$ (in blue) a gap Σ (in red) has been introduced. The forward mapping y with $x' = y(x)$ represents the opening of a gap, its inverse z with $x = z(x')$ represents the closing. Note that $z(\Sigma) = \Gamma$ but $y(\Gamma)$ is not well-defined. (Color figure online)

two images $T, R : \Omega \to \mathbb{R}$ are to be registered; see Fig. 1 for an example. More precisely, we want to determine a function $y : \mathbb{R} \to \mathbb{R}$ such that ideally $T[y] \approx R$, i.e. $T[y](x) := T \circ y(x) := T(y(x)) \approx R(x)$ for almost all $x \in \Omega$. For some applications, y might be assumed to be diffeomorphic, but in the presence of cracks this assumption does not hold.

The similarity of $T[y]$ and R is enforced by minimizing a suitable distance D of the images. As the minimization of D is ill-posed, regularization is required. As examples serve an L_2 distance and a hyperelastic potential for 2D and $\phi = ((v-1)/v)^2$; see [2] for details:

$$D(y) := \|T[y] - R\|^2_{L_2(\Omega)} = \int_\Omega [T(y(x)) - R(x)]^2 \, dx,$$
$$S(y) := \int_\Omega \mathrm{hp}(y(x)) \, dx; \qquad \mathrm{hp}(y(x)) := \sum_{i,j} |\partial_i y_j(x)|^2 + \phi(\det \nabla y(x));$$

Weighting the data fidelity and the regularization with parameters α and β, the generic approach (G) is to minimize the total energy

$$J^G_{\alpha,\beta}(y) := \int_\Omega \alpha \, [T(y(x)) - R(x)]^2 + \beta \, \mathrm{hp}(y(x)) \, dx; \qquad (1)$$

for details and generalizations see [9] and references therein. Note that the specific ingredients are irrelevant and the special choices are only for presentation reasons; our framework is general.

The parameters α and β control the weights of the parts. Typical choices are $\alpha = 1$ and $\beta = \tau$, τ being the smallest parameter for user-specific criterion such as the deformation being one-to-one is still fulfilled. Spatially dependent parameters may also be used [3,6]. In [3], it is even suggested to automatically adjust the penalty for the handling of non-corresponding structures in images.

In [6], a spatially dependent regularization parameter $\beta = \beta(x)$ is studied. We remark that well-posedness requires $\beta(x) \geq \varepsilon > 0$ for all $x \in \Omega$, but it also guarantees a minimizing element y for $J^G_{\alpha,\beta}$. Furthermore, we remark that the minimizer y is globally smooth and has no discontinuities.

From a physical point of view, the parameter $\beta(x)$ represents the elastic stiffness of a material at a point $x \in \Omega$, where stiffness reflects the rigidity of the material. The less stiff the material is, the easier to deform or stretch it is. A close to zero stiffness allows extreme stretching of material, and due to this, a crack may form, or a hole may close in the material. This interpretation motivates us to define the function β depending on the crack indicator p.

2.2   Registration for Images with Cracks

As outlined above, the generic framework is incapable of registering images with cracks. We, therefore, suggest extending the generic model as follows. The basic idea is to partition the domain Ω into a crack Γ and its complement $\Gamma^c := \Omega \backslash \Gamma$. For the registration on Γ^c, we essentially follow the generic approach, whereas the crack deserves special treatment.

In material science, a crack is an interface along which material breaks apart. The breaking may create a hole in the material. For illustration, we consider the previous example; see also Fig. 1. Here, R is characteristic function of an interval $[-a, a]$ whereas T is the characteristic function of two intervals. With the transformation $\widehat{y}$ in Fig. 1, it holds $T(\widehat{y}(x)) = R(x)$ on Γ^c. Obviously, there is no continuous one-to-one mapping y that creates the gap Σ between the two parts in T. Paying the price for a discontinuous transformation and introducing a crack at $\Gamma = \{0\}$, we see that $\widehat{y}$ is a perfect solution, as it is essentially a translation on Γ^c and thus does have minimal regularization energy.

We may describe a crack set $\Gamma \subset \Omega$ by its indicator or phase field function

$$p : \Omega \to [0, 1], \quad p(x) = \chi_\Gamma(x) \quad \text{(i.e. 1 on } \Gamma, \text{ 0 on } \Gamma^c) \tag{2}$$

The closed subset Γ has Lebesgue measure zero, defines the crack interface, and is a set of jump discontinuities for y; see [4] for details. Since Γ has Lebesque measure zero, information for y on Γ is not required.

If the crack and thus p is known a priori, we would simply pick the parameters α and β in (1) depending on p, such that $\alpha(p) = \beta(p) = 0$ for $p = 1$, and we end up with a generic registration problem on Γ^c. However, in our new approach, we aim to estimate the transformation and the crack simultaneously. To this end, we add an additional dissipation energy for the cracks in (1). The overall energy, which is now to be minimized with respect to (y, p) thus reads

$$J^C_{\alpha, \beta, \gamma}(y, p) := \int_\Omega \alpha(p) \, [T(y(x)) - R(x)]^2 + \beta(p) \, \mathrm{hp}(y(x)) + \gamma \, e(p) \, dx. \tag{3}$$

Ideally, $\int_\Omega e \, dx = \int_\Gamma ds$ would measure the $(d-1)$-dimensional volume of the crack. This is similar to the edge set in the approach of Mumford and Shah [10] and known for its challenges. Ambrosio and Tortorelli [1] proposed to use a converging sequence of approximations, where p is differentiable. Roughly speaking,

$$\int_\Gamma ds \approx \lim_{h \to 0} \int_\Omega \frac{1}{4h} p^2 + h \, |\nabla p|^2 \, dx.$$

In our approach, we modify this idea based on concepts from damage mechanics [8]. In damage mechanics, it is assumed that a material dissipates energy during the formation of a crack. This energy is proportional to the area of the crack region in the reference configuration of the domain. Generally, the dissipation energy is expressed as

$$e(p) = p^2 + \ell^2 |\nabla p|^2, \tag{4}$$

where ℓ is the internal length and relates to material properties; see [8] for details.

We remark that the concept of Γ-convergence or dissipation energy can be interpreted as a relaxation of the ideal setting. Rather than working with Dirac measures of the crack, we now have a differentiable phase field p. As a consequence, the proposed model (3) implicitly assumes that the deformation field is continuous and differential everywhere. This is good news as the iterates in our numerical schemes are smooth and differentiable. But it is also bad news, as the discontinuity can only be reached in the limit. In our implementation, we work with a fixed γ and accept an over-smoothed solution.

Our approach is similar to ideas discussed in damage mechanics [8] to handle cracks and in image registration to handle sliding motion [14]. There, the non-smoothness is generally achieved by decreasing the regularization parameter β in the generic case. We remark that our approach is conceptually capable of dealing with sets of measure zero, while the approaches [6,14] are not.

2.3   Parameter Selection Strategy

We now discuss options for the parameters α, β and γ in (3). The weights α and β should ideally be related to indicator functions of the complement of the gap. For our numerical studies, we restrict to the basic choices,

$$\alpha(p) = (1-p)^2, \qquad \beta(p) = \varepsilon + \lambda(1-p)^n, \quad n \in \mathbb{N}, \ \varepsilon, \lambda > 0,$$
$$e(p) = p^2, \quad \text{i.e. } \ell = 0 \text{ in (4), and } \gamma > 0 \text{ constant.}$$

These choices are convex and monotonic functions for α and β. The similarity parameter α is simply a smooth characteristic function for Γ^c. The regularity parameter β is along the same lines. However, we add a global and typically small constant $\varepsilon > 0$, which ensures the existence of solutions for (3). Our parameter λ plays a similar role as the constant parameter τ for the generic case (1) and in our numerical studies, we use the same strategy for picking λ and τ. The power n enables different distributions of the regularization weight. The higher n, the more concentrated is the regularization on the crack complement. As common in damage mechanics [8], we picked $n = 2$ in our experiments.

For the dissipation energy e we again follow [8] and use (4) with the non-physical choice $\ell = 0$, simply to keep the number of tunable parameters small. We remark that we, therefore, have no regularization on the first variation of p on the crack. Physically, the parameter γ reflects the toughness of the material. The less tough the material is, the easier it is to break it. If γ is very big, the energy converges to the generic case, i.e., no cracks at all. On the other side, if $\gamma = 0$, a solution will be $p(x) = 1$ (all is crack) and y is such that $S(y) = 0$. The impact of the weight γ for the dissipation is discussed in our results part.

We remark that for $p \equiv 0$ and proper choices of α and β, the new model coincides with the generic model and is thus a generalization. With this setting, the only degrees of freedom in parameterization is the choices of λ and γ.

3   Discretization and Numerical Optimization

The minimization problem (3) is solved numerically, using the "discretize-then-optimize" paradigm as outlined in the FAIR toolbox [9]. More precisely, the integrals are approximated by quadrature rules, where for the images a cell-centered grid is used. Our discretization of the transformation y depends on the regularization; see [9] for details. In our experiments, we use an elastic regularizer [9] for 1D problems and the hyperelastic regularizer in [2] for the 2D problems, and therefore a nodal discretization for y. The crack indicator function p is discretized on a cell-centered grid.

As common for combined problems, we use an alternating minimization approach. Starting with $p \equiv 0$, we solve for y. This is equivalent to solve the generic problem (1). Using the latest y, we improve p and continue this iteration until our stopping criteria are met. Each sub-problem is solved with the Gauss-Newton scheme using an Armijo linesearch and typical stopping rules; see [9].

We remark that in contrast to the generic case, we do not take full advantage of the FEM approach to compute the hyperelastic regularization energy. The reason is that due to factor β, we do not have an analytic expression for the integral. We use a midpoint quadrature rule for the FEM based hyperelastic potential instead. We also remark that a joint optimization approach for (y, p) may converge to local minima, as typical for combined problems.

Following [9], we use a generic multilevel strategy to smooth out local minima for both 1D and 2D problems. We know that this simplistic strategy may not be optimal in the crack scenario but do not have space to elaborate on the issue.

4   Results

We demonstrate the performance of our new model. The experiment on a 1D example shows the convergence properties of our scheme and manifest that the new model can resolve discontinuous transformations perfectly along the cracks. This is further reaffirmed by our remarkable registration results on a pair of marmoset brain images; the data courtesy of Harald Möller, Max Planck Institute for Human Cognitive and Brain Sciences, Leipzig, Germany.

In all experiments, we use the L_2 or SSD based similarity measure [9]. We choose the elastic regularizer for the 1D studies and the hyperelastic regularizer in [2] for the 2D data. We compare results from the crack capable model (3) with the generic model (1) (denote with subscript C and G, respectively).

In our first study, we demonstrate that our results converge to the solution as the discretization error h reduces. To this end we use the pair of 1D functions as shown in Fig. 1, where an analytic solution $\widehat{y}$ is known. Figure 2 shows the displacement $u(x) = y(x) - x$ for the solution $\widehat{y}$ (and its inverse z) as well as

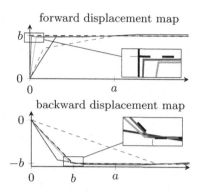

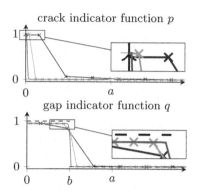

Fig. 2. Detailed results for the 1D performance study; cf. Fig. 1. All functions are symmetric, thus we only show the non-negative parts. Results for the forward pair (y, p) (top) and backward/inverse pair (z, q) (bottom) are displayed. On the left, we show the displacement $u(x) = y(x) - x$ of the solution $\hat{y}$ (black dashed), the numerical solutions y^G and y^C for the generic (red dashed) and new approach (solid) for various discretization levels $h \approx 1/m$; $m = 16$ (blue) $m = 64$ (green), and $m = 256$ (red). On the right we show the corresponding crack indicator functions p and q, respectively. Ideally, $p = \chi_{\{0\}}$, $q = \chi_{[-b, b]}$, and z as in Fig. 1. In our computations, we choose optimal parameter values, such that the estimates y and z have minimal error with respect to analytical solutions, i.e. $\alpha = 1$, $\beta = 0.06$ for the generic approach and $\alpha = (1 - p)^2$, $\beta = 0.06(1 - p)^2 + 10^{-9}$, $\gamma = 0.02$ for the new approach. (Color figure online)

numerical results for the generic and the crack capable approach on different discretization levels. It can be seen that the new approach converges to the true solution: for $m = 256$, the gap is below the discretization error. Note that already on the coarse discretization ($m = 16$), the new approach is superior to the generic approach on finest discretization ($m = 256$).

Our second study demonstrates the superiority of the crack capable model on a dataset of marmoset brain images; see Fig. 3 and its caption for our parameterization. Although the schemes seem to be similar when looking at the closing of the crack induced gap in the transformed images $T(y)$ and also in the difference images, in fact, they produce very different transformations. This is most pronounced on the gap (see top row). For the generic approach, y^G is globally smooth and distributes the gap to a rather thick layer; cf. $T(y^G)$.

On the other side, the crack capable model yields a solution precisely as expected. Its solution y^C shows a discontinuity which is numerically resolved within the discretization error. Moreover, y^C is very smooth on the crack complement. This is also manifested in the hyperelastic potential and the determinant of the Jacobian, where the maximal values of them are 350 and 8 times higher, respectively, with respect to the generic approach.

Also, the crack indicator function p matches our expectations and resolves the crack as a very thin line. We remark that a number of additional areas have automatically been indicated as cracks. In the absence of ground truth, we can neither confirm nor reject these findings. Note that it is generally not easy to determine a crack manually. Therefore, pre-segmentation based registration approaches such as the one in [6] may fail. We remark that the regularization potential and the determinant of the Jacobian from the generic model may also be used as a crack indicator; this is subject of ongoing investigations.

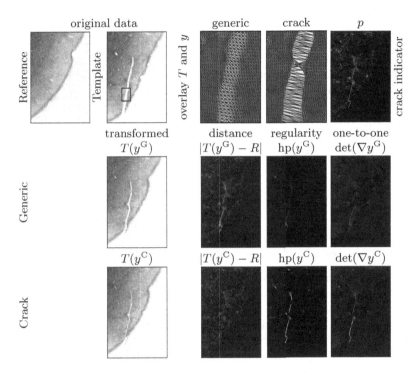

Fig. 3. Results for marmoset brain images. The rows show the reference and the template image (top), result for the generic (middle) and results for the new approach (bottom). For the results, we show the transformed image $T(y)$, the unweighted distance $|T(y) - R|$, the regularity $\mathrm{hp}(y)$, and the determinant of the Jacobian $\det \nabla y$ (from left to right). The top row also displays details of the transformations as well as the crack indicator function p in the new model. As parameters, we use $\alpha = 1$ and $\beta = 500$ for the generic case and $\alpha = (1-p)^2$, $\beta = 500(1-p)^2 + 10^{-9}$, $\gamma = 10^3$ for the crack model, respectively.

5   Conclusion

A novel crack capable image registration framework is proposed. The approach is designed for registration problems suffering from cracks, gaps, or holes. The approach enables discontinuous transformation fields and also features an automatically computed crack indicator function and therefore does not require a pre-segmentation. The new approach is a generalization of the commonly used variational image registration approach [9]. New contributions are an additional dissipation term in the overall energy, a proper balancing of different ingredients, and a joint optimization for both, the crack indicator function and the transformation. The approach is very general and flexible and can be combined with a huge variety of image similarity measures and regularization strategies. It is also not limited to a particular class of applications. For a particular setting, we also propose a parameterization strategy. Results for histological serial sectioning of marmoset brain images demonstrate the potential of the approach and its superiority as compared to a standard registration. Future work address a deeper mathematical analysis of the framework and the exploration of potential applications such as brain shift registration problem.

Acknowledgment. The authors acknowledge the financial support by the Federal Ministry of Education and Research of Germany in the framework of MED4D (project number 05M16FLA) and in part by the European Research Council under grant 291405 (HD-Tomo).

References

1. Ambrosio, L., Tortorelli, V.M.: Approximation of functional depending on jumps by elliptic functional via Γ-Convergence. Commun. Pure Appl. Math. **43**(8), 999–1036 (1990)
2. Burger, M., Modersitzki, J., Ruthotto, L.: A hyperelastic regularization energy for image registration. SIAM J. Sci. Comput. **35**(1), B132–B148 (2013)
3. Drobny, D., Carolus, H., Kabus, S., Modersitzki, J.: Handling non-corresponding regions in image registration. In: Handels, H., Deserno, T.M., Meinzer, H.-P., Tolxdorff, T. (eds.) Bildverarbeitung für die Medizin 2015. I, pp. 107–112. Springer, Heidelberg (2015). https://doi.org/10.1007/978-3-662-46224-9_20
4. Francfort, G.A., Marigo, J.J.: Revisiting brittle fracture as an energy minimization problem. J. Mech. Phys. Solids **46**(8), 1319–1342 (1998)
5. Haber, E., Heldmann, S., Modersitzki, J.: A framework for image-based constrained registration with an application to local rigidity. Linear Algebra Appl. **431**, 459–470 (2009)
6. Kabus, S.: Multiple material variational image registration. Ph.D. thesis (2007)
7. König, L., Derksen, A., Heldmann, S., Papenberg, N., Modersitzki, J., Haas, B.: Deformable image registration with guaranteed local rigidity, vol. 115, pp. S197–S198. Elsevier (2015)
8. Marigo, J.-J., Maurini, C., Pham, K.: An overview of the modelling of fracture by gradient damage models. Meccanica **51**(12), 3107–3128 (2016). https://doi.org/10.1007/s11012-016-0538-4
9. Modersitzki, J.: FAIR: Flexible Algorithms for Image Registration. SIAM, Philadelphia (2009)
10. Mumford, D., Shah, J.: Optimal approximations by piecewise smooth functions and associated variational problems. Commun. Pure Appl. Math. **42**(5), 577–685 (1989)
11. Okano, H., et al.: Brain/MINDS: a Japanese national brain project for marmoset neuroscience. Neuron **92**(3), 582–590 (2016)

12. Pace, D.F., Aylward, S.R., Niethammer, M.: A locally adaptive regularization based on anisotropic diffusion for deformable image registration of sliding organs. IEEE Trans. Med. Imaging **32**(11), 2114–2126 (2013)
13. Pichat, J., Iglesias, J.E., Yousry, T., Ourselin, S., Modat, M.: A survey of methods for 3D histology reconstruction. Med. Image Anal. **46**, 73–105 (2018)
14. Schmidt-Richberg, A., Werner, R., Handels, H., Ehrhardt, J.: Estimation of slipping organ motion by registration with direction-dependent regularization. Med. Image Anal. **16**(1), 150–159 (2012)
15. Schmitt, O., Eggers, R.: High contrast and homogeneous staining of paraffin sections of whole human brains for three dimensional ultrahigh resolution image analysis. Biotech. Histochem. **73**, 44–51 (1997)

Author Index

Aggrawal, Hari Om 163
Andersen, Martin S. 163
Andersson, Jesper L. R. 141
Ashburner, John 122
Astolfi, Pietro 3
Avants, Brian 91
Avesani, Paolo 3

Bastiaansen, Wietske A. P. 34
Bastiani, Matteo 122
Bertelsen, Mads F. 141
Bertó, Giulia 3
Breman, Hester 122

Choi, David 67
Christiaens, Daan 111, 131
Cordero-Grande, Lucilio 131

Deprez, Maria 111, 131
Drobny, David 67

Ebrahimi, Mehran 153
Eck, Judith 122
Edwards, A. David 131
Edwards, David 111

Fritz, Levin 122

Goebel, Rainer 122
Gori, Pietro 3
Grande, Lucilio Cordero 111
Greenblatt, Elliot 91
Grigorescu, Irina 111, 131
Grothausmann, Roman 23

Haas, Benjamin 44
Hajnal, Joseph 111
Hajnal, Joseph V. 131
Heldmann, Stefan 44, 57
Hesterman, Jacob 91
Honegger, Jonas 44
Hutter, Jana 111, 131

Isaac, Amanda 67

Khrapitchev, Alexandre A. 141
Kirschke, Jan S. 81
Klein, Stefan 34
Knudsen, Lars 23
Koning, Anton 34
Kuckertz, Sven 44

Lange, Annkristin 57
Lange, Frederik J. 141
Lu, Xuesong 103

Manger, Paul R. 141
Mars, Rogier B. 141
McCormick, Matt 23
Menze, Bjoern H. 81
Modat, Marc 67, 131
Modersitzki, Jan 163
Molero, Ester 81
Morgas, Tomasz 44
Mühlfeld, Christian 23
Mulders, Joost 122
Müller, Henning 12

Navarro, Fernando 81
Ng, Eric 153
Niessen, Wiro J. 34

Olivetti, Emanuele 3
Ourselin, Sébastien 67

Papenberg, Nils 44
Peters, Judith 122
Pietsch, Maximilian 111
Pyles, John 122

Qiao, Yuchuan 103

Ranzini, Marta 67
Roebroeck, Alard 122
Rousian, Melek 34

Sekuboyina, Anjany   81
Smith, Stephen M.   141
Steegers-Theunissen, Régine P. M.   34

Tournier, Jacques-Donald   111
Tustison, Nicholas   91

Uus, Alena   111, 131

Vercauteren, Tom   67

Waldmannstetter, Diana   81
Wiestler, Benedikt   81
Wodzinski, Marek   12

Zukić, Dženan   23

Printed in the United States
By Bookmasters